The Myth of Self-Reliance

STUDIES IN FORCED MIGRATION
General Editor: Dawn Chatty, Refugee Studies Centre, University of Oxford

This series, published in association with the Refugees Studies Centre, University of Oxford, reflects the multidisciplinary nature of the field and includes within its scope international law, anthropology, sociology, politics, international relations, geopolitics, social psychology and economics.

For a full volume listing, please see back matter.

The Myth of Self-Reliance

ECONOMIC LIVES INSIDE A LIBERIAN REFUGEE CAMP

Naohiko Omata

berghahn
NEW YORK · OXFORD
www.berghahnbooks.com

First published in 2017 by
Berghahn Books
www.berghahnbooks.com

© 2017, 2020 Naohiko Omata
First paperback edition published in 2020

Library of Congress Cataloging-in-Publication Data
Names: Omata, Naohiko, author.
Title: The myth of self-reliance : economic lives inside a Liberian
refugee camp / Naohiko Omata.
Description: New York : Berghahn Books, 2017. | Series: Studies in forced
migration ; volume 36 | Includes bibliographical references and index.|
Identifiers: LCCN 2017012307 (print) | LCCN 2017014646 (ebook) | ISBN
9781785335655 (eBook) | ISBN 9781785335648 (hardback : alk. paper)
Subjects: LCSH: Refugee camps--Ghana. | Refugees--Liberia--Economic
conditions. | Refugees--Ghana--Economic conditions.
Classification: LCC HV640.4.G45 (ebook) | LCC HV640.4.G45 O43 2017
(print) |DDC 362.8709667--dc23
LC record available at https://lccn.loc.gov/2017012307

British Library Cataloguing in Publication Data
A catalogue record for this book is available
from the British Library

Printed on acid-free paper

ISBN 978-1-78533-564-8 (hardback)
ISBN 978-1-78920-810-8 (paperback)
ISBN 978-1-78533-565-5 (ebook)

Contents

Illustrations

Figures

Illustrations

Tables

Acknowledgements

Since I have started this research project, a huge number of people have helped me in many ways. In the first instance, I would like to express my deepest gratitude for the dedicated support of Tania Kaiser and Laura Hammond. Their guidance, advice and encouragement have significantly helped me to progress and complete this research. I would also like to extend my warm thanks to Alexander Betts, Dawn Chatty and other colleagues at the Refugee Studies Centre, University of Oxford, who gave me insightful advice and constructive feedback on my work.

In Ghana and Liberia, I received numerous forms of assistance from Liberian refugees and returnees, and throughout my fieldwork I learnt a great deal from them. Their friendship, interest and participation made this research possible. Their life was marked by uncertainty and full of difficulties. But they agreed with the aim and scope of my research project and sacrificed their time and energy to assist me in my studies. It is impossible to list by name all of those who assisted my fieldwork on the ground. However, I am particularly grateful to my five research assistants: Joseph, Shetha, Benjamin, Kevin and Pennie. Also, I would like to give thanks to my co-residents in Buduburam, Philip and Sam.

I would also like to extend my gratitude to the following institutions; UNHCR in Ghana and Liberia; the Ghana Refugee Board; the Liberia Refugee Repatriation and Resettlement Committee; the Institute of Statistical, Social and Economic Research at the University of Ghana; the Embassy of Japan; and the Japan International Cooperation Agency. During fieldwork, I benefited immensely from their hospitality and generosity despite their busy schedules.

I would like to thank my funders, without whom the research would not have been possible. Principal funding came from the World Bank, with additional fieldwork grants from the University of London and from the School of Oriental and African Studies.

My particular thanks go to Kenji Hiratsuka, Tomoo Nakamura, Hideyuki Morie, Jeff Crisp, Elena Fiddian-Qasmiyeh, Niels Hahn, Nina Weaver,

Yasuko Kusakari, Artemy Izmestiev, Akihiro Fushimi and Akiko Tatsuta. I would not have been able to complete this project without their continued encouragement and assistance. Special thanks also go to Marion Berghahn, Caroline Kuhtz and Sasha Puchalski, as well as other staff at Berghahn Books, who helped this book appear in its current shape through their dedicated support and hard work.

Portions of Chapter 3 previously appeared in the *Community Development Journal* 48(2), 2013. Parts of Chapter 5 previously appeared in the *Journal of Refugee Studies* 26(2), 2013, and the *Journal of Ethnic and Migration Studies* 39(8), 2013. My thanks go to the journal editors for permitting me to incorporate these materials into the book.

Finally, I would like to dedicate this book to those who currently live as refugees and asylum seekers in adverse and uncertain situations around the world. May your voices be heard and your experiences be highlighted.

Abbreviations

AREU	Afghanistan Research and Evaluation Unit
CBO	camp-based organization
DAR	Development Assistance for Refugees
DFID	Department for International Development
ECOWAS	Economic Community of West African States
GH₵	Ghanaian cedi
GRB	Ghana Refugee Board
HH	Household
IP	implementing partner
LRRRC	Liberia Refugee Repatriation and Resettlement Committee
LRWC	Liberian Refugee Welfare Council
MoI	Ministry of the Interior
NCS	National Catholic Secretariat
NGO	non-governmental organization
SLF	sustainable livelihoods framework
UN	United Nations
UNHCR	United Nations High Commissioner for Refugees
USCRI	US Committee for Refugees and Immigrants
WRC	Women's Refugee Commission
WFP	World Food Programme

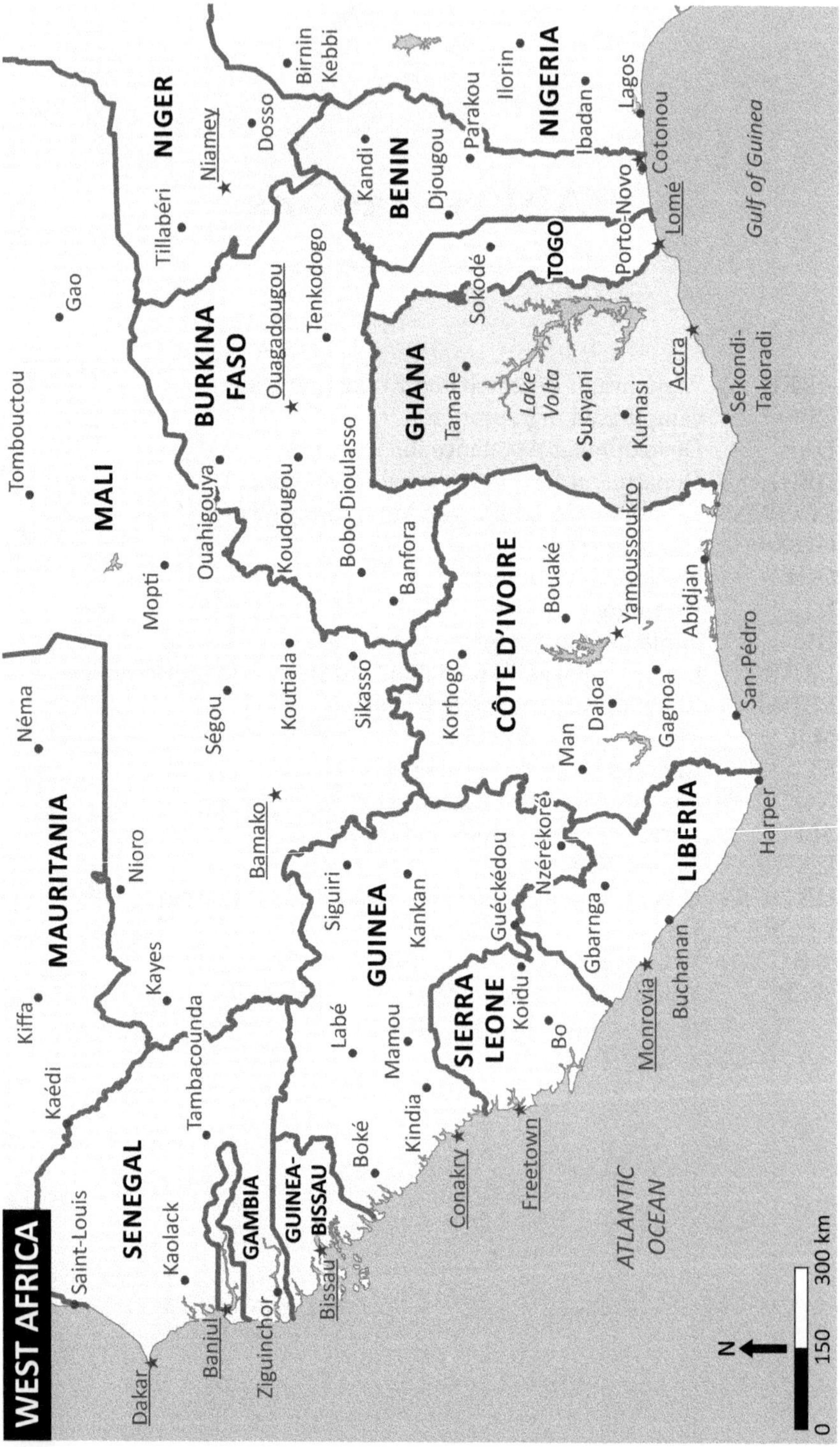

Map 0.1 West Africa (courtesy of Michael Borop, sitesatlas.com).

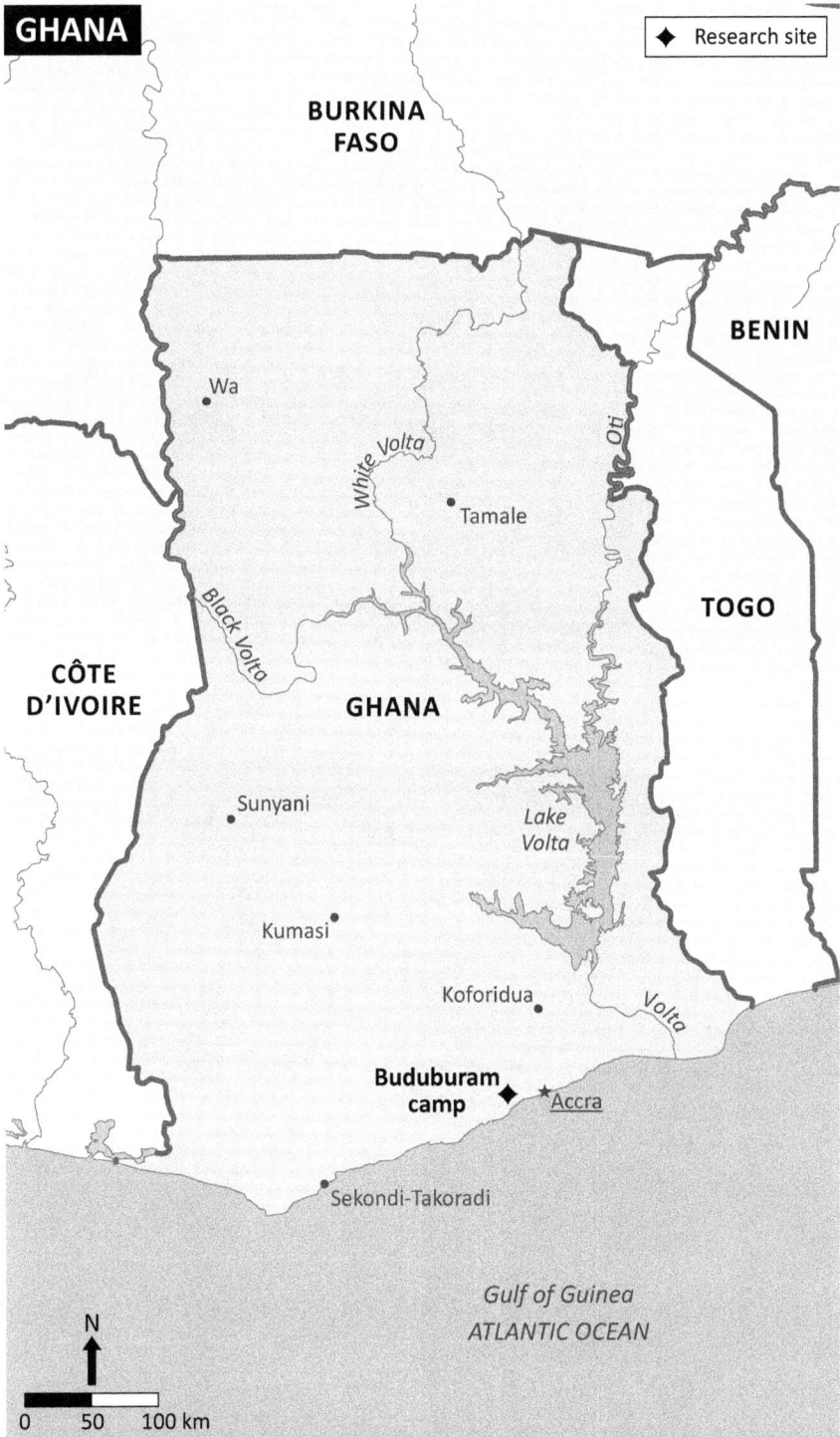

GHANA

Research site

BURKINA FASO

BENIN

Wa

White Volta

Oti

Tamale

TOGO

Black Volta

CÔTE D'IVOIRE

GHANA

Sunyani

Lake Volta

Kumasi

Koforidua

Volta

Buduburam camp

Accra

Sekondi-Takoradi

Gulf of Guinea
ATLANTIC OCEAN

N

0   50   100 km

Map 0.2 Buduburam refugee camp (courtesy of Michael Borop, sitesatlas.com).

Introduction

Buduburam

An Exemplary Refugee Camp?

Integration? NO!
Repatriation? PLUS USD 1,000 YES!
Resettlement? WHY NOT?

—Banner used during refugee protests in Buduburam camp

In early 2008, Liberian refugees in Buduburam refugee camp in Ghana attracted the attention of both the national and global media. Some 100 Liberian women refugees started protesting against the Office of United Nations High Commissioner for Refugees (UNHCR) at the entrance of the camp to firmly reject a local integration plan for Liberian refugees in Ghana. Instead, refugees demanded either third-country resettlement in the industrialized North or repatriation to Liberia with $1,000 for each individual (the repatriation cash grant from UNHCR before 2008 was $5 per person).[1] As the refugee protests continued for nearly two months, the number of participants in the demonstrations grew to several hundred as more and more Liberian refugees supported the protestors' messages. The series of demonstrations provoked the Ghanaian government to describe the demonstrations as 'a threat to the security of the state', and there resulted about 630 arrests and sixteen cases of deportation to Liberia.

Depicted as a 'bustling African village', the thriving economy in Buduburam camp amazed first-time visitors. Owusu, for example, states: 'The camp community is lively … Signs of commerce are evident everywhere, and the main street bustles with life as one walks through the "camp"' (Owusu 2000: 7; see also Antwi 2007; Codjoe et al. 2013; Dzeamesi 2008; Tete 2005). When I visited the camp for the first time in 2005, I was also struck by the vibrant commerce. There was a variety of economic activities inside and around the camp, such as fast-food restaurants, mobile-phone shops, mini-kiosks selling daily goods, internet cafés, clubs and bars, beauty salons and so on.

Due to the presence of active refugee commerce, UNHCR often commended the refugees in Buduburam as 'self-reliant', and the camp as an exemplary model in which refugees sustained themselves through robust businesses, boasting that the organization had facilitated their economic success by gradually withdrawing its assistance over the period of exile. The reputation of Buduburam as a self-sufficient camp was also supported by external researchers. In particular, Dick (2002a, 2002b) has published two influential reports highlighting refugees' robust businesses inside the camp.[2] In those reports, she argues that despite some challenges, on the whole, Liberian exiles in the camp had been able to assist themselves adequately in the face of UNHCR's withdrawal of support.

When I embarked on field research in 2008, many UNHCR staff in Ghana still supported this perspective. A female UNHCR programme officer confidently said to me:

> Refugees in Buduburam are doing very well. Many of them are running trading businesses. Between 2000 and 2002, UNHCR significantly reduced assistance for Liberians so they had to find a means of surviving on their own and of helping themselves ... Now Buduburam is the biggest economic hub in the camp area. Many refugees are having good life there.[3]

However, the economic vibrancy of the camp and the 'good life' claimed by UNHCR did not appear to correlate with the refugees' desire to be locally integrated in Ghana. Despite the renowned reputation of the camp, why did hundreds of refugees protest so adamantly against UNHCR's local integration plan? Didn't these refugees enjoy decent living conditions? On the surface, there was indeed a wide range of economic activities visible in the camp. But did a variety of economic activities mean a correspondingly high level of economic well-being? Behind the façade of a vibrant economy, how were refugees living in this 'successful' refugee camp?

Several scholars have published insightful studies exploring different economic aspects of Liberian refugees in Buduburam camp (e.g. Dick 2002a, 2002b; Dzeamesi 2008; Hardgrove 2009; Porter et al. 2008). To date, however, the existing work has not presented convincing or sufficient data on the nature of refugee livelihoods and their socio-economic conditions. Therefore, the central aim of this book is to put the putative economic success of Buduburam camp under intensive scrutiny and to reveal the diversified realities of the refugees' livelihood strategies and living conditions.

While this study probes into refugees' economic lives inside the camp, it also demonstrates how different groups of refugees navigated various difficulties during their prolonged exile, as well as in the aftermath of repatriation and following invocation of the Cessation Clause of refugee status. This book is based upon a decade work with Liberian refugees. My first visit to Buduburam camp dates back to 2005. I worked as a livelihood advisor for an NGO operating inside the camp until the end of 2007. In 2008 and 2009, I returned to Buduburam as a researcher and conducted research in Ghana and Liberia for thirteen months. At that point, the Buduburam refugee population was already entering the final phase of formal refugee life due to the intense pressure surrounding plans to repatriate the camp's inhabitants to Liberia. In 2012, UNHCR invoked the cessation of refugee status of Liberian refugees. Between 2012 and 2013, I conducted a follow-up study with my refugee interviewees in the face of the ending of their 'official' refugee life. By following the same refugee households over several years, this book sheds light on refugees' voices and lived experiences in protracted forced displacement, which rarely reach the main policy arenas of the international community.

Growing Interest in Refugees' Livelihoods and Self-Reliance

The issue of refugees' economic autonomy in Buduburam is of wider significance for the global refugee regime. Interest in promoting the livelihoods of refugees and their 'self-reliance' began to emerge as a pressing agenda in forced-migration policy and the academic arena around the beginning of this century (see Crisp 2003a; Milner 2014). This emergence is largely due to the failure of UNHCR to provide effective solutions for the numerous protracted refugee situations in which refugees have been in exile for at least five years.

One of the essential mandates of UNHCR is to find durable solutions for refugees, usually glossed as voluntary repatriation, local integration or third-country resettlement. Despite some large-scale repatriation programmes in the 1990s, significant numbers of refugees throughout the world did not return home because of continuing insecurity and instability in their country of origin (Crisp 2006: 11–12). Their integration in a host country did not take place either. The majority of refugees have not been granted permanent residential status in their first asylum country as their host state perceives refugees as a burden on the country (USCRI 2004: 44).

Meanwhile, the chance of being resettled in a third country in the developed world has remained extremely limited for the world's refugee population. Especially after the terrorist attack in New York on 11 September 2001, the pressure on asylum in the industrialized North has been reinforced and has further slimmed down resettlement opportunities for refugees (Koser 2007: 235; Van Hear 2011: 8). At the end of 2015, at least half of the world's refugee population was estimated to be in protracted exile, with the average length of time spent in exile estimated to be approximately twenty-six years (UNHCR 2016).

What is worse, as refugee situations become protracted, levels of international relief are normally reduced or entirely cut off (Jacobsen 2005: 2) because UNHCR and donor communities tend to focus on high-profile refugee crises in which people are either fleeing or repatriating in large numbers (Crisp 2003b: 9). As a result, assistance programmes for long-term refugee situations are frequently deprived of adequate funding. With the declining financial commitment of international donors, UNHCR is increasingly unable to provide essential needs for prolonged refugee populations (Jamal 2000: 3). In the face of mounting budgetary shortfalls, UNHCR has been required to find a remedy for these trapped exiles in long-term 'care-and-maintenance' circumstances (Crisp 2003a).

Due to these systemic pressures, there has been growing interest within the international refugee regime in promoting the development of livelihoods for long-term refugees so as to encourage economic 'self-reliance'.[4] UNHCR broadly defines self-reliance as 'the social and economic ability of an individual, a household or a community to meet essential needs in a sustainable manner' (UNHCR 2005a). Its guiding philosophy can be summarized as: refugees have the skills, capacity and agency to stand on their own and be able to sustain themselves without depending on external humanitarian aid (Jacobsen 2005). This concept has become an increasingly visible part of UNHCR's approach and rhetoric towards refugee assistance and protection (Crisp 2004). For example, UNHCR's 'Handbook for Self-Reliance' states that self-reliance is 'an integral and underpinning part of any durable solutions' (UNHCR 2005a), which should be promoted in all phases of refugee assistance.

However, the promotion of refugees' self-reliance is fraught with some fundamental problems. As non-citizens of the host country, refugees in developing regions are confronted by a number of survival challenges in often inhospitable environments. According to the 1951 UN Refugee Convention, refugees must be accorded the same status as nationals with regard to the right to engage in wage-earning employment. Typically, however, refugees' right to work is significantly constrained by various bureaucratic or regulatory impediments imposed on refugees by the host government, including lack of access to work permits and restrictions on the freedom of movement (see Horst 2006a; Jacobsen 2014; Kaiser 2007; Kibreab 2003; Werker 2007). In addition to formal regulations, ample evidence indicates that refugees' access to economic resources such as land, rivers, lakes, and forests is constrained through informal regulation by local host populations (Bakewell 2014; Bascom 1993; Rogge and Akol 1989).

Furthermore, the majority of protracted refugee situations in the world are located in countries with impoverished populations, where even local host communities themselves are often unable to satisfy their fundamental needs (Meyer 2006: 11). Existing studies pose a fundamental question concerning whether it is feasible to expect refugees to be able to economically sustain themselves within exceptionally constrained environments.

Despite these fundamental challenges for refugees, UNHCR and its partner agencies have traditionally approached the issue of livelihoods and self-reliance from a technical perspective, primarily focusing on the provision of income-generating projects, micro-finance programmes and vocational training (Crisp 2003a).[5] While this technical perspective is important, provision of such support makes sense only when refugees are given an enabling environment to pursue economic autonomy in a host state.

More problematically, there are to date no systematic and rigorous criteria for measuring refugees' self-reliance in the international refugee regime. UNHCR often perceives refugees as 'self-reliant' when they are managing their lives without external assistance. But what requires careful scrutiny is whether refugees living without aid are necessarily 'meeting their basic needs in a sustainable manner and with dignity', as defined by UNHCR (UNHCR 2005a). Additionally, the absence of assessment criteria means that there is a risk that the promotion of self-reliance could be abused to justify a reduction in external support for refugees. Among refugee-policy makers, the notion of self-reliance is very often positioned in polar opposition to 'dependency' – a state in which people rely heavily on and expect continued assistance, consequently undermining people's own initiatives (Harvey and Lind 2005). If dependency is induced by continuous provision of aid, the promotion of self-reliance is assumed to be automatically achieved by decreasing assistance for refugees. However, the relationship between dependency and self-reliance vis-à-vis external aid is not an inverse correlation. As noted above, when refugees' basic rights are severely restricted, self-reliance may not be attainable in the first place, regardless of whether refugees receive external support or not.

Given the ubiquity of protracted displacement and the dwindling availability of aid, enhancing economic independence for refugees is undoubtedly a critical issue of concern. Yet it remains unclear to what extent refugees can build sustainable livelihoods and achieve economic autonomy in the face of identified challenges. Drawing on both qualitative and quantitative research, this in-depth study of Liberian refugees in Buduburam camp seeks to shed light on this question and the fundamental problems outlined above.

Key Concepts of the Book

This section provides an overview of the principal concepts that the book draws upon: namely, refugee livelihoods, the role of social networks in

refugees' economic strategies, and their repatriation and economic reintegration. While this book mainly focuses on refugees' economic survival
inside the camp, it also explores the lived experiences of refugees' return
and economic readjustments. These are pivotal experiences that refugees
inevitably confront after extended displacement. While surveying the literature, the section highlights important analytical and empirical gaps.

Livelihoods in Forced Migration

The analysis of livelihoods in general has been enriched by a range of
institutions and scholars in development studies, poverty alleviation and
agricultural economies (see Ellis 2000; Francis 2000; Helmore and Singh
2001; Scoones 1998, 2007). Among various livelihood-oriented analytical
frameworks, perhaps the most widely known is the sustainable livelihoods
framework (SLF) of the UK Department for International Development.
Drawing upon Chambers and Conway's definition of livelihoods, the SLF
presents five types of livelihood assets, and illustrates how they are shaped
and mediated by external vulnerabilities and structural and procedural
factors such as law and regulations (DFID 1999). The essence of this
framework is its focus on the strengths and potential of poor people and
the strategies that they employ to make a living – rather than highlighting
their vulnerabilities and needs (Farrington et al. 2002: 2).

The development of the SLF and the ensuing emergence of similar
livelihood analytical frameworks has influenced researchers dealing with
refugees' economic activities (see de Vriese 2006; Horst 2006a; Korf
2004; WRC 2011; Young et al. 2007). The SLF has also substantially influenced UNHCR's livelihood policy and programming. According to its
'Livelihood Operational Guidelines' (UNHCR 2012a), UNHCR employs
the SLF as its organizational central framework to understand the livelihoods of displaced populations.

The research drawn from the SLF and similar analytical approaches
has given some useful insight into refugee livelihoods, but critical gaps
remain. For instance, the majority of existing studies gloss over socio-
economic diversity among refugee populations, and thus fail to elucidate
or draw attention to important differences in refugees' economic statuses and strategies. In any community or population, different people
suffer, survive or prosper in diverse ways, adapting to the environment
in which they find themselves (Le Sage and Majid 2002). Personal characteristics, such as displacement history, family background, education,
language skills and social networks, can have an effect on refugees' livelihoods (Horst 2006a: 9). As this book shows, among refugees living in
Buduburam camp, different individual or household characteristics had
significant consequences for the degree of access to livelihood assets and

subsequent formulation of economic coping strategies. Research on refugee livelihoods should aim to disaggregate the target population to account for such variance.

Also, research drawing upon the SLF and other models often does not sufficiently address the impacts of political and power dynamics on refugees' economic strategies and outcomes (see Ashley and Carney 1999; de Haan 2006; de Haan and Zoomers 2006; Murray 2001). People's livelihoods do not exist within a vacuum, but rather interact within a wider context of political, social, historical and economic conditions. In the case of refugee livelihoods, this complexity is amplified by their specific vulnerabilities and by the political economy of the various stakeholders (Jacobsen 2002; Lindley 2010). Shifts in refugee policy lead to significant changes in refugees' existing subsistence, but this is an overlooked analytical and empirical gap in the literature. Over the duration of this study, Liberian refugees in Buduburam camp confronted changing circumstances that were imposed by external authorities, including the tightening of refugee policies by the host government, intense repatriation pressure and the cessation of their refugee status. Incorporating the impacts of these pivotal incidents on the economic lives of refugees was essential for the current research project.

Moreover, the SLF model does not adequately capture the complex web of social connections that are inherent and indispensable for the refugees' economic activities. In the face of often challenging situations, refugees are reliant on their personal and social ties, and must constantly mobilize these contacts in order to achieve better access to resources (Amisi 2006; Andrews 2006; Doron 2005; Hamid 1992; Hammar 2014). As previous research on Liberian refugees in Buduburam camp has also indicated the particular importance of various types of network for subsistence (see Dick 2002a, 2002b; Porter et al. 2008; Tanle 2013), the analytical point of departure in this book is to look into the livelihood strategies of refugees through the lens of their social networks.

The Role of Social Capital in Refugees' Economic Lives

According to Halpern (2005), the birth of mainstream academic interest in the concept of social capital dates back to the 1980s, but the notion of social capital gained particular ascendancy in the mid 1990s with Putnam's work. In his study of civic associations in Italy, Putnam (1993a) approaches social capital in terms of community cohesion and argues that denser amounts of social capital are the essential differentiating factor of regional governments' and communities' success.

Although the concepts of social capital and social network remain popular in social science research, these terms are often criticized as being nebulously defined. For instance, Putnam conceptualizes social capital as 'features of social life – networks, norms, and trust – that enable participants to act together more effectively to pursue shared objectives' (Putnam 1996: 1). Coleman broadly defines social capital by its function as 'a variety of different entities, with two elements in common: they all consist of some aspect of social structures, and they facilitate certain actions of actors within the structure' (Coleman 1988: S98). This vagueness has generated confusion and criticism around the use of these concepts (see e.g. Fine 2001: 11–12; Portes 1998: 5). In particular, equating social capital with the resources acquired through it can gloss over a difference between possessors, sources and resources of capital, and may lead to a tautological explanation. Portes highlights the risk of obscuring this difference:

> Saying, for example, that student A has social capital because he obtained access to a large tuition loan from his kin and that student B does not because she failed to do so neglects the possibility that B's kin network is equally or more motivated to come to her aid but simply lacks the means to do so. Defining social capital as equivalent with the resources thus obtained is tantamount to saying that the successful succeeded. (Portes 1998: 5)

Among various definitions of social capital in the academic arena, perhaps the most durable one was presented by the French sociologist, Pierre Bourdieu. He posited this elusive concept as 'the aggregate of the actual or potential resources which are linked to possession of a durable network of more or less institutionalized relationships of mutual acquaintance or recognition – or in other words, to membership in a group' (Bourdieu 1986: 51). This definition makes it clear that social capital is decomposable into two elements: first, the sum and quality of resources; and second, the social relationships that allow individuals to access these resources (Portes 1998; Siisiainen 2000). Bourdieu's original definition emphasizes that the volume and quality of assets are dependent on the very potency of the social networks that one can effectively mobilize (Bourdieu 2005: 2, 198).

Due to refugees' specific vulnerabilities as non-citizens in the host country and little access to relief aid, social networks play a vital role in their economic lives in protracted contexts. As ample evidence shows, mutual assistance between different refugee households constitutes one of the principal livelihood strategies in prolonged refugee settings (Golooba-Mutebi 2004; Grabska 2005; Palmgren 2014). These examples of support within refugee populations are often referred to as a sign of refugees' communal resilience to survive effectively in times of stress, crisis and emergencies (Doron 2005: 184).

Refugees' networks also often go beyond national borders. In the recent literature on forced migration there has been a number of studies that have highlighted the role of transnational connections and, *inter alia*, the significance of access to remittances for refugees' economic survival (Al-Sharmani 2004; Doocy et al. 2011; Jacobsen et al. 2014; Lindley 2006, 2008, 2010; Monsutti 2005). These financial transfers from abroad are often viewed as not only a source of additional income for the recipient household but also a potential resource for contributing to poverty reduction in the recipient communities.

Despite the increasing focus on the role of social capital in refugees' livelihoods, the existing literature alarmingly obscures some important aspects of this capital. For example, as Devereux and Sabates-Wheeler (2004: 14) warn, there is a 'dark side' to informal assistance networks. It is widely acknowledged that charitable help sometimes causes a sense of defeat and shame in recipients of such aid (Davies 1996: 37; Devereux 2003: 16). In addition, some scholars see the formation of mutual support in deprived communities as an inescapable response to crisis and social breakdown (Griffiths et al. 2005; Zetter et al. 2005). Especially during times of severe scarcity of resources, the burden of assisting others can result in tension or resentment between members (Mosoetsa 2011). Without understanding these negative aspects entrenched in internal assistance practices, researchers can end up painting overly positive pictures of resilience, cohesion and benevolence among refugees.

More importantly, the elusive and intangible nature of social networks is often turned into a 'catch-all' concept. Since everyone has some form of social capital, it is very likely that researchers will come up with evidence that social networks play a role in refugees' economic activities. But it is necessary to differentiate the effects and roles of social capital for refugees with different socio-economic statuses and different institutional contexts. In his development of the original concept of social capital, Bourdieu aimed to highlight how different social classes form and reproduce themselves in relation to one another, with corresponding implications for different types of privilege, inequality and oppression (see also Fine 2006).

Over a protracted period of exile, each household in Buduburam constructed their own portfolio of resource networks, which played an essential role in sustaining their survival in the camp. Nevertheless, there was considerable internal differentiation in the extent and potency of social networks among households. While some had privileged access to socio-economic assets through their personal connections, others could draw upon only limited resources from their contacts. Crucially, internal differentiation in their social capital was often related to their lives prior to displacement. Drawing upon detailed analysis, I elucidate the differences inherent in the relational networks of households, and draw attention to the importance of historical inequalities and privileges from the pre-displacement period vis-à-vis refugees' socio-economic status during exile.

Repatriation and Economic Reintegration after Prolonged Exile

My field research overlapped with a period involving the large-scale repatriation of refugees from Ghana to Liberia, enabling me to expand the scope of the study and follow refugee returnees to their homeland in order to gather data on their economic reintegration back in Liberia.

Refugees' repatriation and reintegration have been under-theorized areas in forced migration. This limited theoretical attention is largely due to both a lack of data and some common myths or tropes within forced-migration policy that assume that return to the homeland is always the best solution for refugees. This belief is predicated on the assumption that post-repatriation life in the country of origin will necessarily be better than a life in exile (Hammond 1999: 230). Previous studies, however, paint less positive experiences for returning refugees undergoing processes of reintegration (Eastmond and Ojendal 1999; Lindley 2011; Marsden 1999; Omata 2013a; Rogge and Akol 1989). Among various difficulties, establishing a new economic base after lengthy exile is a particularly onerous challenge (see Jackson 1994; Kaun 2008; Stefansson 2004; Tapscott 1994).

On the other hand, some researchers have reported relatively auspicious cases. Sorensen (2000: 197), for example, in his discussion of the repatriation of Eritrean refugees from Sudan, reports that returnees managed to restore their livelihoods and improved their living conditions in a relatively short time, mainly because of an extensive range of coordinated support from refugee-assisting agencies as well as from the Eritrean government.

Although the current scholarship suggests considerable variations in levels of economic integration among returnees, the causes of these differences remain poorly understood. By drawing on the wider migration literature, however, some plausible hypotheses can be formed. For instance, if the nature of repatriation, especially after decades of exile, does not lead to a 'homecoming' in a familiar setting, but rather leads to 'a new life cycle in an unfamiliar environment' (Black and Koser 1999: 11–12), this implies a significant role for social networks in facilitating transitions following repatriation. In migration literature, the importance of personal or ethnic ties in arrival destinations is extensively documented; these linkages facilitate migrants in adjusting to a new place by helping them to find accommodation and employment opportunities, and to access social and economic information (Koser 1997: 600; Massey et al. 2008: 43; Poros 2001: 245; Vertovec 2009: 39). This book thus looks into refugees' repatriation through a social network lens and attempts to account for variations in levels of economic integration among returnees.

Also, in the existing literature, refugees' repatriation and reintegration are rarely investigated in relation to their exilic experiences. However, refugees' return decisions, and even the process of their economic reintegration, are deeply linked to their socio-economic conditions during exile and their livelihood networks (Omata 2013a, 2013b). Therefore, it is essential to examine repatriation and economic readjustment as a continuation of their experiences and resources during protracted displacement, rather than as an event that is independent from previous asylum experiences. Because I followed Liberian returnees from Ghana, I was able to observe and contextualize their economic transition upon return in relation to their socio-economic lives during exile.

Having obtained the 'best' durable solution, how did returnees perceive their post-repatriation life in Liberia compared to their experiences during exile? Upon return, were they able to construct meaningful economic foundations and ties in a new environment? Did the returnees improve their degree of 'self-reliance' upon repatriation? Were there any observable differences in the degree of economic reintegration? If so, what factors differentiated their economic adjustments? Did their personal networks, as I hypothesized, play a crucial role in their economic reintegration? I had a privileged opportunity to explore these compelling questions with returnees to Liberia from Buduburam, and discuss these research findings more extensively in Chapter 5.

A Note on Research Approaches and Methods

The Impact of the 2008 Refugee Protests in Buduburam

I commenced fieldwork for this study in 2008 during a period in which the Ghanaian government was tightening its refugee policy against the remaining Liberians in Ghana. This policy shift was triggered by the refugees' large-scale demonstrations against the UNHCR's promotion of local integration as a solution for Liberian refugees in Ghana, as explained above.

The consequences of these protests did not end with the arrest and deportation of demonstrators by the host government. The Ghanaian authorities took Liberians' refusal to be integrated into the country as an unacceptable insult to the hospitality of the government, which had accommodated them for nearly two decades. Incensed by the demonstrations, the minister of the interior, Kwamena Bartels, made an official statement on 1 April 2008 that all Liberian refugees should go back to

Liberia (MoI 2008). The government of Ghana subsequently expressed its intention to significantly reduce the residual number of Liberians in the country, as well as to break up Buduburam camp into more manageable, smaller pieces and to disperse the refugees to other parts of Ghana. The Ghanaian government also asked the UNHCR to apply the Cessation Clause to the refugee status of the residual Liberians in the country. Apparently, the protracted life of Liberian refugees in Buduburam was entering its final phase.

Concurrently, a tripartite committee comprising the governments of Ghana and Liberia and the UNHCR was formed in April 2008. By agreement, the UNHCR commenced the orderly voluntary repatriation of camp residents to Liberia in April 2008, involving an increase in the financial incentive offered to returnees, which went from $5 to $100 (for a person below the age of 18, the amount was $50).

Liberian refugees in Buduburam had been unwilling to repatriate to Liberia despite the UNHCR's previous efforts to promote a repatriation programme (Essuman-Johnson 2011: 117). This time, in 2008, the reaction of the refugees changed after seeing the deployment of much tougher measures by the Ghanaians. Under strong pressure from the national authorities and international refugee regime to repatriate, many Liberian refugees decided to leave Ghana for Liberia. According to UNHCR internal statistics, more than 9,000 Liberians, about 40 per cent of the Buduburam refugee population, returned to Liberia between April 2008 and March 2009 under the UNHCR's repatriation package (UNHCR 2009).

These policy shifts had an important impact on my research. At the outset of my fieldwork in Ghana, this latest repatriation programme was ongoing, and many of my interviewees were choosing to repatriate. Given the magnitude of repatriation, as noted above, I extended my fieldwork period so as to follow repatriating refugees from Buduburam back to Liberia, allowing me to study their post-return economic reintegration.

My Life as a Researcher in Buduburam

During thirteen months of research between 2008 and 2009, in order to obtain a better understanding of Buduburam refugee life, I lived inside the camp with two male Liberian refugees for over ten months. My co-residents were Philip and Sam. Philip was in his mid thirties and Sam was in his early twenties. Philip ran his own camp-based organization (CBO), providing school education for refugees in Buduburam camp, and also worked as a pastor. Initially I thought that both Philip and Sam were unmarried. Sam was, but later I found out that Philip had a wife and son, even though they had never lived in Ghana as refugees. He had met his wife in Liberia and had got married there before he left the country in 1999. His wife and son had stayed in Liberia throughout the country's civil war, which lasted from 1989 to 2003.

The relationship between Philip and Sam was not clear to me at first. Due to their hierarchical relation, I first assumed that they were related. There was, however, no biological tie between them. Sam had at one time been a student at Philip's school, but he had had to stop his schooling as he was unable to afford to pay his tuition fees. Impressed by Sam's school performance, Philip had personally helped him continue his schooling. In exchange, Sam had started working for Philip as a housekeeper. When I started fieldwork in 2008, Sam had finished his high-school education in the camp some years earlier, but had continued working for Philip.

During the research, I attempted to adopt a similar lifestyle to that of camp residents. For instance, I always bought daily necessities and food such as vegetables, fish, meat and pasta from shops owned by Liberian refugees. I frequently ate out at canteens and fast-food stands and enjoyed (warm) beer at bars inside the camp. I shared the latrines and open shower space used by refugee residents. I purchased prepaid mobile-phone cards from refugee sellers, and used internet cafés in the camp whenever I needed to access my e-mail. In early 2009, our house faced a shortage of water when the tank we were using ran dry. I could perhaps have purchased water from other tanks but I did not do so. Instead, as my co-residents did, I minimized water usage and only took a bath once in a while.

In addition, I tried to become familiar with the Liberian refugee community as an external researcher. In particular, I did a lot of 'hanging out' (Rodgers 2004: 48) with refugees, which was not necessarily directly related to the research project. I participated in a youth football team as an assistant coach. Whenever the team played a game, I went to watch and cheered them on. Together with other football coaches, I occasionally went to a 'theatre' in the camp to see international football matches. Watching football was for my personal interest. Nevertheless, as football was undoubtedly the most popular sport for Liberians, I came to meet many refugees there. Also, I joined church prayers on Sundays whenever I was invited by refugees. There was always a moment when new church-goers were introduced to those gathered at the beginning of prayer meetings, and social hours after the meeting. Church visiting was thus a useful way to introduce myself and to explain what I was doing to many refugees at the same time.

Although I encountered numerous inconveniences, living with refugees in the camp returned tremendous rewards. For example, I could expand my contacts with refugees through my co-resident, Philip. Owing to his activities in the camp through his CBO and church, Philip had wide networks including other Liberian residents, and he put me in touch with other key refugee informants. Also, I was able to garner a clear sense of living costs in the camp as I understood the exact prices of household items and services, including food, water, clothing, transportation, internet access and pre-paid phone credit. This local knowledge proved to be essential, especially when I started to gather quantitative data from refugee households.

Data Collection

The main empirical data, including both qualitative and quantitative data, was collected during thirteen months of research in Ghana and Liberia between 2008 and 2009. During this period of fieldwork in West Africa, I conducted a total of some 400 interviews with refugee households and non-refugee stakeholders, including staff members of the UNHCR, government officials in charge of refugee issues and Ghanaian villagers living in the area of the camp.

In addition to a large volume of qualitative data, in the later stages of fieldwork I gathered a significant volume of quantitative data on sources of income and food, and on patterns of expenditure from sample households. As few previous studies of Liberians in Buduburam provide any convincing quantitative data on their economic status and living conditions, I considered it important to complement my qualitative data with numerical evidence.

After my departure from West Africa in late 2009, I maintained regular communication with my refugee interviewees. Especially after the announcement of the Cessation Clause for Liberian refugees, I conducted intensive follow-up interviews by telephone and Skype with residual households in Ghana between 2012 and 2013.

During data collection, I faced myriad ethical dilemmas. Provision of financial reward for interviewees was one of these challenges. Before beginning the fieldwork, I made a clear decision not to give financial compensation to any interviewees for their participation in the study, regardless of their living conditions. At a first interview, I articulated this rule to my interviewees and asked whether they were still comfortable about being interviewed by me. When I explained this no-financial-compensation rule to interviewees, several refugees asked me what benefit my research would bring to them if I was not financially compensating them. In response to such an inquiry, I explained that my research project would in the end aim to generate a better understanding of the present refugee population among external stakeholders, and would eventually contribute to better policies for forced migrants in the future.

As the research progressed, however, I began to feel less comfortable with this prepared explanation. Extended interaction and participation in the daily life of the community deepened my understanding of the imminent and daunting challenges faced by refugees on a day-to-day basis. Importantly, for some households in the poorest economic category, their main concern was how to cope with the day at hand and the next few days. What they needed was immediate access to some material assistance such as cash and food, not vague hints about potential benefits which might in the future be brought to them or others like them as a consequence of my research. This dilemma continued to afflict me throughout fieldwork. In fact, I breached this rule several times with some interviewees. I made charitable donations to some refugees when I saw the urgency of their situation, such as when their children were suffering from severe malaria or typhoid but they did not have money for medical treatment.

Another ethical dilemma I confronted was how to deal with people's traumatic experiences during interviews. As I collected oral histories from refugees about their pre-flight life in Liberia, my questions had the potential to trigger some painful and negative memories and experiences. This moment often abruptly popped up during an interview; my interviewee's facial expression would suddenly turn gloomy and the tone of their voice lowered. Whenever I realized that an informant was uncomfortable or in distress, I immediately told interviewees that they did not have to say anything if it was uncomfortable for them. I also knew that I was in no position and had no capacity to assist them with the possible consequences of remembering such traumatic events.

In some cases, however, they continued to speak with long periods of silence, and sometimes tears. For example, Daniel, a thirty-five-year-old male refugee, spoke to me for nearly three hours about his and his family's traumatic experiences in Liberia; he was severely tortured by rebel soldiers, and his wife was raped by insurgents. He showed me his wounded knees because the rebel soldiers had hit his knees with their guns repeatedly. While he was talking, I listened to him without interruption. After listening to these bitter and graphic episodes, I was lost for words and remained speechless. At the end of his talk, he said: 'Thank you for listening and for your time and patience ... I haven't shared this story for many years. You are the first person in Ghana who sacrificed such long hours with me'.[6]

Paying attention to these negative signs often enables researchers to discover the different layers of refugees' experiences, which are not expressed in words. When 'negative evidence' (Ghorashi 2007: 126) such as a moment of silence or crying surfaced during an interview, I patiently tried to understand what was behind it. These unexpectedly long interviews consequently changed my daily interview schedule because it was so difficult for me to cut them short. At the same time, I felt a moral obligation to accept people's negative experiences as part of my research. As a consequence, I stopped viewing the interviews I conducted as simply a source of data from which I could extract a specific piece of information that I needed for my research.

Outline of the Book

This book consists of seven chapters. Chapter 1 sets out the research context of the book. It begins by providing general information about Buduburam camp and the demographics of the camp population, as well as distinctive features of Buduburam life. It moves to a brief explanation of Liberia's ethno-political landscape during the pre-civil war period, and the entrenched monopoly of economic and political power among Americo-Liberians – descendants of former liberated American slaves. This historical inequality is significant for understanding refugees' current socio-economic conditions in exile. The chapter also summarizes the root causes which brought about the forced displacement of Liberian refugees to Ghana, and finally highlights the increasingly inhospitable environment in which Liberian refugees have found themselves in their prolonged exile.

Chapter 2 presents an overview of livelihood activities employed by the Liberian refugee population in Buduburam camp. As my research progressed, the idealized image of Buduburam as an exemplary economic model sustained by refugee businesses started to fall apart. The research revealed that a key livelihood resource for refugees in the camp was not their commercial activities; instead, refugees highlighted the significance of access to overseas remittances as a main determinant of economic well-being. The chapter elucidates how remittances have contributed to sustaining the Buduburam refugee economy by introducing the concept of 'remittance clusters' to illustrate systematically how remittances 'trickle down' to non-recipients of remittances. Crucially, however, not all refugees had access to these social networks, and about half of the camp residents lived hand-to-mouth, relying on various types of mutual or charitable support from other refugees. By illustrating livelihood strategies employed by different groups of refugees, the chapter demonstrates the diverse realities of refugees' survival strategies and indicates the economic stratification behind the façade of a thriving economy.

With a wealth of quantitative evidence, Chapter 3 shows how refugees with different economic statuses made ends meet in the camp. Using an adaptation of the household economy approach, it presents a detailed analysis of the income sources, food consumption and patterns of expenditure of refugee households. The numerical data confirm that there is considerable economic inequality induced by access to remittances, and demonstrate which refugee households are managing and which are not, at what cost and under what conditions. The research also illustrates the ways in which refugees in the camp share and transfer resources to assist each other through various forms of relational networks. While the refugees' informal support is often painted as a sign of communal resilience or solidarity, mutual assistance among the poverty-stricken refugees in Buduburam was better characterized as 'shared destitution' (Leliveld 1991). Throughout the chapter, the quantitative data is brought to life by compelling narrative accounts describing how a 'decent life' exists alongside the grinding poverty in Buduburam camp.

Given the significant economic divisions within the Buduburam refugee population, Chapter 4 probes into the roots of inequality by employing a historical approach. Drawing upon life-history analysis, it first focuses on the wealthiest refugee groups and demonstrates the ways in which their social and economic privileges in Liberia have contributed to bringing them large sums of money through remittances. The chapter also investigates the difficult prewar life of indigent refugees in the camp, and illustrates the structural inequalities between richer and poorer refugees within the same refugee population. By situating refugees' current economic differences in the specific historical contexts of Liberia, the chapter unveils the hidden implications of class and privilege that are reflected in refugees' socio-economic status and livelihood strategies during exile.

Chapter 5 turns to refugees' experiences of repatriation and economic reintegration in Liberia. The chapter begins by looking into the dilemma of decision making about repatriation. For the majority of Liberians, the decision to repatriate after their protracted sojourn in Ghana was a much more complicated task than the original decision to seek asylum. Drawing from the study of returnees from Buduburam, the research shows the continuity of inequality from exile into post-repatriation life. In particular, the chapter looks into the different degrees of economic reintegration in the country of origin, and analyses what the factors are that underlay these variations. By 'following the people' on their repatriation journey, the findings reveal the relationship between people's economic status in exile and the level of reintegration upon repatriation, and they further challenge the idealization of repatriation as the 'best' solution for all refugees.

Returning the focus to Buduburam camp, Chapter 6 sheds light on how the remaining Liberian refugees in Ghana responded to the ending of their refugee status. In January 2012, the UNHCR announced the cessation of the refugee status of remaining Liberian refugees globally, given the restored peace and stability in Liberia. The remaining 11,000 Liberian refugees in Ghana were left with two options: either repatriate before the invocation of the Cessation Clause by the end of June 2012, or stay in Ghana to be locally integrated as citizens of the member countries of the Economic Community of West African States (ECOWAS). Again, depending largely on their socio-economic resources, the refugees responded differently to the sudden closure of their formal refugee status. Whereas some wealthier refugee households had more options and finally decided to repatriate to Liberia, those with scarce resources were often 'forcibly immobilised' (Lubkemann 2008a) in exile. Drawing upon follow-up interviews in 2012 and 2013, the chapter highlights the diverse reactions of refugees and sheds light on their dilemma, unfixedness and uncertainty in the face of the ending of their official refugee life. It also looks into ECOWAS-based integration and poses some crucial questions about the sustainability of this sub-regional 'solution'.

The concluding chapter revisits the feasibility of the self-reliant camp model in prolonged displacement. It unveils the role of UNHCR politics and interests behind the promotion of the self-reliant image of Buduburam. The chapter also addresses the neoliberal discourses that underpin and support the sector-wide promotion of refugees' self-reliance and the interest in the role of social networks. By integrating the findings, the final chapter offers a theoretically and empirically informed understanding of refugees' livelihoods, remittances, social capital and return migration in protracted contexts.

Notes

1. All dollar amounts are in US dollars.
2. Dick (2002b) is a report commissioned by UNHCR as part of its Protracted Refugee Situations Initiative. Therefore, to a certain extent, it is reasonable to think that the views presented in the article might have been influenced by staff members of the funding agency.
3. Interview, Accra, September 2008.
4. Related to the concept of self-reliance, some scholars explore the notion of 'self-sufficiency'. For instance, Fiddian-Qasmiyeh (2015) argues that there are diverse understandings of self- sufficiency. In the present book, I will use both self-reliance and self-sufficiency interchangeably.
5. Elsewhere, UNHCR's assistance programmes for refugee self-reliance tend in practice to be reduced to professional qualifications and income-generating techniques without taking the condition of refugees' rights and entitlements into consideration (see e.g. UNHCR 2007).
6. Interview, Buduburam, October 2008.

1

'Guests Who Stayed Too Long'

Refugee Lives in a Protracted Exile

This chapter provides the research context of this book. It first sketches out both the demographic and geographic information of the camp and its residents, as well as distinctive features of Buduburam refugee life. Then, in order to contextualize refugees' current living conditions in Ghana, the chapter takes a chronological approach, starting from Liberia's prewar era and moving though its civil war and on to refugees' displacement history, and then to their prolonged exile in Ghana. In particular, it details the recent socio-political environment surrounding the Liberian refugees in Buduburam.

Buduburam Refugee Camp: Location, Demography and Governance

The total number of Liberian refugees in Buduburam camp reached a peak of about 42,000 in 2003, but when my fieldwork began in 2008, the number of Liberian camp residents had fallen to about 18,000, in addition to a small number of refugees from other West African states. This Liberian refugee population had been listed as one of the thirty-eight major protracted situations by UNHCR (2004a: 10). There were no longer any makeshift tents in the camp as most of the refugees' houses had already been converted by refugees themselves into permanent structures built with bricks and cement.

The area of the camp was approximately 140 acres, although the camp boundary had never been defined clearly. Over time, due to the continuous influx of refugees from Liberia, refugees had spread beyond the designated site of the camp. Thus, in some areas surrounding the camp, the Liberian refugee population coexisted with local villagers.

Buduburam refugee camp was in a semi-urban area, approximately a one-hour drive from Accra, the capital of Ghana. The camp was established on one of Ghana's main highways, which follows the coastline of several West African states, making the camp relatively accessible. The semi-urban location of the camp had both advantages and disadvantages in terms of making a living. For refugees who were engaged in trade, the relative proximity of Accra was a major advantage for them, allowing them to purchase goods from markets there. Conversely, the locality constrained refugees' access to natural assets such as arable land and rivers. In and around the camp area, cultivatable land and natural water were very limited, reducing the options for subsistence farming.

The Ministry of the Interior is the governmental body responsible for issues regarding refugees in Ghana. Established in 1995 under the 1992 Ghana Refugee Law, the Ghana Refugee Board (GRB) was delegated to act on behalf of the ministry for the management of activities relating to refugees in the country, such as refugee status determination and refugees' welfare. For dealing with daily activities in the camp, the GRB officially mandated the camp management team as an on-site representative body of the GRB. To assist in carrying out the wide range of responsibilities assigned to the camp management team, there was the Liberian Refugee Welfare Council (LRWC), a formal leadership structure comprised of appointed members from the Liberian refugee community in Buduburam camp. Along with a chairperson appointed by the Ghanaian camp commandant (sometimes called the 'camp manager' by refugees), the LRWC board was composed of two co-chairpersons and four executive members.

Due to the frequent influx of Liberian refugees to the camp during the fourteen years of Liberia's civil war, the refugee community in Buduburam became quite diversified, with different tribal groups from both urban and rural backgrounds. It is said that there are sixteen identifiable indigenous ethnic groups in Liberia (Bøås 2015: 60; Olukoju 2006: 3), in addition to a small number of miscellaneous groups and the Americo-Liberians – descendants of liberated American slaves.

Because the Liberian civil war involved several ethnically based armed groups, there had been strong ethnic rivalry inside the camp. According to refugees who had lived in the camp since its foundation, tensions between different ethnicities in the camp reached a peak during the second half of the 1990s when military factions based on ethnicity mushroomed in Liberia. Some residents even began organizing camp-based political parties, which were mostly linked to specific tribes. However, the Ghanaian camp commandant saw the danger of increasing ethnic animosity between the refugees, and most of these political affiliations were subsequently dissolved.

At the time of my fieldwork, acute tension between different ethnic groups seemed no longer to exist or was at least largely diluted. At a micro-level, nevertheless, tribal solidarity of course remained among the camp residents and sometimes played an important part in their daily economic coping strategies. In particular, mutual help between members of the same tribal group or clan was widely observed. Additionally, as legacies of ethnic and political affiliations in the camp, county-based organizations still existed. Liberia consists of fifteen counties, which are mostly populated by specific ethnic groups. Within the camp population, those from the same county organized themselves and selected their own representative and executive body. Being part of these ethnic groupings often had economic implications for members as some of these organizations sometimes provided welfare support for their fellows when in an economic predicament.

Local Host Communities in and around Buduburam

The Gomoa district in which Buduburam camp was located is known as one of the poorest districts in Ghana (Porter et al. 2008: 235). Interviews with the local community confirmed that the area used to be a tiny village in what was virtually bush country, with very little commercial activity. There was unanimity among the Ghanaian interviewees that the development of this local area began after the arrival of Liberian refugees.

Despite the development induced by the influx of Liberian refugees, the economic level of local inhabitants had remained quite low. There were no official economic statistics at the district level in Ghana. According to my interviews with a Ghanaian bishop who had been living in the area since 1993, only a handful of local people could spend more than $1 per day for their own consumption besides food. When I asked twenty local villagers the question 'Who is better off, Ghanaians or Liberian refugees?' all but one answered that Liberians were better off than local Ghanaians.

Although the majority of the local people were considered poorer than the refugees, they did have some livelihood advantages over the Liberian exiles. Unlike refugees, they did not need to obtain permission from the government to apply for formal employment. Also, Ghanaians had better access to local markets, as refugees were often restricted to selling goods inside the camp area alone. Crucially, knowledge of local languages was a major asset for running local businesses as a command of English in the Buduburam area was not very strong.

The predominant livelihood activity of locals was the small-scale trading of groceries and other daily household items. Right next to the camp entrance, there was a Ghanaian market where many Liberians purchased their daily food and other necessities from Ghanaian traders. According to local merchants, the most important customers for Ghanaian retailers in the area were undoubtedly Liberian refugees residing in the camp. Edgar, a Ghanaian owner of a pharmacy in a village adjacent to the camp, told me:

> Normally, I receive twenty customers per day. Ten out of the twenty are Liberians [refugees]. A Liberian normally spends more money than a Ghanaian customer ... Before [repatriation started], I received many more Liberian customers. At its peak, I received almost fifty [Liberian customers] in one day ... In this area, all Ghanaian shop owners are benefiting from Liberians' money.[1]

I also saw other signs of interaction between refugees and Ghanaian villagers in the camp area. For example, many churches in and around the camp had both Liberians and locals in their congregations. Some friendly football matches were played between refugees and Ghanaian hosts. In the youth population, I observed several cases of intermarriage and dating between Ghanaians and refugees.

Whereas these observations and testimonies implied peaceful coexistence between local villagers and Liberian refugees, there was a view that, in recent years, the general relationship between Liberians and local people had cooled considerably, or even deteriorated. During my interviews with Liberian refugees, I occasionally heard complaints against Ghanaians. Some refugee business people said that economic transactions were almost entirely unilateral: only Ghanaian business people were benefiting from Liberian customers but not vice versa.

Also, I frequently heard from both refugees and local villagers about a land-related conflict between refugees and locals on excretion in the 'Gulf', a bushy area which many Liberians used as a latrine. In the camp, the use of public toilets was fee-based, so refugees without cash used this area regularly. In the local host community, this bushy area was perceived as a sacred place, and using it for excretion was seen as a disgrace and a huge insult against the (local) spirit. So whenever they found Liberians excreting there, Ghanaian villagers arrested and punished them violently. These incidents indicated that there was at least a certain level of tension between locals and refugees.

Distinctive Features of Buduburam Camp Life

Fee-Based Camp: 'Nothing Is Free!'

'Nothing is free in this camp!' I heard this sentence repeatedly from Liberian residents. This was indeed true. As briefly mentioned above, refugees in

Buduburam camp had to pay for basic services, including water, using a public latrine, medical treatment and electricity: for instance, 5 pesewas (3 to 4 cents) for a small bucket of water and 5 pesewas for each use of a public latrine. In addition, if a refugee was living outside the originally al-located camp area, they had to pay rent to a Ghanaian landlord. Monthly rent was roughly 10 GH₵ ($7) but normally refugees were required to pay at least twelve months' rent in advance.

Education in the camp was no exception. The annual tuition fee in 2008/9 for Buduburam Refugee Community School, the largest school in the camp, was 45 GH₵ ($33) for a twelve-year-old student and 202.50 GH₵ ($150) for a eighteen-year-old student. Vocational training in the camp also required registration fees and the cost of any materials used (for example, buying cloth to learn sewing skills).[2] At the time of my field-work, the only apparently free service for refugees was the provision of a food ration by UNHCR and the World Food Programme (WFP) for targeted vulnerable groups of refugees such as those who were chroni-cally ill or HIV positive. This food assistance programme was in any case terminated in late 2009.

An experienced UNHCR field officer in Ghana told me that making Buduburam a fee-based camp had led to (or had created) 'a strong drive for refugees to make a living on their own'.[3] But for the majority of Liberian exiles, it was a major source of frustration or even distress to have to meet their own basic living expenses (see also Hardgrove 2009: 489). Many refugees asked me whether it was normal for refugees to pay for everything in other refugee camps outside Ghana.

The fee-based camp life had inevitably created disparities among ref-ugees in their ability to access services. For example, households with limited financial capacity could not provide even primary education for their children and were unable to receive necessary medical treatment. Chapter 3 will provide a detailed quantitative analysis of how fee-based camp management burdened refugees and forced them to compromise on their fundamental needs.

Freedom of Movement and Access to the Camp

Host governments in the Global South often shackle refugees' mobility outside camps to prevent them from melting into the host economy and fuelling competition with locals or taking away employment opportunities from them (Werker 2007: 471). However, unlike many refugee-receiving countries in Africa where refugees' mobility is constrained, the Ghanaian government in principle respected the freedom of movement for refugees as enshrined in the 1951 UN Refugee Convention. Liberian refugees could go virtually anywhere in Ghana without restrictions. There was a local police station right next to the camp entrance but the police officers paid little attention to people's entry to and exit from the camp.

The open-entry character of Buduburam camp made the camp accessible to people other than Liberian refugees, such as non-refugee Liberians, Ivorians, Sierra Leoneans, Nigerians and, of course, Ghanaians. I occasionally met non-refugee Liberians who were visiting their relatives or friends living in the camp. According to my interviews with camp-based Liberian refugees, after the resumption of the repatriation programme in April 2008, the influx of non-Liberian refugees, and particularly Ghanaians, intensified. These Ghanaians were coming into the camp and occupying vacant homesteads where repatriated Liberian refugee families used to live.

Buduburam: A Transit Point?

Buduburam camp was often referred to as a 'transit point' by both refugees and non-refugee actors. Whilst the term could be interpreted in several different ways, one of the meanings was related to trading activities carried out by Liberians. Taking advantage of freedom of movement, there were some Liberian business people who were using the camp as a transit centre for their sub-regional businesses.

The other, perhaps the most common, use of this expression was mainly among non-refugee stakeholders. The staff members of UNHCR tended towards the view that Liberian refugees in Buduburam camp chose to come to Ghana only for third-country resettlement rather than as a result of fleeing war or persecution. When Dick interviewed a UNHCR representative in 2000, the representative said to her, 'Liberians are staying in Ghana because of the resettlement programme' (Dick 2002a: 48). These types of simplistic interpretation of the reasons why remaining refugees continue to stay in Ghana apparently remained consistent over the years. In one of my interviews with a UNHCR programme officer, she explained: 'Liberian refugees came to Ghana for resettlement purposes. But now there is no resettlement opportunity for them. I don't understand why they are still staying in Buduburam camp'.[4]

From this point of view, the camp was perceived as a 'springboard' to a better life in developed countries in the North. During my research, indeed, I interviewed a good number of Liberian refugees who did come to Ghana for the purpose of resettlement. Because of the historical affiliation with the United States, in particular, the sentiment towards this 'dreamland' had spread into the Buduburam refugee population, and many Liberians thus saw the United States as a destination or the best place to live. Although UNHCR repeatedly emphasized that an avenue to resettlement had been closed for Liberian refugees, a considerable number of refugees, especially young people, still believed that the door for travelling to the Global North would open up again in the future.[5]

While I certainly acknowledged the popularity of resettlement among the camp's residents, at the same time I remained uncomfortable generalizing about 18,000 refugees in the camp as simply 'resettlement seekers'. I was also uncomfortable with the implication that these refugees had not experienced persecution or exposure to violence in Liberia. As I shall show in this book, however, there were many Liberians who had to flee to Ghana to escape threats to their physical security and dignity.

The Importance of Networks in Buduburam Daily Life

Life in Buduburam camp was governed by a complicated web of human relations and social institutions. From these interactions, personal connections beyond immediate kinship often emerged as an important source of resilience in the daily economic life of refugees.

The Virtue of Sharing: Mutual Support Networks

During my fieldwork, whenever I came back from interviews to my shared house in the evening, I almost always found some refugees in our small living space. They came to meet my co-resident, Philip, one of the respected refugee community leaders. Almost always they invited me to eat with them, and I usually joined them. After eating, these visitors normally stayed to chat and watch TV for about an hour. Then they returned to their own homes at around 8 or 9 p.m. Some of Philip's long-term friends came to eat at our place virtually every day. Their visits were very naturally accommodated – as if they were expected to come and eat there. Philip once explained to me that he always told Sam, his housekeeper, to prepare some extra food for these guests. I soon realized that these informal social activities had economic implications as well.

In the conventional definition, a household is a group of co-residents who draw upon a common pool of resources and function as a basic economic unit. However, a household often becomes fluid in a mobile population such as refugees, where people are often attached to several groups at the same time and are accustomed to sharing various resources with non-family members (Clark 2006: 3).

The household among the Buduburam refugee population certainly went beyond a group of co-residents. Inside the camp, the sharing, lending and borrowing of resources such as food, water and petty cash frequently took place between different households or between individuals linked through various connections such as kinship, clan, school and church membership. Whilst kinship was still a common element that cut across many refugee households, non-biological members were also accommodated as part of a household in some cases. As I shall show throughout this book, the transfer and exchange of resources between these refugees, especially underprivileged ones, were embedded in their daily survival strategies.

Religious Life: Churches as Spaces for Network-Building

In Buduburam camp, Christianity was the predominant religion, although Islam and traditional beliefs were also present on a smaller scale. According to statistics assembled by the LRWC in 2009, there were seventy-eight churches and one mosque in the camp. During fieldwork, I normally did not set up interviews with refugees on Sundays because going to church was almost a customary practice for many refugee households. There were also a certain number of refugees who commuted to Ghanaian churches outside Buduburam camp. After church prayers in the camp, 'social hours' always followed and the church served as an arena for people's social life as well. Refugees cooked and ate together. They shared their happiness, dreams, frustrations and plight with each other over Liberian dishes.

Besides the provision of religious services, churches often played a role in assisting Liberian refugees in the camp.[6] Especially in the early stage of their exile in Ghana, some of these faith-based organizations were engaged in providing social services, including vocational training and dealing with trauma (Dovlo and Sondah 2001: 207–8).

Furthermore, churches provided a space for networking. The active involvement of local Christian organizations contributed to connecting Liberian refugees with the host community and with Christian institutions abroad. Dick's (2002a: 34–35, 53) work also underlines the significance of churches as a means for Liberian refugees to access additional financial and material resources through social networks. The role of faith-based organizations in refugees' economic life will be highlighted in later chapters.

The Causes of Displacement: Liberian Prewar History and the Civil War

Buduburam refugee camp had a history of more than two decades. Despite their prolonged exile, refugees' camp life could not be divorced from the pre-displacement period in Liberia. In order to contextualize the economic lives of refugees in exile and the aftermath of repatriation and the cessation of refugee status, understanding Liberia's historical background, including Liberia's formation and prewar social structure, is essential. Therefore, this and the following sections provide a chronological account of refugees' displacement: from Liberia's prewar ethno-political landscape and its civil war to protracted exile in Ghana, including the attitudinal shifts among non-refugee stakeholders.

For the vast majority of Liberian refugees, the direct cause of their forced displacement was the fourteen-year civil war that began in 1989. The roots of this conflict, however, were deeply embedded in the formation of Liberia as a country in the early nineteenth century (Sesay 1996: 37). In 1821, Liberia was founded by interests in the United States as a means of resettling liberated American slaves, who were subsequently called Americo-Liberians. In the new country, the group of emancipated slaves from the United States established a political strategy of division between themselves and other, 'uncivilized' natives (Bøås 2015: 61). The Americo-Liberian 'elites' severely marginalized the indigenous population and ruled the nation as quasi-imperial masters until the late twentieth century (Adebajo 2002: 21; Ellis 2007: 43; Nmoma 1997: 3). Native Liberians were relegated to second-class status and were given only very limited access to social, political and economic power. As the subsequent chapters highlight, this historical inequality is significant for understanding the diverse realities of refugees' socio-economic conditions in exile, and even their post-refugee lives.

Accumulated frustration and anger towards the ruling elite paved the way for Samuel Doe, an indigenous military officer, who took over the country in a military coup in 1980. The insurgency led by Doe brought to an end the entrenched Americo-Liberian monopoly of power. Nevertheless, Doe's ruling regime was characterized by incompetence, corruption and cruelty (Cleaver and Massey 2006: 179). In a process often criticized as 'new tribalism', Doe started filling important government posts with people from his own ethnic group (Bøås 2015: 64; Sesay 1996: 37). Doe's regime experienced multiple coup attempts and a lack of support from the majority of Liberian citizens. Meanwhile, Charles Taylor, a former minister of Americo-Liberian origin who had fled Liberia for the United States, established an anti-Doe military movement during his exile. In December 1989, Taylor's army advanced into Liberia from Ivory Coast to oust Doe from power. This incursion marked the opening of the brutal fourteen-year civil war in Liberia (Cleaver and Massey 2006: 179–80).

Among Africa's numerous wars and conflicts, the Liberian war has been seen by some as one of the most destructive. In addition to more than 200,000 fatalities, it displaced one-third of the population internally or externally (Jackson 2006: 16–18). After 1990, owing to the protracted conflict, many uprooted Liberians intermittently sought refuge in Ghana, which at the time was deemed the most stable state in the sub-region. Because Ghana and Liberia do not share a border, Liberian refugees reached Ghana by sea, by road and on foot, through intervening countries, primarily Ivory Coast.[7]

Prolonged Exile, Aid Fatigue and Repatriation Pressure

Facing the incessant arrival of displaced Liberians, in 1990 the Ghanaian government organized an ad hoc committee and set up a refugee reception centre adjacent to Buduburam village, and this was the origin of the Buduburam refugee camp. In the very early phase of refugee inflows, the Ghanaian villagers generously provided food, water and blankets for displaced Liberians, which considerably contributed to refugees' survival during the emergency phase (Dick 2002b: 12). In 1991, UNHCR started supplying cooked meals, water, mattresses, blankets, charcoal and other necessities to the refugees. Tents were set up to accommodate the displaced Liberians. Around early 1993, UNHCR, in partnership with WFP, commenced the distribution of dry food rations. Cooking utensils were also provided to refugee households to enable them to cook at home. At this time, dry food rations were distributed to all refugee households in the camp. The basic needs of the Liberian refugees were, in general, met in the initial emergency phase of their exile in Ghana (Essuman-Johnson 1995, 2011).

As the exile of refugees extended due to the prolongation of the Liberian civil war, the environment surrounding the refugees became gradually inhospitable, and the refugees were encouraged by UNHCR to return to their home country. This trend strengthened especially after the ceasefire agreement of 2003. The internationally backed peace accord in 2003 helped the donor community to forge a consensus about Liberia's restored peace and stability. Thereafter, UNHCR started actively promoting the repatriation of refugees, whose number had risen to a peak of 42,000 in Ghana (UNHCR 2004b: 6). Between 2004 and 2007, UNHCR organized a large-scale repatriation promotion programme for Liberians in the sub-region and encouraged their return to Liberia. But because many were cautious about returning to the precarious political and economic situation in their country of origin (see also Agblorti 2011: 5; Essuman-Johnson 2011: 118), the number of repatriates from Ghana reached only 7,000 during the three-year repatriation programme. At the end of 2007, about 27,000 Liberian refugees remained in Ghana, which made the country host to the largest number of Liberian refugees in the world at that point (UNHCR 2008: 78). Given the limited success of UNHCR's promotion of repatriation, the Ghanaian administration expressed grave concern about the large number of Liberian refugees remaining in the country (Salducci 2008: 12).

As widely observed in protracted refugee situations worldwide, the volume of relief aid for Liberian refugees dwindled over the period of people's extended exile. According to Loescher (2001: 321–22), in the late 1990s the amount of funding from donor states for protracted refugees in Africa had already started declining, and refugees in West Africa, including Liberian refugees, were the principal losers as a result of the shortage. After the 2003 ceasefire agreement, the volume of aid for Liberian refugees was further cut. As the Liberian civil war had become a 'finished' issue in international politics, the global community's interest in assisting residual Liberian refugees was already very small. During an interview with UNHCR's senior programme officer in Ghana, he frankly confirmed that there was no more funding for Liberian exiles in Ghana as it was very difficult for UNHCR to 'sell this refugee population' to any donors.[8]

The dwindling financial support of the donor community also affected the provision of basic services and facilities in the camp. As described above, at the time of my study, camp residents were paying fees for basic services and items such as water, electricity and even using a public latrine. UNHCR provided subsidized services for medical treatment and primary education, but refugees still had to cover a large proportion of these expenses on their own.

Alongside the increasing emphasis on repatriation and the declining financial commitment of the donor community, UNHCR rapidly downscaled support for the livelihoods and welfare of residual refugees in Ghana. For instance, according to the director of one of the UNHCR implementing partners (IPs) operating in Buduburam, his NGO had previously provided a micro-loan programme for refugee entrepreneurs, designed to help refugees start new businesses in Ghana. But as the repatriation of refugees had to be prioritized in its assistance programmes after 2004, the organization had to close down its micro-finance project. Instead, the NGO focused on the provision of vocational skills such as carpentry and masonry to assist repatriates in contributing to Liberia's reconstruction process upon their return.

Ambiguous Legal Status: 'Are We Really Refugees?'

Despite more than a decade of exile, the legal status of Liberian refugees in Ghana remained unclear, and this had a profound impact on many aspects of their lives. At the inception of my fieldwork in 2008, in addition to around 18,000 refugees who were formally 'registered' with UNHCR, there was an unknown but considerable number of non-registered

Liberians living both in and outside the camp. Whilst there were no official statistics, UNHCR had previously estimated that there were over 4,000 of them (UNHCR 2004c: 161).

The large number of 'invisible' Liberian refugees emanated from UNHCR's sloppy registration exercises (see Omata 2011a). In August 2003, UNHCR and the GRB conducted a one-off comprehensive registration exercise for all refugees in Buduburam camp (UNHCR and WFP 2006: 11). Liberian refugees who had arrived in Ghana before the registration exercise and who managed to show up for it were granted prima facie refugee status and given a UNHCR ID card. After the registration exercise there was no update of new arrivals, meaning that those who arrived after it or who missed it never had an opportunity to receive an ID card.

Unregistered refugees without an ID card were excluded from any forms of protection and assistance provided by UNHCR. For instance, they were denied access to the UNHCR/WFP free food ration for vulnerable refugees, even if they met the vulnerability criteria. Unregistered refugees did not benefit from the subsidized medical services for refugees in the camp. They were unable to access vocational training programmes organized by UNHCR's IPs to learn new livelihood skills. Even if they decided to resume a new life in Liberia out of desperation, only the formally registered ID cardholders were able to access the UNHCR repatriation package to assist them in returning to Liberia.

Although UNHCR ID cardholders were formally granted refugee status in Ghana, even then they were perplexed about their legal status because of statements on their ID cards. The front of the card contained the refugee's picture and a serial number, and their name, date of birth, date of issue, sex and nationality. But the reverse contained the following contradictory statement with the signatures of both GRB and UNHCR officials: 'This card is for registration of asylum seekers. The card neither confers nor implies recognition of refugee status under international or domestic law. This card does not entitle the holder to any individual benefit from either UNHCR or the Government of the Republic of Ghana'.

In Ghana, even formally registered refugees were unable to prove or claim their refugee status by presenting any kind of document, since the UNHCR ID card was the only official item given to individual refugees. In fact, the unclear refugee status was a long-standing concern for Liberian refugees in Ghana, and was one of the major reasons why they adamantly resisted the local integration plan. Andrew, a Liberian refugee who had been living in Ghana since the early 1990s, expressed his view on his ambiguous refugee status: 'I think the reason why UNHCR and the Ghanaian government refuse to give us full refugee status is that if it is given to us, it will entail rights to better welfare for us. Then they will have more responsibilities for us. I believe this is what these stakeholders are afraid of'.[9]

UNHCR's Withdrawal Strategy

With the unsatisfactory results of the repatriation programme and very limited availability of resettlement opportunities for Liberian refugees, in about 2007 UNHCR shifted its focus to the local integration of the residual Liberian refugees in Ghana (Salducci 2008: 6). Nevertheless, the refugees strongly resisted local integration when they learned of UNHCR's intentions, leading to a series of refugee protests in Buduburam refugee camp, as explained in the previous chapter.[10]

Nonetheless, the series of refugee protests had little impact on UNHCR's integration plan. During my fieldwork between 2008 and 2009, UNHCR was quietly but gradually moving towards withdrawing from this long-term refugee population in Ghana. UNHCR's scenario for withdrawal envisaged two phases: first, reduce the number of Liberian refugees as much as possible by means of ongoing repatriation; second, bring in a local integration scheme for the remaining refugees in Ghana. In an interview with UNHCR's senior programme officer in August 2008, he explained frankly to me that:

> UNHCR cannot maintain the status quo of the care and maintenance stage of Liberian refugees any more. What UNHCR can do for them is to encourage and support their repatriation to Liberia ... Now the new stage of repatriation is ongoing. Four thousand refugees repatriated since this April [2008]. Our plan is to reduce the number of Liberian refugees to the level at which local integration would be more effective. The current number of refugees is too large for the Ghanaian government to feel comfortable to accept local integration.[11]

Given this exit strategy, between 2008 and 2009, UNHCR continued to put pressure on the remaining refugees in Ghana to repatriate, at times appearing almost threatening in their attempts. After extending the original deadline of the repatriation scheme from August 2008 to November 2008 and then to March 2009, UNHCR posted an announcement on bulletin boards inside the camp that it would terminate its food rations for vulnerable groups at the end of June 2009. The statement concluded: 'Refugees are therefore encouraged to make informed decisions about their future, including opting for voluntary repatriation before the deadline of 31 March 2009'. UNHCR's strategy appeared to work well, as the Buduburam refugee population was reduced by 40 per cent through the repatriation of more than 9,000 Liberians under this 'voluntary' programme.

Whereas the first part of UNHCR's scenario for withdrawal generally succeeded, by decreasing the number of refugees in Ghana, the second part did not. Not only the Liberian refugees, but also the government of Ghana – the key stakeholder in the local integration of refugees – expressed strong resistance to UNHCR's integration scheme and subsequent exit plan. In many refugee-receiving countries in the Global South, local integration is often a 'forbidden or evaded solution' due to the potential cost of integrating refugees (Hovil 2014). Similarly, the Ghanaian government saw that local integration of Liberian refugees would likely impose an increased burden on the government. In an interview with the secretary of the GRB, he described UNHCR's plan for local integration without detailed follow-up strategies as 'wholesale local integration for residual Liberians'.[12] The tone of the secretary's comments was ironic but acrimonious, corroborating the existence of acute tension, or at least major disagreements, between UNHCR and the host government over the issue of the residual refugees.

Despite resistance from both the Ghanaian government and the refugees, UNHCR completed its exit strategy in 2012. At the very beginning of 2012, UNHCR announced the cessation of refugee status of remaining Liberian refugees globally, given restored peace and stability in Liberia. The Liberian refugees in Ghana were left with two options: either repatriate before the invocation of the Cessation Clause by the end of June 2012, or remain in Ghana to be locally integrated as citizens of member countries of the Economic Community of West African States (ECOWAS). Chapter 6 provides more details of this significant moment, and specifically highlights refugees' diverse responses to the end of their 'formal' refugee life.

Making a Living within Constraints

As their exile grew longer, it became necessary for most of the refugees in the camp to make a living under increasingly adverse conditions. While humanitarian aid for Liberian refugees in Buduburam had sharply decreased, the formal and informal restrictions on making a livelihood remained and new restrictions emerged. Arguably, Ghana had been applauded by UNHCR as an exemplary model state regarding refugee protection. UNHCR wrote:

> Ghana has exemplified a number of objectives outlined in the Global Consultations and the Agenda for Protection, having ratified all the relevant refugee conventions, enacted national refugee law, and established a body for the determination of asylum claims. The refugee protection

regime has been substantially reinvigorated by new procedures for refugee status determination and other protection activities. (UNHCR 2004c: 160)

In contrast with this positive reputation, the Ghanaian administration had actually set up several bureaucratic impediments to refugees' economic activities, similar to those in other refugee-hosting countries in the Global South. For instance, refugees were required to obtain work permits from the government for formal employment, but this cumbersome process took several months, discouraging local employers from hiring refugees (also see Hampshire et al. 2008; Tanle 2013). The Ghanaian government did not recognize professional qualifications obtained in Liberia, such as those for doctors, nurses and teachers (Dick 2002b: 18; Porter et al. 2008: 238). Therefore, these professionals had to take their training again in Ghana to receive an official certificate from the Ghanaian authorities, an option which was not affordable for the majority of refugees. Also, certain types of employment such as taxi-driving and hairdressing were not open to foreigners, including refugees. These restrictions virtually excluded refugees from formal employment and forced them to work in informal sectors.

Even in the informal sector, refugees faced 'invisible' barriers erected by local people. Initially, the host community's generosity to displaced Liberians played an important role in helping refugees to survive during the emergency phase. In later years, however, many Ghanaians started seeing Liberians as their competitors as the refugee presence became pro-tracted (Agblorti 2011: 7). In local markets around the camp, Liberian refugees were not allowed to trade without paying so-called entry fees to Ghanaian market leaders. Even if refugees managed to pay these entrance fees, the xenophobic attitude of locals often limited refugees' income-generating activities in these markets. For example, Ghanaians did not buy goods from refugees if they found that they were Liberians, even though they were selling the same items as local traders (also see Hardgrove 2009: 486). There was a general perception among Ghanaians that Liberian refugees were better off than local people in neighbouring areas because of refugee businesses in the camp (Porter et al. 2008: 245). This perception had given rise to reluctance among locals to purchase from Liberian traders.

Given these formal and informal restrictions on their livelihoods, the economic activities undertaken by Liberian refugees were inevitably confined to inside and around Buduburam camp. This also meant that the customers of refugees' businesses were camp residents and a small number of nearby villagers.

As the period of asylum extended to nearly two decades, the refugees in Buduburam were treated as 'guests who stayed too long' by the host government and UNHCR. Apparently, when the main fieldwork of this book started in 2008, the occupants of Buduburam camp were already entering the final phase of their formal refugee life; UNHCR was closing off support for them and the host government was requesting their return to Liberia. Several years after Dick's insightful work in 2002, Porter et al. (2008: 236) questioned whether refugee self-reliance in Buduburam was still viable given the livelihood constraints and the lack of humanitarian assistance.

In the face of these unfavourable conditions, were all of the 18,000 refugees still able to achieve the self-reliant status claimed for them by UNHCR? Who failed and who managed, and at what cost? Drawing upon the empirical evidence, the following chapters will provide the answers to these compelling questions.

Notes

1. Interview, Buduburam, May 2009.
2. These vocational training programmes were provided by UNHCR and its implementing partners as free services. However, because the programmes did not cover the cost of materials, refugees who were not able to purchase them had to sit and watch other people's training. During my research I frequently observed such cases.
3. Interview, Accra, September 2008.
4. Interview, Accra, July 2009.
5. According to the sub-regional refugee coordinator of the US Embassy in Ghana, at the point of this study the only resettlement criterion to be applied to Liberian refugees wanting to move to the United States was family reunification, but new applications had already been suspended since 2006 due to recurrent fraud. Another possibility for migrating to the United States was to apply for an immigration visa, but this option was only available for refugees who had either parents, children or a spouse already living there.
6. See Fiddian-Qasmiyeh (2011) for the role of faith-based organizations in assisting refugees.
7. According to my interviews, a significant number of refugees first sought asylum in Ivory Coast, but they were forced out of the country because of intensified insecurity due to its internal conflict and because of acute animosity towards Liberians due to Charles Taylor's involvement in the conflict.
8. Interview, Accra, June 2009.
9. Interview, Buduburam, January 2009.
10. See Holzer (2012) for details of the refugee demonstrations.
11. Interview, Accra, August 2008.
12. Interview, Accra, July 2009.

2

Economic Lives in Buduram

With its brightly coloured houses, busy market, well-stocked supermarkets, corner shops, jewellery stores, hair salons, video clubs, cinema, churches, temples and mosques, it feels more like a small town than a refugee camp. Painters, musicians and cafés help enrich life in buzzing Buduram.

—UNHCR, 'A Tale of Two Camps'

Many donors, UNHCR staff members, and students visited us. But they just looked on the surface and never entered deeply inward. Please look into our life closely.

—Refugee representative of a community-based organization in Buduram

This chapter investigates the livelihood strategies of Liberian refugees in Buduram camp. Despite the challenging environment, refugees did establish their own economy. Whilst UNHCR highlighted refugee commerce as a sign of their economic success, a closer look suggests that in fact these business activities are of limited profitability. Instead, the importance of access to overseas remittances emerges as a key determinant of refugees' economic well-being. By illustrating livelihood strategies employed by different groups of refugees, this chapter demonstrates the diverse realities of refugees' survival and indicates the economic stratification behind the façade of a thriving economy.

Refugees' Commercial Activities in the Camp

Over-Concentration of 'Easy' Businesses

UNHCR's description of Buduram camp as 'bustling' is supported by the presence of a variety of business activities inside the camp. On one of the busy main streets, a visitor sees kiosks selling everyday goods, mini-theatres showing cable TV programmes, rental DVD shops, barbers, boutiques and tailoring shops, as well as a number of street vendors selling cooked food, used shoes and clothes. Because of the constant need to communicate with fellow refugees in and outside the camp, sellers of prepaid mobile phone cards were ubiquitous. I also saw other niche businesses such as a mortician, a home-made malaria drug seller and a mentor (who would provide religious lectures to other refugees for payment).

There were some positions in institutional employment, including teachers or administrative staff at the camp schools, and employees of UNHCR and its implementing partners (IPs). Those without specific livelihood skills often made a living by doing household work for other refugees. Agricultural work was less common, since, as noted earlier, the semi-urban environment of Buduburam camp meant there were limited agricultural activities due to little land availability and lack of access to natural water and irrigation.

Among the diverse camp businesses, by far the most common economic activities were selling drinking water and fruit (oranges and pineapples) and collecting used plastic containers of drinking water for resale. Due to the long dry season and scorching equatorial sun, water and juicy fruits were indispensable for the daily life of camp residents. In Ghana, sterilized water was sold in a small plastic bag for drinking. Since refugees dump these plastic bags all over the camp, many refugees walked around picking them up to sell Ghanaian recycling companies.

In addition to the existence of considerable demand, another reason why so many refugees were involved in these income-generating activities was that these businesses could be founded with relatively small financial capital and no specific skills – which is why they were referred to as 'easy' livelihoods by refugees in the camp. This low entry threshold, in turn, resulted in an over-concentration of refugees with limited assets in the area of accessible income-generating activities. One day, I counted the number of water sellers on the main street inside the camp. Within a radius of about twenty metres, I was able to locate three or four.

Vending small packs of water barely made them any profit, however. According to these retail water sellers, after working for a whole day under a scorching sun, their daily profit rarely went beyond 2 GH¢ ($1.48). One of them told me that this was just 'survival money' for her household, which included two school-age children. The market for fresh fruit was completely over-saturated too. Those who were engaged in these most common livelihood strategies were mostly refugees with few economic resources and marketable vocational skills, and they were all competing for a slice of the same pie.

As the heavy concentration of people in less capital-intensive businesses implies, in Buduburam camp one of the major impediments making a living was a lack of access to financial capital, which prevented them from embarking upon or expanding their business activities. As refugees were virtually excluded from the lending services of formal financial institutions in Ghana, micro-loan programmes were one of the few potential avenues to accessing financial assets for those without adequate resources. In line with the repatriation efforts of UNHCR in recent years, almost all of the assistance programmes to encourage business in Ghana had already closed down by the time of my field research. The sheer lack of access to financial capital trapped many refugees in 'easy-to-start' but less profitable subsistence activities.

Successful Businesses in the Camp

Throughout the fieldwork period, I purchased most of my daily necessities and services from refugee-owned shops inside the camp. However, in an early phase of research, it was not easy for me to ascertain which commercial activities were making a good profit. When I asked refugees which businesses were lucrative, they gave me different examples, such as restaurant ownership, mini-market trading, teaching and working for UNHCR's IPs. But perhaps the most frequent reply to my questions about successful businesses was running internet cafés.

In the camp area, there were three or four internet cafés owned by Liberian refugees. During my fieldwork, I regularly used these to check my e-mail, and found them usually crowded with refugees. Many of the customers were young Liberians who were communicating with relatives or friends abroad. Some of them were seeking financial help via the internet, registering themselves with so-called 'friend-searching websites' and looking for potential sponsorship from people they had never met (see Omata 2011b).

I became close to John, the refugee owner of one of these internet cafés. He had commenced his business in 2007 with remittance assistance from relatives and friends living in the United States. His internet café was open twenty-four hours a day, seven days a week. He had thirteen computers with internet access, one printer and one phone. According to John, when the café was busy, he received more than 100 customers a day, and his monthly turnover was about $1,000, which gave him a monthly profit of about $300 after deducting the maintenance costs.

Evidently, these businesses were quite profitable due to the endless need of refugees to stay in touch with their family or friends outside the camp, or to seek internet sponsors. Owing to the need for a large financial capital outlay and computer knowledge, however, ownership of these businesses was monopolized by a handful of 'privileged' refugees with access to such resources.

Mobility as a Livelihood Asset

De Haan and Van Ufford (2002: 4) have pointed to multi-directional mobility as a characteristic of West African livelihoods. Indeed, a good number of Liberians took advantage of the relative freedom of movement in Ghana and the sub-region for their economic subsistence. For instance, there were refugees who bought second-hand clothing in Accra's markets and sold it in the camp. Several Liberian women were moving back and forth between Buduburam and Tema, a harbour city near Accra, where they made money braiding hair. In order to save the cost of travelling, these women normally stayed in Tema for a week or so and slept outside while they were there.

Some refugees were engaged in cross-border livelihoods in the sub-region. There was a shuttle bus service between Buduburam camp and Monrovia, the Liberian capital. This transportation business was formally registered with the Ghanaian government and the Ghana Private Road Transportation Unit, and was run by Liberian refugees. Refugee mobile-phone sellers went to Nigeria, where they could purchase new or used phones 25 per cent cheaper than in Ghana, and they then sold them in the camp. Taking advantage of the well-organized second-hand car markets in Togo, some refugees were running businesses selling cars in the sub-region. They received an order from Liberia and went to Togo to buy used vehicles, and then drove them all the way to Liberia. Because of freedom of movement between the member countries of the Economic Community of West African States (ECOWAS), they did not need a visa to move between countries.[1] As an indication of their extensive mobility, there were some unofficial (illegal) FOREX bureaux inside the camp.

My co-resident's family was one of these mobile households. As described above, Philip – one of my two co-residents – had a wife and son in Liberia, but they occasionally visited Philip in Ghana. During my stay at his place, his wife came to Ghana for about three weeks using the shuttle-bus service between Ghana and Monrovia. The main purpose of her visit was to purchase used clothing in Accra (Ghana had a cheap but good-quality used clothing market, which served the sub-region) to sell at her own shop in Monrovia. She had been in this transnational trading business for the previous seven years and came to Ghana a few times a year. Philip himself occasionally moved back and forth between Ghana and Liberia as his wife did. While I was in Ghana, he took a three-week trip to Liberia with members of the Liberian diaspora living in the UK to link them with some potential business partners.

While certain refugees enjoyed the freedom of movement and open-entry rules of Buduburam, the number of these mobile entrepreneurs, especially those involved in transnational cross-border movement, was rather modest due to the specific livelihood skills necessary for such enterprises. Most of the transnational traders used to be engaged in similar types of sub-regional trading before displacement from Liberia, and were equipped with pre-existing business knowledge and networks. Also, the cost of transportation between the camp and neighbouring West African states was roughly $100, which was not easily afforded by refugees with limited economic resources.

Refugee Businesses: Evidence of Economic Success?

Buduburam refugee camp has been portrayed as an exemplary case of self-reliance, with the active informal economy operated by refugees used as a primary explanatory factor for their economic success. A column written by a UNHCR staff member in 2006 applauded refugees' entrepreneurship and painted Buduburam as an economically successful model. The author of the column writes: 'UNHCR and its local and overseas partners have helped to create the conditions that have allowed people to recreate their former lives, but it is above all the spirit of entrepreneurship and community – and the expertise of its inhabitants – that drives Buduburam' (UNHCR 2006).

Whilst UNHCR tended to see causal links between refugees' businesses and their economic prosperity, refugees themselves opposed this idea. With a few exceptions, such as owners of internet cafés, the testimonies of refugee entrepreneurs suggested that camp businesses were not as successful as they appeared to UNHCR officers, or to previous researchers.

Emmanuel, a former Liberian government official who sought refuge in Ghana in the early 1990s, ran a mini-supermarket selling daily necessities such as soap, drinking water, canned food and bread. Although his shop appeared to be popular, he revealed the challenges of making a good profit from his business: 'I have been in this business for so many years but I am just running this shop. I cannot make good profits from this business … There are six or seven shops like mine in the camp area. They are also selling almost exactly the same items … Competition is harsh here'.[2]

The limited profitability of camp businesses was echoed by other refugees, especially in the face of the decreasing camp population due to repatriation. Patricia, a single mother with a seven-year-old daughter, ran a popular hair salon inside the camp. When I visited her place for a scheduled interview, there were several customers waiting for her hairdressing service. But she lamented that the revenue generated by her salon had been on a downward trend for last few years, and sales had dropped steeply after April 2008 due to the repatriation of her most frequent customers. With decreasing revenue from her business, after deducting food and necessary non-food expenses, she complained that very little cash remained in her pocket. During an interview in July 2009, she appeared to be very uneasy as she needed to think soon about securing her daughter's tuition for the next academic year, starting in September.

In 'bustling Buduburam' there was indeed a wide range of commercial activity undertaken by refugees. While camp businesses appeared to be vibrant, most of them seemed to struggle to generate a meaningful profit, except a handful of capital-intensive enterprises such as internet cafés and transborder trading. If refugee businesses were not the central driver of the economic success of the camp, what had sustained the daily lives of refugees in Buduburam? The following section will investigate the significant role played by overseas remittances in underpinning the camp economy.

Access to Remittances: A Crucial Variable in Wealth Differentiation

Perceptions of wealth (and poverty) vary by locality and community (Devereux 2003; Hulme and Toye 2006; Moore et al. 1998). During the first three to four months of my field research, I frequently asked my refugee informants, 'What kind of people do you think are better off or wealthy in the camp?' Before fieldwork, like UNHCR and some previous researchers, I had assumed that the most common response would refer to 'those who own businesses'. However, the actual answer turned out to be 'those who have relatives or friends abroad' – because of the financial remittances received from them.

Right in front of the camp entrance, there were two Western Union branch offices. One morning, around 8 a.m., I was walking past these offices; they were not yet open but I saw ten or more people standing outside them, waiting. Because of their distinctive pronunciation of English, it was clear to me that most of them were Liberian refugees. According to camp residents, the majority of remittance beneficiaries received their overseas financial assistance through one of these two branches. These were of course open to everyone, including local villagers, but according to both branch managers, recipients were predominantly Liberian refugees.

The first Western Union branch in Buduburam was opened in 2005, immediately followed by the other in 2006. The Ghanaian manager of one of the branches commented as follows during an interview:

N.O.: Why did you start your branch here [in Buduburam]?

MANAGER: Before, many refugees were coming from the camp to Kasoa branch [a town located in a neighbouring district]. We knew there was massive demand for banking for refugees living in the camp.

N.O.: How many customers do you receive per day?

MANAGER: The number of customers per day is sixty to seventy now, but before we used to have 120 to 150 when the camp was packed.

N.O.: Are your customers Liberian refugees?

MANAGER: Yes, 99 per cent are Liberians. I can easily tell from their English accent. Also, in this area, very few locals have relatives abroad.[3]

In order to understand the importance of remittances to the economic life of the camp population, I obtained statistics from both of these Western Union branches concerning, first, the average amount of the monthly remittances, and second, the average number of monthly transactions handled by the two branches over the previous five years. Table 2.1 shows the aggregated data.

Table 2.1 can be read in two ways. With a steep drop in the number of monthly transactions, the monthly average amount recorded a sharp decline

Table 2.1 Monthly remittances and transactions through Western Union branches, Buduburam.

Year	Monthly average of total remittances received ($)	Fluctuation from previous year (%)	Average number of monthly transactions	Fluctuation from previous year (%)
2005	676,536	–	6,720	–
2006	806,402	19	7,756	15
2007	857,245	6	6,502	-16
2008	791,926	-8	6,876	6
2009	442,819	-44	3,736	-46

Source: Western Union branches in the Agricultural Development Bank and the Trust Bank, Buduburam.

Note: Each of the two Western Union branches is hosted inside Buduburam branches of other banks: the Agricultural Development Bank and the Trust Bank respectively. The remittance figures were provided to the author through the remittance service section of the headquarters of each bank.

in 2009. Even so, a monthly total of $442,819 in remittances is certainly not a negligible amount given the shrinking support provided by the international refugee regime to the refugee population. If the monthly average is multiplied, the annual total of remittances for 2009 came to more than $5.3 million, which is a considerable amount. The UNHCR annual budget for the whole of Ghana was only $6.1 million in 2008 (UNHCR 2008: 199).

Whereas almost all of the refugee interviewees agreed that access to financial remittances from abroad was a chief determinant of economic well-being within the refugee population, they also emphasized the considerable differences in the size, frequency and regularity of remittances between recipients. According to one refugee, who had access to sporadic remittances,

> There are differences even among remittance recipients, so you can't group us into one. For instance, some refugees regularly receive money, as if [the money sent was] their monthly salary; but others like me receive it only once in a while … Also, we receive different amounts of money. In my view, if one receives $100 regularly, every month, that person is better off or very much self-sufficient unless he has an extravagant life style.[4]

In addition, there was general consensus among the refugees that while remitters could potentially be anyone, substantial remittances were almost always sent by immediate kin such as recipients' parents, children, spouses and sometimes siblings. Many camp residents explained that there was in general a 'sense of obligation' in Liberian culture, requiring kin to assist each other. Compared to remittances from these closest biological links, financial support from extended family members such as uncles, aunts and cousins or friends was perceived as sporadic and unreliable, and involving smaller amounts, because of the weaker sense of obligation on the part of the remitters. The differences in the quality of overseas remittances will be explored throughout the book.

'Buduburam Is Living on Remittances'

At the time of my research, Shetha was in her mid thirties and had been living in the camp with her husband and son since 1996. She was a well-respected female refugee leader with multiple roles in the refugee community: she was a teacher at a refugee school and a project coordinator of a camp-based organization. Until her family's repatriation to Liberia in February 2009, she worked as one of my research assistants. A series of dialogues with Shetha gave me a number of crucial insights. As an example illustrating the importance of transnational ties for the camp-based refugees, she told me the following story:

At my church, we always pray for those living abroad. These include people in Liberia, other neighbouring countries and Western countries. But we put particular emphasis on those resettled in Western countries ... When church members lose their family members, it is always announced at the church. The news of death of family members in Liberia of course makes people feel sad. But the news of death of family members in the US or other Western countries is much more sensational and shocking to us. We all deplore: 'why did a person in the US need to die?' The level of our disappointment is much higher. We all know remittances from our fellow Liberians living in developed countries are our lifeline.[5]

Indeed, during fieldwork, many Liberian refugees stated that 'Buduburam is living on remittances'.

Households Living on Overseas Remittances

If a household is privileged to have access to a consistent flow of remittances over a long period of time, the family can often entirely depend on this financial assistance without being involved in other income-generating activities. Josh, one of the camp leaders in his early sixties, had been in Ghana since the 1990s. His main source of income was financial remittances from his wife and children, who had moved to Western countries:

I receive assistance from my family members abroad. My wife [59 years old], my daughter [40], my son [38], are living in the US, North Carolina. My youngest son [36] is in Canada. They assist me. ... My youngest son used to be in Buduburam. He fortunately got a scholarship and went to Canada in 1999. Now he is working there. He has his wife and son living in the camp. He remits to his wife regularly and she cooks for me every day. He also sends money to me sometimes ... Thank God, [because of the assistance] I don't have many problems here. Whatever I receive from my family, I can spend all for myself. My life is OK.[6]

In this case, Josh was both a direct and indirect beneficiary of remittances. Although he never revealed the amount of his remittances to me, it was evident that with access to multiple remitters in the United States and Canada, he had not had any welfare problems or concerns about meeting basic living needs in his daily life.

The Use of Remittances in the Buduburam Context

The existing literature indicates different uses of remittances by recipients. Remittances can strengthen the economic capabilities of recipient households with scant financial resources by being directly invested in small-scale businesses and other income-generating activities (Durand et al. 1996: 423; Orozco 2003: 12; Taylor 1999: 69). Similarly, some refugee recipients in Buduburam camp capitalized on remittances by establishing their own enterprises. For instance, John, the owner of the successful internet café mentioned earlier, mobilized $2,500 from his relatives and friends abroad to purchase his thirteen personal computers and to install other necessary internet infrastructure items to start his business. In John's case, remittances certainly gave him a greater level of 'power and choice' (Horst 2006b: 7).

Conversely, in the context of forced displacement, some scholars have noted that these financial resources are predominantly used to meet the daily expenses of households for such things as food, clothing and health care, rather than for saving or investment (see e.g. Lindley 2008; Suleri and Savage 2006). In Buduburam camp, many refugees said that financial resources from abroad were almost entirely used to meet the daily expenses of households rather than for investment. According to a senior refugee community leader in his early forties: 'The majority of remittance recipients get only modest amounts of money from abroad on an irregular basis. Remittances [to Buduburam camp] are more or less for their upkeep … I don't think people can make saving or investment from remittances'.[7]

These findings were initially perplexing or almost contradictory to me. As can be seen in Table 2.1, on average, $800,000 used to flow into the camp through Western Union branches on a monthly basis. Were remittances equally distributed among the refugee population? Or did a small group of refugees – including Josh, whom I mentioned above – received most of the money while a large number of occasional recipients shared a tiny proportion of the rest? The next chapter will explore this question with quantitative evidence.

'Wasted' Remittances or Spill-Over Benefits?

A good number of refugee interviewees, particularly those not in receipt of remittances, lamented that remittances were often 'wasted' on extravagant purchases. Morris, one of these critics, had been living in Buduburam since 2001. With a bachelor's degree in religious studies from the University of Liberia, he was seen as a 'mentor' among the refugee population by other Liberians. From his years of observation of other refugees, Morris told me:

> So many Liberians misused the money from relatives or friends in this camp. I know some cases that they lied to their parents to get remittances like, 'Oh, I got sick so please send money', or 'I want to go to vocational school so send tuitions'. But when they received money, they spent all money for drinking, buying clothes and playing with girls.[8]

Whilst Morris's view was generally shared by many interviewees, other refugees gave me a different perspective. They believed that the 'wasted' money was a crucial resource for sustaining the camp economy. Anita, the owner of a mini-bar in the camp, explained that many of her frequent customers were remittance recipients and that the money that they spent on drink and food at her bar was a source of income for her and her employees. When I interviewed Anita at her bar, she told me: 'Their lavish spending is often criticized but it is also true that they made others able to live on their remittances. If they kept their money for saving, the entire camp would immediately dry up!'[9]

Indeed, as her comments indicate, the majority of refugee businesses in the camp were heavily reliant on the remittance recipients as their main customers. The money sent from abroad was redistributed in the Buduburam economy through the consumption practices – regardless of whether they were extravagant or not – of the primary recipients, and sustained refugee enterprises.

'Remittance Clusters': The Redistribution of Remittances Inside the Camp

In Buduburam, remittances rarely stayed within the nuclear family of those that received them. Instead, the money was spent and benefited underprivileged households who had no direct access to remittances. Whereas secondary benefits of remittances within communities have been extensively reported in existing studies (Orozco 2004: 12; Taylor 1999: 70), there are two major gaps in their analyses. First, the current body of research largely fails to systematically illustrate how and among whom remitted money is shared. Second, human dynamics in the process of redistribution of remittances remain under-researched and poorly understood.

Within the Buduburam refugee population, remitted money was redistributed between different individuals and households through intricate webs of personal connections. Drawing from my observations and interviews with refugees, I developed the concept of a 'remittance cluster', defined as a group of refugees headed by someone in direct (both regular and irregular) receipt of remittances, and also comprising those not in receipt of remittances as indirect beneficiaries of remittances. I employ this notion as a means of systematically analysing how remittances 'trickle down' through social networks within the camp's refugee community. This concept also helps to capture the social dynamics, pressures and complex relationships between primary and secondary recipients of remittances.

The Anatomy of Remittance Clusters: The Case of Victoria

High-income households with constant access to remittances almost always supported individuals or households without direct access to them. According to Grace, who was supported by substantial remittances from her husband in the United States, she frequently provided financial assistance for three or four friends and also regularly gave away some food to them. A remittance cluster was also formed around those with relatively smaller remittances, such as Victoria.

Victoria received between $50 and $100 every month from her husband, who had settled in Norway in 2005 and worked as a cleaner in a hotel. Because the remittances were not enough to support her entirely, Victoria also sold oranges and drinking water in the camp. She did not have any immediate family members in Ghana but was living with two other families: Justina (Victoria's husband's childhood friend from Liberia) and her three children, and Anita (an eight-year-old girl, Victoria's husband's cousin's daughter). Victoria was the head of this remittance cluster, and other members made occasional financial and material contributions (see Figure 2.1).

In Victoria's case, the relationship between herself and others was relatively straightforward since Justina and Anita were her husband's childhood friend and an extended family member respectively, as her testimony below explains.

Justina is my husband's long-time friend since childhood in Liberia. They are both from the [same] small village in Grand Gedeh [one of Liberia's counties] and grew up together like a real family. I came to know her in

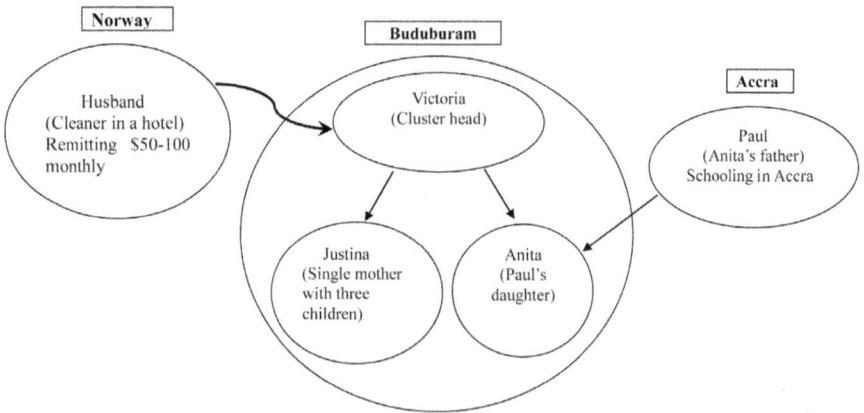

Figure 2.1 Victoria's remittance cluster

the camp through my husband ... She often came to my place to beg for food and money. She has three kids but no spouse ... I know how tough her life is so I took her in [in 2008]. Now she is selling oranges like I am doing. Sometimes she contributes small money to me.

Anita is a little girl. Her father is Paul. He is my husband's cousin. They [Paul and Victoria's husband] were close to each other [before Victoria's husband left] ... Anita's mother broke up with Paul and returned to Liberia. Paul is now in Accra for his study. He got a small scholarship from one of the camp-based organizations ... Paul left Anita to me in November 2008. My husband said we should take care of her ... Paul doesn't contribute to our household except Anita's school fees so all other expenditures are on me ... Before last November, a different relative was taking care of Anita but this person returned to Liberia.[10]

I observed and analysed many remittance clusters within the camp population but it is hard to generalize about the nature of the relationships between those of the same cluster. Evidently these clusters were not limited to kin relationships. If someone's steady boyfriend or girlfriend was a remittance recipient, there would almost always be support between these two. I also observed that these clusters were formed between members of the same tribe or clan, schoolmates, work colleagues and members of the same women's group.

Sometimes, a remittance cluster involved beneficiaries who are unknown to the primary remittance recipients and their remitters. At one point during fieldwork, for example, I came to understand that several different refugees were linked as part of one remittance cluster. Angela got irregular financial support from abroad and gave away a proportion of her remittances to Dora, her female colleague in a camp-based organization. Dora shared this pecuniary resource in the form of food with George, Dora's neighbour in the camp who came from the same village in Liberia. George occasionally brought his 'brothers' to Dora's place when they were having difficulties in securing their food. Neither Angela's remitter nor Angela herself was familiar with George and his friends at all.

Whereas there were a variety of relationships in this wealth redistribution structure, a tacit principle among refugees was that if someone is fortunate enough to find a remittance sponsor or gets regular support from a different remittance cluster, they should not stay in the same assistance umbrella. One of the women who headed a cluster told me that she used to assist three female-headed households in her neighbourhood but that she had recently stopped providing small amounts of cash and food to one of them as this woman had found an internet sponsor and had started receiving some financial assistance from this person.

Social Dynamics within Remittance Clusters

Viewed positively, the existence of remittance clusters in Buduburam camp signified safety nets for their members and was evidence of an interconnectedness between Liberian refugees. Although this is an accurate representation, there are also some complicating dynamics involved in the existence of clusters. For instance, a number of refugee interviewees, both male and female, pointed to issues involving expectations of sexual relationships between direct remittance recipients and those assisted by them. According to a Liberian refugee pastor in Buduburam, an artificial relationship or fake marriage was an economic coping mechanism for some people. There were two implications in this comment. First, indirect beneficiaries were often placed in a vulnerable position, where it was hard for them to resist the sexual demands of cluster heads. Second, some of those who were not in receipt of remittances deliberately set out to develop relationships with primary remittance beneficiaries in order to access their financial assets.

In refugee settings, single mothers sometimes agree to unattractive marriages or partnerships with men as their survival strategy (Andrews 2006: 76; Kaiser 2007: 310). During a focus-group interview with female-headed households in the camp, one participant with four children shared her story:

> First, they [her ex-partners] promised to support me, but after I got pregnant they left ... I was then living in deplorable conditions. I was seeking someone who can help me so I accepted the relationship ... If you don't have anyone to help you, your life in the camp is so tough. When our children are without food or medication for many days, it is hard for us to resist the relationship with promises.[11]

Some of the refugee interviewees who were part of a remittance cluster were fed up with the arrogance of their cluster heads. During an interview with Emerson, a twenty-three-year-old ex-unaccompanied minor, he expressed his frustration about some wealthy refugees although he frequently got indirect benefits from those in primary receipt of remittances.

N.O.: What do you think of rich refugees?

EMERSON: In this camp, money is power. Some Liberians receive a lot of money from the US. They behave like a king!

N.O.: How do they behave?

EMERSON: They make orders to other people. They said to me, 'Hey, go and get water' and, 'You, come here and buy phone credit for me'. They are like my boss.[12]

During my research, I frequently saw Emerson hanging around with his wealthy friends at bars or watching football games at mini-theatres in the camp. While I could not observe any hierarchical relationship between Emerson and these rich friends, he indicated that he suffered from an emotional conflict between his resentment of these perceived hierarchies and the financial circumstances that necessitated such relationships. Although some refugees without direct access to remittances strategically forged friendships or relationships with primary remittance recipients to access their financial resources, they often had to confront a sense of frustration or disgrace in formulating these connections.

Charity or Pressure to Share Remittances?

Cluster heads with access to remittances had their own views about those who relied on them. I asked primary remittance recipients why they shared resources with others although there was no biological link between them. Their common initial response was to say that they felt pity for those who did not have external support. In addition to this, however, many of them later revealed that it was difficult not to share with neighbours in the camp when one had resources from outside and other refugees were aware of it. They admitted that there was a degree of peer pressure from neighbours.

In her work on rural communities in Kenya, Francis notes that in a setting in which poverty is widespread, those with better asset profiles are often required to redistribute their resources:

> In a world where most people are very poor, people with slightly more resources had to make a choice. If they recognized the claims their kin and neighbours made on them, they would be locked into redistributing their incomes. The only way to withdraw from the web of redistribution was to withdraw socially and look elsewhere for one's own networks. (Francis 2000: 156)

Earlier, I briefly mentioned Angela, a twenty-five-year-old unmarried refugee. She was 'locked into' sharing her assets with others due to pressure from her neighbours. Angela received sporadic remittances of about $100 every one to two months. In addition to Dora, Angela occasionally gave food or small amounts of cash to some impoverished female-headed households with multiple children in her neighbourhood. In earlier interviews with Angela, when I questioned her about why she shared these limited remittances with non-biological family members, she told me that it was because they were all single mothers living in conditions of harsh poverty and that she felt particularly pressed to assist them as much as possible. But in subsequent interviews, she shared some of her bitter experiences with them:

> If I cook something and don't share with neighbours, they will call me a 'mean girl'. ... One evening, one of my neighbours was passing by my place and saw me cooking food. She asked for some food. I said to her it is not enough so I can't share today. Then she cursed me! From the next day, this woman stopped talking to me. She didn't talk to me until I prepared some food for her. Then she became friendly to me again ... Among my neighbours, there is an expectation of me because I am supported by someone abroad. If I let them down, they will exclude me.[13]

Cases like this demonstrate that it is possible for needy refugees to utilize peer pressure on well-off refugees in order to force them to share portions of their resources, sometimes resulting in feelings of guilt or fears of ostracism among well-off refugees.

The Breakdown of Remittance Clusters: The Global Financial Crisis and Repatriation

While remittances served as an underpinning of the camp economy, the remittance-based economy was gradually destabilized during my fieldwork. As Diaz-Briquets and Perez-Lopez (1997: 414) point out, the volume and frequency of remittances can be very volatile due to the employment conditions of remitters, particularly during a period of economic downturn. Because of the impact of the global financial crisis in 2008, I came across many cases in which remittance beneficiaries had recently lost their financial support due to the unemployment of remitters abroad.

For instance, Marian's household had a decent life due to a monthly remittance of $150 from her resettled elder sister in the United States until her sister lost her job as a helper at a nursing home in late 2008. Marian had two sons, aged twelve and seven, and the costs of their tuition were entirely covered by the financial support she received from her sister. After this support was suspended, both of her children had to stop their schooling. Although Marian had a small tailor's shop inside the camp, it did not generate an adequate income for all the basic necessities for her family. When she was chatting with me, she said, as if she was telling herself: 'Even if you have a family member abroad, you gotta be careful. All of sudden things can go bad for you ... One day you will find yourself income-less'.[14]

For indirect beneficiaries of remittances, the ongoing repatriation scheme was a source of major concern as the departure of cluster heads was tantamount to the loss of important spill-over benefits. Olga and her five school-age children, perhaps one of the most impoverished households in the camp, lost their important patron, Elsie, due to Elsie's return to Liberia:

> Elsie, my neighbour, was helping my family with food, clothing for kids, and small money. She sometimes helped my children's tuitions. She had

her husband in the US so she was receiving remittances constantly. But she left for Liberia in April 2008, right after the demonstrations. After her departure, our life got really tough. [Without her help] I can no longer send my children to school.[15]

During my research in 2008 and 2009, I repeatedly heard of similar stories from others who were part of remittance clusters. As shown in Table 2.1, when more than $800,000 was being remitted to people in the camp, remittances in Buduburam to a certain extent underpinned the livelihoods not only of direct recipients but also of a large number of indirect beneficiaries through spill-over benefits.

However, direct access to remittances – a product of transnational social networks – belongs to an individual recipient, not to the Buduburam refugee community. Once relatively well-to-do refugees began returning to Liberia, the camp economy was significantly undermined and posed particular survival challenges for those attached to remittance clusters. As illustrated here, the rapid repatriation, which was intensely promoted by UNHCR, generated profound negative impacts on Buduburam livelihoods as its by-product.

The Role of Internal Networks for Buduburam Livelihoods

One day I was talking to Korlison, the principal of the refugee school in the camp. At one point he commented on the nature of economic support among Liberians:

> Liberia is a small country with only three million people there. It is an interrelated society. Our notion of extended family is very broad so we have so many brothers, sisters, uncles and aunts. We form very intimate relations with each other and support one another even in the camp. I would say this interdependence is part of Liberian culture.

Other interviewees supported this view. Besides international connections for remittances, I observed various cases of refugees mobilizing personal or social relations to make ends meet. In particular, for those households with little access to transnational networks, these connections were indeed their lifelines. The following examples illustrate refugees' social networks inside and outside the camp, and their impacts on people's subsistence.

The Formation of New Bonds for Survival

The creation of new connections following displacement is often observed among refugee communities. In fact, some of these ties turn out to be between fictive kin and can become an important avenue for material and psychological assistance between refugees (see Al-Sharmani 2003, 2004; Amisi 2006; Andrews 2006).

Various types of new relationship emerged among non-related members in Buduburam camp. Richard, a twenty-seven-year-old male refugee, was the sole survivor of his family from the Liberian civil war. Richard's father was an influential chief in their home county and was known to be close to the former president, Samuel Doe, an affiliation that caused Richard's parents and other family members to be deliberately targeted by the rebels during the war. Richard alone managed to escape from Liberia, and in 1996 he reached Ghana, where he knew no one. He told me how he had been assisted by a senior member of his tribe during the initial stages of his life in Ghana.

N.O.: Why did you come to Ghana?

RICHARD: I had no plan to come to Ghana. I just jumped a boat [from Monrovia] and it took me to Ghana. After my arrival in Ghana, I came straight to the camp.

N.O.: Did you know anyone in the camp?

RICHARD: No, no one.

N.O.: So how did you manage? You were only fourteen years old.

RICHARD: First, I slept outside. I then searched inside the camp to find someone I may know. In doing so, I happen to meet an elder Liberian, Mr Sunday, who is from the same tribe. I explained my situation to him. He knew my father very well. He kindly accommodated me in his place.

This pattern of developing entirely new ties with people from the same tribe or clan was frequently observed in the camp. Especially for young refugees who had lost family members due to the civil war, support from members of their tribe upon arrival in Ghana often played a critical role in enabling them to survive in exile.

N.O.: Did he give you any other assistance?

RICHARD: Yes, he became my father in the camp. He was feeding me and sending me to school. Between 1996 and 2000, I was living in the same house with his family.

N.O.: Was he a rich person?

RICHARD: He was not working. But he had a brother in the US and was receiving remittances regularly so he could help me.

But this family-like relationship between Richard and the senior clan member ended abruptly with Mr Sunday's return to Liberia:

N.O.: Why did you move out of his place in 2000?

RICHARD: Mr Sunday repatriated to Liberia. His brother in the US suddenly passed away. He lost his income source so could no longer afford to stay in the camp without working. He decided to go back.

N.O.: Why didn't you go with him?

RICHARD: Initially, he was saying to me that he would observe the situation in Liberia and come back to the camp to pick me up. So I was waiting for him to return but he never returned.[16]

Richard's story reveals that this kind of semi-kinship was often of limited durability, as physical proximity was a sine qua non of maintaining this type of bond. Similarly, other refugees reported that once non-related members were resettled in a third country, their relationships with people still in the camp withered over a few years as they embarked on their new life in a new destination. These testimonies suggest that the enduring sense of obligation in these relationships might not be as strong as that between real blood kindred.

Building Livelihoods from Personal Contacts: The Case of James

In the camp, refugees' livelihood strategies changed during exile depending on the expansion and contraction of their personal connections. James, a twenty-five-year-old male, reached Ghana in 1994 via Ivory Coast without any of his immediate family. Below is a summary of interviews carried out with him about his livelihood trajectory between 1994 and 2008 to illustrate how he continued to build on his evolving support networks in the camp.[17]

Between 1994 and 2001, when James grew from an eleven-year-old boy to become a teenager, he relied on ties built during his flight from Liberia:

My village in Nimba [a county in Liberia] was attacked by the rebels. My family got scattered ... I escaped through bush and jungle and ended up in Ivory Coast. I did not know where I was going. I just joined other people running away from the rebels ... People escaped together from Liberia, they helped me during flight. This was a group of several Nimbanian families from the same area ... We decided to leave Ivory Coast for Ghana because it was very dangerous. I just followed other adults. After several weeks, we reached the [Buduburam] camp.

A few weeks later, one of these families found a house in the camp and accommodated me in one of their rooms ... This family started farming with other refugees so I started helping them with gardening [Irish] potatoes and potato leaves. I also helped them sell these crops ... But our gardening was not very successful. The farm land was tiny. It was often stopped because of dry weather and lack of water. We also did other petty works for money. During these years, I could not go to school at all. Just surviving ...

In 1998, my foster family left Ghana as the peace agreement was made in Liberia [this peace accord was broken later]. But I did not go with them ... After they left, my life became very hard. I did many things for food, like fishing frogs, gardening, washing and cleaning for other people ... These years [1998 to 2001], I really struggled to survive. I didn't know many people in the camp.

In Buduburam camp, new bonds between refugees who had not known each other before displacement often emerged while fleeing together from violence. Like James's example, some of these ties remained during exile and often played a critical role in enabling some refugees to survive in the camp.

James's personal connections in this early phase, however, were of limited potency and coverage. His foster family generously accommodated James in their household but they were unable to provide non-food necessities such as school. Since James was almost entirely dependent on this family, the eventual departure of the family immediately reduced his access to daily necessities.

Around 2002, James's life slowly improved as he expanded his connections, and from then until 2007 his connections with other Nimbanian refugees grew.

At that point, I had already lived in the camp for several years. I came to know more people [from the same ethnic group in Nimba county]. These friends and families sympathized with me and helped me in many ways ... I started spending more time in washing other people's clothing and cleaning up their house. These housekeeping works became my main income sources.

When I cleaned up their house, I was usually invited to eat together with them. They sometimes gave me some extra money. I accumulated money and went to school. At school, I made more friends. Some of them also helped me ... But when my money was finished, I had to stop schooling ... I could eat somehow but it was hard for me to make enough saving for school tuitions from these chores.

About three years ago [in 2005], I met Mr Freeman. My best friend in the camp knew Mr Freeman very well and introduced me to him ... He is a mature Liberian refugee from the same area [as me] in Nimba county. He used to live in the camp but got married to a Ghanaian woman and started living in Accra. But he visited the camp very often ... Freeman was working for an NGO in Accra ... He liked me and understood my situation. He

offered me a job. I started working at his home in Accra every two weekends as a housekeeper.

Before working at Freeman's place, my monthly income was between 10
and 15 GH₵ [$7 to $11]. Freeman gave 10 GH₵ every two weekends so I
made 20 GH₵ [$15] per month just from him. My life improved ... I con-
tinued to do housekeeping works in the camp during weekdays and worked
for Freeman over weekends.

During his exile in Buduburam, James's 'social world' (Marx 1990) gradually expanded and provided the medium for livelihood opportunities
that enabled him to survive in Ghana. But the repatriation programme
between 2008 and 2009 undermined James's Buduburam-based survival
strategies, and he found himself, in his mid twenties, once again in an in-
secure position, this time due to the departure of his sponsors.

Things changed so much this year [2008]. After [the] refugee demo, many
people started leaving Ghana. My helpers [James's client families who were
giving him housekeeping work] in the camp also left. I used to work for six
or seven families but now only one is remaining in the camp. I could no
longer make money and obtain food from housekeeping works. Everything
suddenly became upside down ...

It became difficult for me to live in the camp. So I asked Freeman to help
me. He said yes but told me I should go back to Liberia next year. I moved to
Freeman's place in July [2008] as a housekeeper. Freeman and his wife support me with food, accommodation and fees for computer school [Freeman
recommended that James acquire computer skills before repatriation in
order to get employment in Liberia]. But Freeman will only assist me until
the end of this year [2008]. Then I have to go back to Liberia ... I was not
planning to return yet. If I am with sponsors, I want to stay in Ghana.

When the Ghanaian government and UNHCR pressurized Liberians
to repatriate and most of James's clients departed, his subsistence based
on Buduburam connections was significantly undermined. In the face
of increasing adversity, James was compelled to repatriate to Liberia in
January 2009. During fieldwork in Liberia, I met him in Monrovia. I shall
come back to the post-repatriation life of James in Chapter 5.

Connections with the Ghanaian Community

Some researchers have pointed to the catalytic role of refugees' links
with host communities and local institutions for constructing their livelihoods (see e.g. Andrews 2003; Kaiser 2006). In the camp, churches often
served as a space in which bonding occurred between Liberian refugees
and the local population. Some Liberians built their livelihoods around

connections with the Ghanaian community, and some joint enterprises between refugees and Ghanaians from the same church emerged. These relationships were largely based on mutual business interests in exploring benefits from the purchasing power of the refugee community. The example of a wholesale water business described below was a typical case.

As I have written above, there were a great number of retail drinking-water sellers in the camp, and almost all of them purchased the water they sold from Liberian brokers who were connected with Ghanaian water companies. Prince, a Liberian male in his early thirties, was one of a few water wholesalers in the camp. He embarked on this business with his Ghanaian partner in 2004. The following excerpts from interviews with him highlight how his church linked him with the Ghanaian business community.

> I think there are two or three local water companies in this area. They normally have Liberian wholesalers residing in the camp. There are perhaps three or four [Liberian wholesalers] like me in this camp ... I got closer to a Ghanaian water producer through my church. This church has its headquarters in Ghana. I was a member of this branch church in Liberia. When I visited the headquarters in Accra, I met him. He wanted to expand his business inside the camp. So he brought water to me to sell in the camp. To sell inside the camp, it is better to have Liberian distributors.

Prince worked as a middleman to connect this local businessman to the camp population. The business ran well due to the incessant demand for water among camp residents.

> I buy one sack [thirty small bags of sterile water] at 50 pesewas [35 cents] and sell it [to refugee retailers] with a 10 pesewas [7 cents] margin. This varies depending on the season, dry or rainy. In this camp, water is always in high demand. Especially in 2004, the camp was really packed. When we brought 500 sacks to the camp, all sacks were sold out in less than three hours [making about $35 profit]. The pace of sale is now slower. Now 500 sacks may take two to three days [to sell].
>
> In this kind of small-profit business, you have to be a wholesaler. Retailers can't make money. Imagine one sack of water is 60 pesewas [42 cents] and they sell it at 100 pesewas [70 cents]. After selling one sack [thirty small bags] of water, their profit is just 40 pesewas [28 cents]. Even if they manage to sell ten sacks [300 small bags] per day, their profit is 4 GH¢ [$2.80]. This is nothing. If they are only selling water, it is hard to sustain themselves.[18]

Prince's wholesale enterprise seemed to be constantly making substantial revenues because of little competition in the wholesale water business. In early 2009, Prince invested his profits from this enterprise in a second business, a small kiosk shop inside the camp.

Mutual Help within Isolated Groups

From their own experiences, Liberian refugees were very cognizant of the importance of being well connected with other refugee households, host communities, churches and especially those living abroad. To put it another way, refugees knew the high risk of being isolated from other households in the camp. Certain groups within the camp were nevertheless unwelcome among the rest of the refugee community, and consequently struggled to build their support networks with others. For instance, according to two commercial sex workers living in the camp, their neighbours were very aloof towards them due to the nature of their livelihood: 'My neighbours know what I am doing in Accra. I know they don't like my work ... They don't want to talk to me. Only greetings ... It is not easy for me to make friends with other residents in the camp'.[19]

Another excluded group in Buduburam camp was comprised of former combatants. Throughout fieldwork in Ghana, I often heard strong expressions from refugee interviewees of aversion to ex-soldiers. Many camp residents stigmatized them and saw them as 'troublemakers' or 'criminals', and kept their distance from them.

Whilst these groups of commercial sex workers and ex-combatants were isolated from the other refugees, they formulated their own mutual support networks with those in similar situations in order to cope with challenges. According to Campbell (2001), in South Africa, commercial sex workers' survival largely relied on support from their colleagues, especially in times of illness, hunger and death of family members. Sex workers in Buduburam camp employed similar strategies, and would take turns to go to Accra for their business, sharing some of the money they earned with those who stayed to take care of the children left behind.

In the case of former soldiers, they normally gathered in three particular quarters called 'gaps' or 'ghettos' where only those with a similar background were allowed to enter. Accompanied by other ex-soldiers, I was introduced to leaders in each of these three 'gaps' and was permitted to conduct several interviews with people there. Most of them came to these zones every day. One boss named Edwin explained how these 'gap' networks played an important role for these marginalized people: 'In "gaps", we are like one big family. We carry one another's burden. If I am in trouble, I go to "gap" and ask for help. We consult each other and discuss and share the problems. I feel most assured and eased when I am here'.[20]

This was a safety net developed by ex-combatants. While I was interviewing some members within these 'gaps', I frequently observed that they were giving away some portions of their food to others and sharing their cigarettes with other smokers.

Conclusion: The Importance of Social Networks and Remittances in Buduburam

Each refugee household in Buduburam built its own social world of relatives, neighbours, friends, local people and institutions, inside and outside the camp. There were, however, variations in the extent and strength of these networks between different households, and the quality of social assets affected the way refugees' formulated livelihood strategies in the camp. Transnational ties giving access to remittances were undoubtedly invaluable assets, which not only assisted the primary recipients but also the indirect beneficiaries through remittance clusters. Furthermore, financial resources from abroad also contributed to the informal refugee businesses in the camp. Indeed, as many refugees said, remittances were a 'lifeline' for the refugee community in the face of decreasing international support.

But, critically, not all refugee households in the camp were incorporated into these remittance clusters or even had access to the spill-over benefits that remittances could bring. Poorer households benefited very little from the remittances circulating in the camp. For their survival, the majority of these indigent refugees were engaged in 'easy' livelihoods such as selling drinking water and fruit, but were unable to produce a meaningful income from them, despite years of effort.

During the fieldwork period, due to drastic changes in people's living environment, the remittance-based economy in the camp was collapsing. A considerable number of remittance recipients in Buduburam lost their support from abroad due to the unemployment of remitters as a result of the global economic slump in 2008. In addition, under strong pressure to repatriate, it seemed that many remittance recipients decided to return to Liberia. Their departure further reduced the influx of financial support into the camp, resulted in the erosion of remittance clusters and significantly destabilized the Buduburam refugee economy.

The findings of this chapter raise questions about the legitimacy of the self-reliant reputation of the Buduburam refugee population. In particular, although UNHCR had applauded the thriving commerce inside the camp as a sign of refugees' economic autonomy, the refugees' comments belied UNHCR's interpretation. Instead, refugees' testimonies emphasized the significance of remittances for the camp economy and indicated the economic inequality within the camp population – even before widespread repatriation had begun. Which view, that of refugees themselves or of UNHCR, is the more accurate description of the camp's economic life? The next chapter considers this crucial question through an analysis of quantitative data.

Notes

1. In theory, these refugees were required to present their passport when cross-ing the borders of ECOWAS states, but in reality many managed to pass through by showing their refugee ID card or paying a small bribe.
2. Interview, Buduburam, November 2008.
3. Interview, Buduburam, May 2009. Another reason why the manager could confirm that the predominant recipients were Liberian refugees was that refugees are required to show their UNHCR ID card whenever they receive remittances at these branches.
4. Interview, Buduburam, October 2008.
5. Interview, Buduburam, January 2009.
6. Interview, Buduburam, February 2009.
7. Interview, Buduburam, April 2009.
8. Interview, Buduburam, November 2008.
9. Interview, Buduburam, December 2008.
10. Interview, Buduburam, March 2009.
11. Focus-group interview, Buduburam, April 2009.
12. Interview, Buduburam, April 2009.
13. Interview, Buduburam, November 2008.
14. Interview, Buduburam, March 2009.
15. Interview, Buduburam, November 2008.
16. Interview, Buduburam, February 2009.
17. These interviews with James took place in Buduburam between September and December 2008.
18. Interview, Buduburam, May 2009.
19. Interview, Buduburam, June 2009.
20. Interview, Buduburam, June 2009.

3

The Household Economy
in the Camp

The higher amounts of remittances from external sources may be expected to make a significant difference to the overall welfare of the receiving households.

—Adriana Castaldo and Barry Reilly, 'Do Migrant Remittances Affect the Consumption Patterns of Albanian Households'

I have no helpers outside. So unfortunate … My main income source is collecting recyclable plastic bags for sale. My children are also collecting them in the camp … They need to work [to supplement the household income].

—A refugee single mother with five children in Buduburam

Drawing primarily upon qualitative research, the previous chapter demonstrated the importance of various types of support networks, including access to transnational remittances, for refugee livelihoods, and also indicated considerable economic stratification within the camp population. This chapter delves quantitatively into the findings from Chapter 2 and reveals how refugees with different economic statuses made ends meet. Were all refugee households able to meet their basic needs? How significant were remittances for refugees' economic life compared to their businesses? Did spill-over benefits of remittances enable indirect beneficiaries to meet their basic needs? How were households without access to even secondary benefits of remittances surviving? This chapter provides numerical responses to these questions and sheds light on the realities of refugees' living conditions behind the veneer of 'bustling Buduburam'. I have used an adaptation of the household economy approach in order to present a detailed analysis of the income sources, food consumption and patterns of expenditure of refugee households.

Administering the Household Economy Study

The household economy approach is instrumental for drawing a holistic picture of the way that people obtain things they need to survive such as food and cash. This method is typically conducted as part of a quick appraisal by consultancy teams who are assigned to carry out livelihood assessments of people within a relatively short period of fieldwork. In order to increase its reliability, accuracy and effectiveness, I commenced this quantitative study after having spent five to six months with refugees in the camp and having already sketched a fair picture of the economic structures of the Buduburam refugee community.

In this quantitative study, I asked the heads of sample households to record the following four categories of data about their own household.

1. Acquisition of food (types of food eaten, how they obtained them, how much they paid, including cooking costs);
2. Sharing of food (if they shared food with non-household members, then what and with whom they shared);
3. Sources of cash (how much cash they obtained and in what way);
4. Patterns of non-food expenditure (what else did they spend money on besides food).

The study was conducted over a period of three to seven months, depending on respondent households, since I needed longer to establish relationships with some refugees before asking them to participate. Because none of the sample households were engaged in agriculture for subsistence, I assumed that there would be very little seasonal variation in their income, food acquisition and expenses.

Wealth Breakdown and Selecting Sample Households

As explained in Chapter 2, my initial study of the camp established that access to remittances from overseas was a major factor that led to the stratification of economic status in Buduburam. By employing a method of wealth breakdown, with support from my refugee research assistants and other key refugee informants, I therefore established four different economic categories: high, middle, low, and very low income groups, largely based on degree of access to remittances.

Households in the high- and middle-income groups, constituting roughly 10 per cent and 30 per cent of the whole camp population respectively, were direct recipients of overseas remittances from relatives and friends in developed countries. The critical difference between the high- and middle-income groups was the amount of money remitted as well as its regularity and frequency. Those in the low- and very-low-income groups, respectively forming about 40 per cent and 20 per cent of refugees in Buduburam, did not have direct access to overseas remittances. The coping strategy of these lower economic groups was to combine various income-generating activities that produced only meagre incomes. For these underprivileged groups, whether they could get charitable support from wealthier refugees or not was critical for their daily life. Households in the very-low-income group had very little to no access even to secondary benefits of overseas remittances, which placed them at the bottom of the wealth distribution in the camp.

After a series of meetings with my research assistants, we came up with a list of relevant households that fitted the criteria of these wealth divisions. After careful triangulation, we finally chose eighteen sample respondents on the basis of four different economic categories. These preparatory efforts contributed considerably to enhancing the representativeness of the sample households and to reducing sampling bias, despite the relatively small sample size.

Since the accuracy of data and consistent recording were a sine qua non for this study, I carefully chose households that I trusted for the samples.[1] Before asking them to record their household economic data, I had already conducted several interviews with members of each household. From these interactions, I had a sense that they had forged a certain level of mutual trust with me and appeared to be comfortable participating in my research – for example, they showed up on time for interviews and expressed definite interest in what I was doing with the research. After having selected candidate households, I explained to the members of these households the specific purpose of the quantitative research. I continuously observed a no-pay policy with the selected families. I only provided notebooks and pens for recording. At the end of their data recording, however, I gave them a small amount of cash as a token of my gratitude since they had recorded the data in most cases for several months.

Table 3.1 presents the demographic profile of the eighteen respondent households. I obtained data from four households from the high-income group, five households of middle-income status, five households of low-income and four households of very-low-income status.[2] I also tried to represent the social diversity of the refugee community in the camp. The size of household varied from one to eight persons, with an average of 3.5 people per household. The gender of the head of the household was balanced: seven male and eleven female. The length of their exile in Ghana varied between six and nineteen years. They were selected from diverse ethnic backgrounds.

Table 3.1 Demographic profile of the eighteen sample households

HH #	Name of HH head	Economic status	Number of HH members		Male or female head	Years in Ghana	Ethnicity
			Adult	Child (under 12)			
1	David	Very low	2	3	Male	11	Kpelle
2	Emily	Very low	2	4	Female	6	Grebo
3	Olivia	Very low	1	4	Female	6	Krahn
4	Stephanie	Very low	1	1	Female	7	Vai
5	Christiana	Low	4	0	Female	7	Kpelle
6	Emerson	Low	1	0	Male	9	Krahn
7	Esther	Low	1	2	Female	8	Krahn/Kru
8	Matilda	Low	1	2	Female	9	Vai
9	Richard	Low	3	2	Male	13	Sappo
10	Angela	Middle	1	0	Female	11	Krahn/Sappo
11	Joanna	Middle	1	1	Female	8	Vai
12	Mike	Middle	5	3	Male	19	Sappo
13	Martin	Middle	1	0	Male	16	Kru
14	Patricia	Middle	1	1	Female	11	Krahn
15	Jennifer	High	5	2	Female	19	Americo-Liberian
16	Jones	High	6	0	Male	9	Americo-Liberian/Sappo
17	Grace	High	1	0	Female	13	Americo-Liberian/Lorma
18	Terry	High	1	0	Male	13	Kru

Source: Household economic survey conducted by the author.

Snapshot of the Household Economy in Buduburam

Table 3.2 is a summary of monthly expenses and income per household in the different economic brackets in the camp. The table shows much higher level of expenses and income in the high-income households compared with the other three groups. With nearly 500 GH₵ ($370) income, a refugee family in the wealthiest quartile could still have excess cash of 44.7 GH₵ ($33) in their hands after spending 454.60 GH₵ ($336) on food and non-food items in a month.

In middle- and low-income households, both expenditure and income were significantly lower. In middle-income families, expenses per household were 164.60 GH₵ ($122), about one third of that of high-income households, and a household's income was a bit too small to cover their total expenditure. In the low-income category, households ran into greater deficits as their incomes were 76.60 GH₵ ($57), unable to cover their total spending. In the poorest division, the household economy was even further slimmed down. As I shall illustrate later, for those refugees with meagre incomes, the daily survival of household members was an immediate priority. They eked out a precarious living only by fully mobilizing their resource networks and changing their consumption patterns.

In the aggregated data, the food expenditures of the wealthier divisions, particularly the high-income group, may be inflated because those households with access to remittances frequently fed other refugees in the camp. Since it was impossible to separate out the food expenditure for these non-household members in their data, I present the total spending on food in this

Table 3.2 Monthly average income and expenditures per household in GH₵

	High income	Middle income	Low income	Very low income
A. Total income	499.30	160.30	76.60	39.50
B. Food expenditures	188.00	74.20	58.10	27.40
C. Non-food expenditures	266.60	90.40	38.00	10.40
D. Total expenditures (B+C)	454.60	164.60	96.10	37.80
E. Surplus/Deficit (A–D)	44.70	–4.30	–19.50	1.70
F. Average HH size (persons)	3.80	2.80	3.20	4.50

Note: 1 GH₵ is equivalent to $0.74.
Source: Household economic survey conducted by the author.

study. The details of exchange of food between different households will be explained later.

Food Acquisition and Consumption

Daily Diet

Table 3.2 shows large differences in food budgets between richer and poorer households. But how did these differences appear in their actual daily food consumption? With such a limited food budget, what did poorer households eat? I looked into the recording books of the sample households to see the actual content of their diet. As anticipated, there was a marked difference in the kinds of food consumed by the different wealth groups. Comparing food items, the high- and middle-income households enjoyed a good combination of meat, fish, vegetables, rice, pasta, milk and other ingredients in their diets, whereas relatively expensive items such as fish, meat and rice were rarely eaten by low-income families. The food consumption of very-low-income families was much simpler and expensive food items were completely absent.

With a significantly limited budget, very-low-income households regularly had a poor diet. For instance, I frequently found a combination of '*gari*, sugar, water' listed among the daily foodstuffs of impoverished households. *Gari* is coarse-ground, dried-cassava meal sold in small portions in plastic bags, costing usually 20 pesewas (14 cents). These indigent families added water and sugar to *gari* to increase its volume, and then drank it. Some refugees replaced *gari* with corn starch, which was equally cheap. This was one of the cheapest ways of eating in the camp, with a meal costing between 40 pesewas and 50 pesewas (28 cents to 35 cents) in total. This diet filled the stomach and provided some carbohydrates but very little nutrition, and thus was locally called the 'survival diet'. When people could not afford even this diet, drinking water alone was all that was consumed by very poor households. Olivia, the female head of a very-low-income family with four children, described to me how her household managed when they had no food: 'Once or twice or sometimes more in a week, we don't have any food. Nothing … On those days, we don't eat anything but instead we drink water … I learned if we drink a lot [of water], we feel full. After that, we just go to bed'.[3]

A reduction in the quality of diet is a common start to the sequence of a household's responses to a food crisis (Corbett 1988: 1104). In Buduburam, however, needy refugee families, including their children, constantly relied on less nutritious foodstuffs such as a combination of *gari*, sugar and water. Because food insecurity was chronic, they frequently had to resort to such a diet rather than treating it as a temporary reaction to a food shortage. As evidence of undesirable eating patterns in poorer refugee households, a nutrition survey conducted in the camp in 2007 by the National Catholic Secretariat, a UNHCR implementing partner in Ghana, found that nearly 30 per cent of the sampled children were considered at risk of acute malnutrition (NCS 2007: 25).

Sharing Food between Households

Acquisition of food from other households was an essential practice, especially for refugee families in a financial predicament. As I noted above, during fieldwork, some guests usually came to dinner at our shared house – mostly friends of Philip, my co-resident. Among these visitors, some came to our place to eat almost every night, and I later discovered that they were mostly economically underprivileged. Whilst the scale of sharing was hard to quantify, I asked the eighteen respondents to keep a record of what they shared and with whom whenever they gave away food to non-household members. Table 3.3 is a summary of the findings.

Refugees in the relatively well-to-do categories were expected to share their food with other refugees, particularly with those faced with economic adversity. Noticeably, the high-income households shared meals with others for nearly two-thirds of the month and the middle-income households one-third. For instance, Terry, head of a well-off individual household, received a monthly remittance of about 270 GH₵ ($200) from a relative in the United States. He shared his food with his friends and fellow churchgoers who had tougher living conditions for more than twenty of the thirty days of the month. These data again show that overseas remittances were redistributed within the camp from richer to poorer households in the form of food.

Table 3.3 Number of days of giving food to other households in a single month

High-income HH	17.5
Middle-income HH	11.2
Low-income HH	4.7
Very-low-income HH	3.5

Source: Household economic survey conducted by the author.

The WFP/UNHCR Food Ration: Did the Poorest Households Benefit?

During the fieldwork period, UNHCR and the World Food Programme (WFP) were still providing free food rations to vulnerable households containing those who were elderly, chronically ill, children affected by malnutrition, HIV and tuberculosis carriers, and the physically disabled. Of the eighteen sample households, four were recipients of this food assistance: Christiana (low income), Richard (low income), Matilda (low income) and David (very low income). However, it was apparent that not all the households who met UNHCR's criteria for vulnerabilities were receiving assistance.

There were four very-low-income households in the sample but only one of them, David's family, was identified as a vulnerable household by WFP and UNHCR. Of the three poorest non-recipient families, two were non-UNHCR ID card holders, so their existence was not even recognized in UNHCR's registration data. The remaining household was that of Stephanie, a single-mother with a four-year-old daughter, who was making only a sparse income from braiding hair and selling oranges in the camp.

Verdirame and Harrell-Bond have criticized UNHCR's 'immutable vulnerabilities' (Verdirame and Harrell-Bond 2005: 291) and warned against failing to assist refugees actually at risk. Although the plight of Stephanie's household, especially her daughter's poor nutrition status, was more than apparent to every refugee in the camp, they were not selected to receive the WFP/UNHCR food ration. In fact, Stephanie went to the UNHCR office in Accra twice to ask to be added to the list of recipients, but on both occasions she was unable to meet UNHCR protection officers even after waiting for many hours. She could not afford to travel to Accra for a third time, and was also too discouraged to chase the UNHCR further.

Even if a household did receive the monthly food ration, the amount of food was insufficient to feed a household for a month. For example, the following is a list of the contents of the food ration given to a household with four members: salt (one small plastic bag), oil (4 litres), beans (4 cups), corn porridge (4 cups), maize (50 kilogrammes). All four of the households receiving the food ration in this study agreed that the food provided normally lasted two weeks at most. Moreover, since maize was not the staple food of Liberians, recipient families sold a bag of maize to local Ghanaian traders in order to buy rice – Liberians' actual staple food. Due to the much higher price of rice than maize, however, the refugees almost always ended up with a smaller amount of rice.

During the research, I discussed this problem with WFP Ghana. Below is an excerpt from my interview with a WFP programme officer who was in charge of the distribution of the food ration in Buduburam camp.

N.O.: Why don't you provide rice for refugees? That's their staple food in Liberia.

PROGRAMME OFFICER: Simply, rice is more expensive than maize. If we use rice, we then significantly have to reduce the number of beneficiaries. Also, last year, the budget for Liberians further dropped. They need to understand that their support environment has changed. Even this free food ration for vulnerable households is expected to be terminated soon.[4]

As the comment above suggests, WFP was also phasing out assistance for the remaining Liberian refugees in Ghana. According to WFP's project document, written in 2007, the provision of food rations for targeted vulnerable groups in Buduburam was entering a final phase between 2007 and 2009. This document also indicates that the UN country team in Ghana had agreed to disengage from Liberian refugees in the country. In the section on its exit strategy, WFP writes: 'During this last phase of assistance WFP will work in synergy with UNHCR and the UN country team, the Government of Ghana and other partners to ensure a smooth transition and handover of responsibility [for remaining Liberian refugees]' (WFP 2007: 5).

In line with this exit plan, WFP terminated the provision of the food ration in late 2009. Although the amount contained in the food ration was not adequate, for recipient families it still constituted at least one of the avenues for food acquisition or a means of acquiring money to provide for their subsistence by selling its constituents.

Sources of Cash

A Breakdown of Income Sources

In Table 3.4 I have disaggregated the total cash incomes of households in the different economic categories by source.

The high-income households which participated in this survey were almost entirely reliant on remittances from abroad. The consistent flow of transnational support enabled them to live entirely on external financial assistance. For instance, the following is an excerpt from my interview with Jones, a thirty-six-year-old head of a household in the highest income quartile.

N.O.: How are you making life in the camp?

JONES: I teach at Buduburam community school [the largest refugee school in the camp] but this is just a small allowance. The major source of my income is support from my parents.

N.O.: Where do they live?

JONES: They live in Maryland, the United States.

N.O.: How much do they send you?

JONES: $150 per month. My wife also receives $150 from her relative every month so it will be a total of $300 budget for a month. In addition, during Christmas season, I receive $700 to $800 from them.

N.O.: Do you ask them to remit?

JONES: No, every twenty-fifth of the month they send money to us. It is regular.

N.O.: How big is your family [in the camp]?

JONES: Six. Me, my wife and four children.

N.O.: Are your remittances enough for your family?

JONES: Yeah, we are fine.[5]

Sample households in the middle economic stratum all had some income from small-scale businesses or jobs, but remittances and assistance from other refugees exceeded this amount.[6] Since both the low- and the

Table 3.4 Sources of monthly household income

	High income	Middle income	Low income	Very low income
Total monthly income in GH₵ (from Table 3.2)	499.30	160.30	76.60	39.50
Breakdown of income sources				
Business/employment/casual labour	3.0%	15.1%	67.1%	79.3%
Remittances	95.1%	44.2%	0.0%	0.0%
Assistance from other refugees/ institutions	1.5%	36.3%	28.5%	17.2%
Loan	0.0%	4.4%	1.2%	0.0%
Other sources	0.4%	0.0%	3.2%	3.5%

Note: 1 GH₵ is equivalent to $0.74.
Source: Household economic survey conducted by the author.

very-low-income household groups had no direct access to remittances, their very small income mostly derived from multiple casual labouring jobs and support from friends or neighbours.

In the previous chapter, I explored the limited profitability of businesses compared with that of remittances. The household economic study adds quantitative evidence on this issue. Joanna, head of one of the middle-income households, was making an income by selling home-made food and biscuits, but her monthly income from her business was about 25 GH₵ ($19). Meanwhile, she sporadically received a monthly remittance worth on average 40 GH₵ ($30) from her relatives and friends abroad, which made a larger contribution to her household budget.

The Challenges of Savings

The limited profitability of camp businesses in turn indicated that it was extremely difficult for refugee households without constant remittances to save any money. Without capital, sample respondents without access to regular remittances were unable to invest in themselves and pursue their socioeconomic betterment. For instance, Mike was a thirty-nine-year-old male breadwinner of a middle-class household comprised of himself, his wife, niece and five children. He was making ends meet by combining different petty trading businesses, irregular remittances and loans from other refugees. During one interview, he told me how he had been struggling to save some money to obtain a university education in Ghana. When I asked him whether he was approaching his goal, he replied with frustration: 'No! I don't feel like [I am] approaching to my goal at all … I started living in the camp since 1998 but I have no saving. Even for my daily life, I am sometimes relying on credits from other people in the camp. How can I go to university?'[7]

According to his economic data, although his household occasionally received small amounts of remittances from abroad, it was insufficient to cover all the expenditures of eight family members including five children of school age. He also had to allocate roughly 15 per cent of his total income to repaying his debts to other refugees.

Mike's view was repeated throughout the Buduburam refugee community. Except for a handful of wealthy refugees who received constant remittances from abroad, many residents saw little prospect in continuing their current life in Ghana.

No Profits from 'Easy' Livelihoods

In the previous chapter, I described certain types of income-generating activity employed by many low- and very-low-income households: for example, selling drinking water and fruit, picking up discarded plastic water bags for recycling and doing someone else's housekeeping tasks. Many of these households in the camp combined these livelihood activities. But in what Ellis characterized as 'the diversification alternative of the poor' (Ellis 2000: 97), all of their economic activities were low-paid, casual and unskilled jobs. Notwithstanding their long working hours, as the household economic data indicate, these 'easy' businesses generated only tiny amounts of cash on an irregular basis.

Earlier in this chapter, I wrote about Stephanie's family, who were living in dire poverty but were not given the WFP/UNHCR free food ration despite her household's eligibility under the vulnerability criteria. With limited access to financial capital and no specific vocational skills, Stephanie sold fruit in the camp for very meagre profits: 'I sell oranges on the main street in the camp. I purchase a half bag of oranges [about fifty oranges] for 3 GH₵ [$2.22]. This half bag lasts almost one week. When I sell all of them, I make roughly 5 GH₵ [$3.70]. Profit in a week is 2 GH₵ [$1.48]'.[8]

It is also plausible that Stephanie engaged in commercial sex work as an additional survival strategy. In her household economy record book, she would occasionally record a comparatively large sum of income such 15 GH₵ or 20 GH₵ ($11 or $15) in one day. Although she recorded these sums as 'money from hair-braiding' in her data book, the amounts recorded would have been abnormally high for this work. Later I discovered that Stephanie often went to Tema, a harbour town which is a suburb of Accra, where some refugee commercial sex workers went for work. It is likely that these relatively larger income entries were related to these visits, and in fact, most of her close friends and neighbours in the camp were aware that she was engaged in this survival strategy.

Patterns of Expenditure

As can be seen in Table 3.2, there were observable differences in the average expenditure of the different economic groups. In order to get a better idea of households' living conditions, I made a distinction between food and non-food expenses. The empirical studies of Albanian communities carried out by Castaldo and Reilly (2007: 39–41) revealed that households with external remittances allocated a larger proportion of their average budget for non-food items and durables compared with households not in receipt of remittances. Figure 3.1 shows a similar tendency in the sample households in the different economic brackets. As is clearly shown, the wealthier households were, the more non-food expenditures they had.

The higher percentage of non-food expenditure in richer households, and precisely the opposite in poorer households, was predictable. In order to gain a more detailed understanding of non-food expenditure,

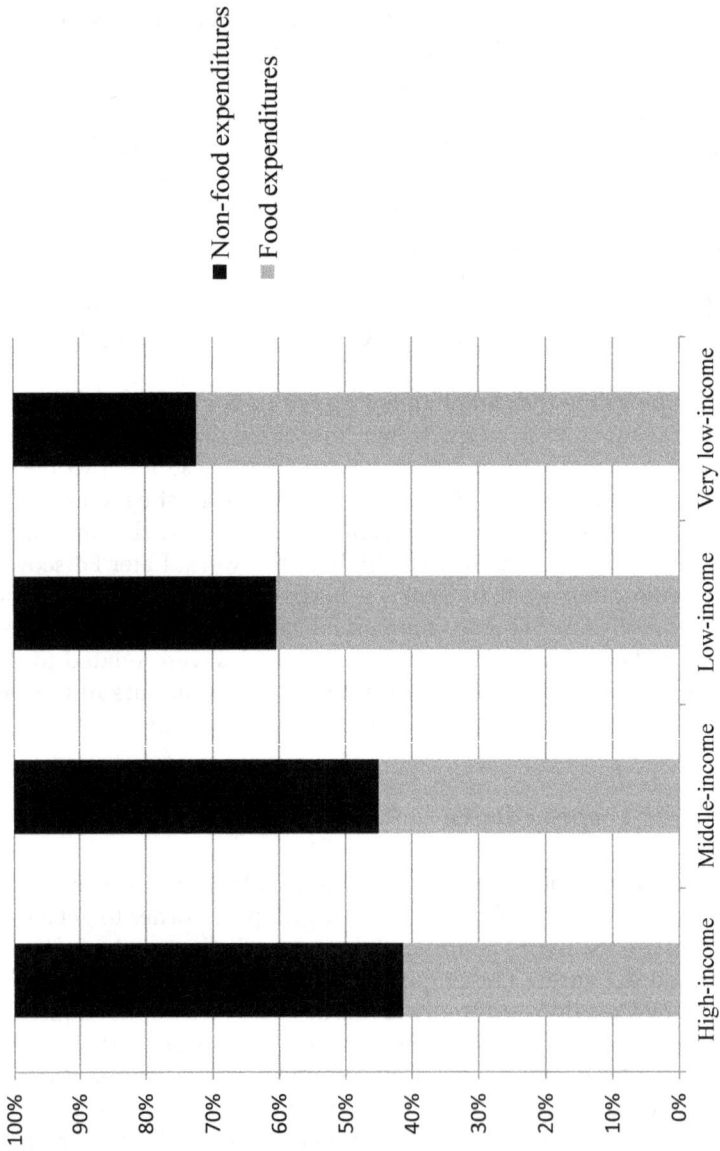

Figure 3.1 Percentage of food and non-food expenditures.
Source: Household economic survey conducted by the author.

I disaggregated the expenses for non-food items and services that the sample households purchased. Table 3.5 shows characteristics in the patterns of expenditure of the eighteen households in the four wealth groups.

A significant difference between richer and poorer households in their expenditure patterns becomes apparent at a glance. In order to illustrate this sharp difference, in the rest of this section I shall compare two cases: Grace's household from the high-income group and Emily's household from the very-low-income category.

Grace's Household: 'I Go To a Hair Salon Every Weekend'

At the time of my interview in 2009, Grace was thirty-five years old. She was a member of one of the wealthiest households in the camp due to consistent financial assistance from her Liberian husband living in the United States, receiving at least 405 GH¢ ($300) every month.

In the camp, the provision of basic services such as water, latrines and electricity was fee-based. For example, one use of a public toilet cost 5 pesewas (3 to 4 cents) and one bucket of water cost 5 pesewas. Regardless of economic categories, all households therefore allocated a proportion of their cash for these daily necessities. Grace was spending roughly 30 GH¢ ($22) every month to cover these expenses.

Like other better-off households, Grace owned a laptop, digital camera, DVD player and iPod. Her mobile phone was an advanced one with many technological features. Large expenditure on phone credit was a distinct characteristic of richer households since they frequently communicated with their remitters abroad. Grace normally allocated 20 GH¢ ($15) for communication every month since she called her husband and other family members in the United States and Liberia every weekend. She also spent some money on taking advanced training courses in such things as computer and interior design at vocational training schools in and outside the camp. For Grace, however, the purpose of taking these courses was not to strengthen her livelihood skills, since she did not need to work because of her reliable remittances. According to her, she went to vocational training school 'to keep herself busy', to avoid being bored.

Another trait of the spending patterns of high-income households was giving away a significant proportion of their cash to other refugees in the camp. As I explained in Chapter 2 in relation to the remittance clusters forged between recipients and non-recipients, well-off Liberians with constant remittances were important providers of cash to other refugees in the camp. As Table 3.5 illustrates, nearly a quarter of the expenditure of remittance-receiving households went on giving help to other refugees.

Table 3.5 Patterns of monthly non-food expenditures per household in GH¢

	High income		Middle income		Low income		Very low income	
	Expenses	%	Expenses	%	Expenses	%	Expenses	%
Daily necessities (i.e. water/latrine/soap)	23.4	8.8%	9.6	10.6%	16.2	42.6%	4.1	39.4%
Business material costs	0.0	0.0%	2.3	2.5%	11.8	31.1%	1.0	9.6%
Electricity/rent	9.1	3.4%	2.9	3.2%	0.5	1.3%	1.7	16.3%
Internet/phone	15.3	5.7%	4.3	4.8%	0.3	0.8%	0.0	0.0%
Education	66.1	24.8%	16.1	17.8%	2.2	5.8%	2.1	20.2%
Giving to others and to the church	62.1	23.3%	13.3	14.7%	2.1	5.5%	0.0	0.0%
Clothing	4.2	1.6%	12.1	13.4%	0.8	2.1%	0.1	1.0%
Debt repayment	0.0	0.0%	6.1	6.8%	1.0	2.6%	0.1	1.0%
Transportation	9.5	3.6%	7.9	8.7%	0.0	0.0%	0.4	3.8%
Medical costs	17.6	6.6%	10.0	11.1%	2.0	5.3%	0.9	8.7%
Miscellaneous	59.3	22.2%	5.8	6.4%	1.1	2.9%	0.0	0.0%
Total non-food expenditures (from Table 3.2)	266.6	100%	90.4	100%	38.0	100%	10.4	100%

Note: 1 GH¢ is equivalent to $0.74.
Source: Household economic survey conducted by the author.

Grace gave away at least 30 GH₵ ($22) per month to her friends and neighbours in various states of adversity.

In addition to charitable assistance, recipients of large remittances often spent a large amount of the money they received on socio-cultural activities in the camp, such as funerals or weddings. In general, these expenses were viewed by them as a necessary expenditure for maintaining the unity of the refugee community. In the case of funerals or weddings of intimate friends, Grace provided much larger sums of money to them than she gave in the form of regular help. In addition to these personal charity payments, she donated 30 GH₵ ($22) to her church every month.

As Table 3.5 shows, well-to-do families spent a significant amount of money on miscellaneous items. Among Grace's non-food expenditures, the most noticeable item was substantial spending on her appearance. According to her data record book, she routinely allocated from 50 GH₵ to 60 GH₵ ($37 to $44) a month to having her hair braided and fixing her nails, as well as purchasing cosmetic items such as hair spray and skin cream. When I visited Grace at her place, she occasionally received a pedicure from a Liberian beautician. I later discovered that this nail salon service cost 5 GH₵ ($3.70) each time, and that she was a frequent customer.

It was her habit to go to a hair salon in the camp every weekend before going to church. One Sunday, when I saw Grace on her way to church, she was in a beautiful African dress and wearing gold bracelets and necklaces. Every Sunday afternoon after church services, it was her customary practice to invite her friends, fellow churchgoers and neighbours for a 'feast' at her place, with a meal and drinks.

Emily's Household: 'I Don't Send My Children to a Clinic Because I Have No Money'

Emily was a single mother with five children. In prewar Liberia, she had lived in a suburb of Monrovia. Emily got married at the age of fourteen and had given birth to three children before being displaced by the civil war. Her husband was killed by the rebels during the war and she fled from Liberia with her children. After spending several years in Guinea and Ivory Coast, she reached Ghana in 2003. After her arrival in Buduburam, she gave birth to another two children, although her partner didn't take care of them and later disappeared from the camp.

Her family's dire living conditions were more than clear to me. When I first interviewed Emily, she was thirty-six years old but she looked much older: she had grey hair and a worn look with many wrinkles, which were perhaps signs of her long plight. According to her data record book, Emily's household was living on only 25 GH₵ to 35 GH₵ ($19 to $26) per month, which she got by gathering and selling discarded plastic bags and from the charity of other refugees. She needed to use most of the income for her family's diet, thus non-food expenditures in her household were very small and simple. The fee-based camp system burdened her family. Every month, the largest expense of 6 GH₵ to 8 GH₵ ($4 to $6) was allocated for paying for fundamental services such as water and latrine use. Her house did not have electricity since she had no money to allocate for it.

In the camp, households in economic difficulties attempted to reduce necessary costs by improvisation, although not always in a desirable or healthy manner. Emily's household collected rain water in buckets for their daily needs, including drinking and cooking. Her family regularly fetched water from the dirty pond behind the camp area, even though using this water resulted in some serious health consequences for her children. To reduce the expense of latrine use, Emily and her children often went deep into the bush around the camp. In an earlier chapter, I described the conflict between local people and refugees over the practice of excretion in one of these bushy areas, often called the Gulf, which was considered a sacred place by some groups of local Ghanaians. One evening, when Emily's daughter excreted in the Gulf, she was caught and severely beaten up by a Ghanaian villager.

As Table 3.5 shows, there was a sharp contrast in terms of educational expenditure between rich and poor families in this camp. Due to lack of financial means, none of Emily's five children were in school. Instead, they picked up discarded recyclable plastic bags to sell in order to supplement their subsistence. For impoverished families, it was very common that children of school age had never been to school while in exile but helped their household with its income-generating activities instead.

Inside the camp, tropical diseases such as malaria, cholera and typhoid were prevalent. During the research period, I observed that members of poorer households became ill more often than better-off ones, which appeared to be natural to me given their very poor diet and the poorer sanitary conditions they lived in. I also came to realize that the symptoms of illness in poorer households lingered for much longer than normal, perhaps because of malnutrition. Despite this, the medical expenses of indigent families were noticeably small. This held true for Emily's household. When I was reviewing her data, I initially thought that she had forgotten to record these expenses, but in reality she was unable to spend any money on these items. Whenever her children caught an illness, Emily had to deal with it by using boiled water, herbs and leaves from trees. According to her, this remedy cleans up the body by making the sick person sweat, but in fact it is damaging to the kidneys and the stomach.[9]

During fieldwork, I set myself a rule not to give financial compensation to my interviewees, but I was always tempted to break this no-pay rule whenever I interviewed Emily. In fact, I breached the rule several times and gave financial assistance when her children had severe bouts of malaria and typhoid and Emily could not afford medical treatment.

Clearly, Emily's family were living on the edge of survival and unable to pay for non-food needs such as medical and educational costs. Her family's (unhealthy) coping techniques resulted in unfortunate outcomes. Her six-year-old daughter, who had been constantly ill, lost her life because of the combination of severe malaria and malnutrition after my departure from Buduburam.

These two cases discussed above, describing the circumstances of Grace and Emily, demonstrate the striking difference in living conditions between wealthier and poorer households in terms of non-food expenditure. This finding held true with other sample families in Buduburam. Whilst high-income households could find money for their own comfort or entertainment thanks to regular assistance via remittances, families in the lowest income quartile were unable to meet even the fundamental needs of daily life.

How Self-Reliant Are the Buduburam Refugees?

Living Costs in the Camp

With the data gathered from the sample households, I estimated the living cost inside the camp. In a guide to using the 'household economy approach', Holzmann et al. (2008: 28) identified two thresholds as benchmarks: first, the survival threshold (income required to ensure food, costs associated with food preparation such as paraffin or firewood, and water for human consumption); second, the livelihood protection threshold (income required to cover medical and schooling expenses, and the costs of sustaining livelihoods above the survival threshold). I calculated the cost for the monthly survival threshold of one household (average 3.5 persons) in the camp as 103.8 GH₵ ($76.81). In addition, I calculated the monthly livelihood protection threshold for a household in the camp as 124.8 GH₵ ($92.35), which was the total of the survival threshold plus 21 GH₵ ($15.54) for medical, educational and livelihood-related expenditures.

Figure 3.2 shows the average income per household of the different economic groups in comparison with the livelihood protection and the survival thresholds. With its substantial remittance assistance, the wealthiest group had far more than an adequate income to achieve the livelihood protection threshold, whilst middle-income households managed to earn just enough to cover this higher benchmark. On the other hand, for those in the low- and very-low-income categories, their monetary income was far below the livelihood protection level and was not even enough to meet the survival threshold level, with a shortage of 27 GH₵ for the low-income group and 64 GH₵ for the poorest group. This means that households in the poorer categories were unable to generate adequate income to meet even their most essential needs in a sustainable manner.

Although actual living costs per household varied widely between refugee households, these thresholds capture an approximation of how much income is needed to manage in Buduburam. I asked all of the eighteen sample households how much money they needed to live decently for one month in the camp. The most frequent figure given was $100 (135 GH₵), which was similar to the amount of the livelihood protection threshold. Since I also lived in the camp throughout my fieldwork in Ghana, I can say that these figures conformed to my own observation and experience.

Importantly, Figure 3.2 calls into question the self-sufficient status of Buduburam-based refugees. Assuming the livelihood protection threshold is equivalent to the cost of securing self-reliance in the camp, households in the low- and very-low-income groups, which constituted about 60 per cent of the entire refugee population, completely failed to meet the threshold. As the case of Emily reveals, impoverished households in the camp had

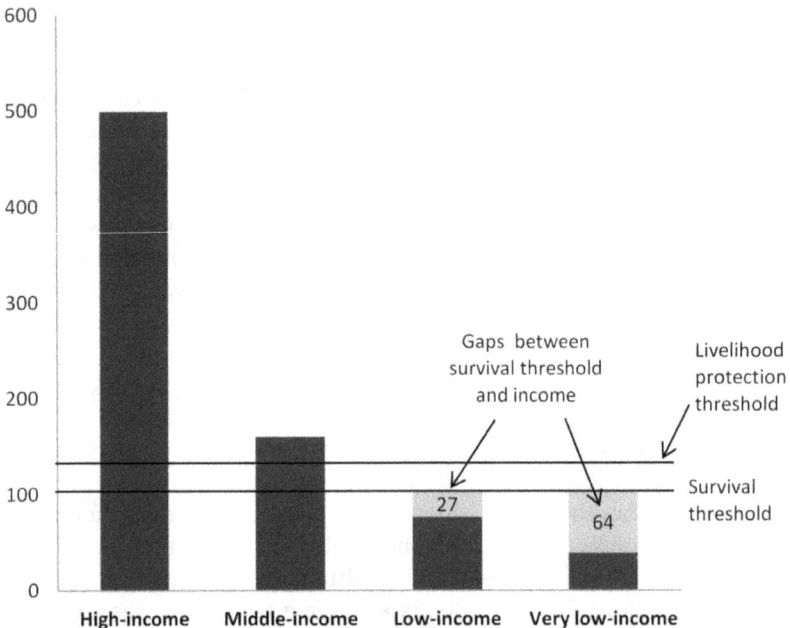

Figure 3.2 Monthly income in comparison with livelihood protection and survival threshold, income numbers given in GH₵.
Source: Household economic survey conducted by the author.

to make trade-offs or simply had to give up even the most fundamental goods or services because of their desperate financial condition.

Understanding Assistance Networks between Refugee Households

Whom Do They Share With?

Using the concept of remittance clusters, as described in the previous chapter, I discussed the significance of mutual support among the camp population. The data gathered for the household economy study provided quantitative evidence on the important roles of networks in the daily life of refugee households. But with whom did refugees share their resources?

There has been considerable debate about whether social capital is a public good that can benefit a wider group of people, rather than the sole property of individuals. Although Bourdieu (1986: 52) sees the existence of social networks as not naturally given but rather a product of investment strategies aimed at establishing social relationships, Putnam insists that 'unlike conventional capital, social capital is a "public good", that is, it is not the private property of those who benefit from it' (Putnam 1993b: 4). In Putnam's interpretation, if one is part of a community in which a norm of cooperation and helpfulness is widespread, one can readily derive benefits from other people's assets even if one does little or nothing to maintain them.

To understand the nature of assistance networks between households in Buduburam, I used the data I collected to trace the relationships between givers and recipients of cash and food. These patterns of connection were hard to generalize and often multiple relationships existed in one household's resource network. In this Liberian community, the ad hoc transfer or exchange of minor resources took place throughout the camp, while constant sharing or giving out of substantial resources was limited to those in denser relationships; this corresponds to Bourdieu's interpretation of social networks as non-public goods.

According to the data recorded by the respondent households, I very often found that the term 'friend' referred to a person with whom they shared or to whom they gave food or cash. However, transfers of major resources did not occur between 'mere friends' but usually required a more significant attachment or bond, such as kinship or long-term romantic relationships. For instance, Martin, one of the participants in the survey, was fed every day by his girlfriend, who received financial support from her brothers in the Unites States. He also received part of her remittance whenever she received some money. As the case of Martin indicates, if someone's boyfriend or girlfriend is a constant remittance recipient, they very often received large spill-over benefits from these heads of remittance clusters. The other types of 'friend' used as a resource avenue encompassed friends from childhood in Liberia and those who had experienced a difficult period together during exile. Mere acquaintance was too weak to induce the significant sharing of limited resources.

Throughout this book, in describing inter-household sharing within the Liberian refugee community, I have intentionally avoided using terms such as mutual support 'mechanism' or internal safety-net 'system'. I do not want to create the impression by using these terms that the assistance networks were structured in the camp population as an automatic system that would indiscriminately assist and sustain any destitute and vulnerable households in a predicament.

Mutual Support or Shared Destitution?

The above examples mainly involve a transfer of resources from high-income and middle-income refugees to low-income and very-low-income ones with no direct access to overseas remittances. Moral responsibility to assist those who were more destitute was also observed among the poverty-stricken refugees and a certain number of low-income households gave away their scarce resources to refugees in the poorest category. But sharing between the bottom two groups sometimes entailed tensions or even engendered conflictual relationships between them. The following case of Kevin and Emily is an illustrative example.

As we saw earlier, Emily headed a household containing five children, and she struggled to secure even the most basic necessities from her meagre income. Emily had a very close association with Kevin's family because Samantha, Kevin's wife, was a childhood friend of Emily's – they came from the same village in Liberia. Kevin worked for one of the UNHCR implementing partner NGOs in the camp. With no access to either direct or indirect remittance benefits, Kevin had to sustain his family, consisting of his wife and five-year-old daughter, on his monthly salary from this NGO.

From Emily's data record book, evidently she and her children were heavily reliant on donations from Kevin in terms of food. During the fieldwork period, I visited Kevin's place frequently and almost always saw Emily's family there. It was a daily habit for Emily and her children to come to Kevin's place to receive portions of meals. Whereas both families faced survival challenges, the economic status of Kevin's family was a bit better due to his regular monthly salary of 50 GH₵ ($37) from the NGO. Cognizant of Emily's dire living conditions, Kevin and Samantha did what they could for Emily's household. However, when I asked Kevin whether it was easy for him to help her and her family, he replied:

Emily and her children come to our place every day. To be frank with you, it is almost like feeding two families ... We provide food and water and sometimes even cash for them ... My organization [the NGO for whom he worked] only gives me 50 GH₵ per month. With this money, we need to eat and send Katrina [Kevin's daughter] to school and assist Emily and her children. This is a big challenge for us.[10]

Emily was more than aware that her family was a burden on Kevin. In an interview, she expressed her strong sense of guilt: 'I know we are troubling Kevin and Samantha. For the last few years, they have been helping us ... I feel so bad but we cannot survive without them'.[11]

Internal support within refugee communities is generally presented to paint positive pictures of their cohesion, solidarity and benevolence. In Buduburam, however, when mutual help took place between poorer families with scarce resources, it was better characterized as 'shared poverty or destitution' (Leliveld 1991: 33) rather than communal resilience. The little money available to a household had to be stretched to support not only household members but also extended relatives, friends and neighbours who were more indigent or equally poor. In these cases, the moral obligation to assist others frequently engendered in caregivers a degree of stress or even frustration with recipients of their aid.

Differences in the Potency of Social Capital

Since social networks in the Buduburam refugee community were not equally accessible to all refugee residents, this led to differentiation in the potency of social assets. For instance, due to a delay in the sending of the scheduled remittance she received, Jennifer's household, a family in the high-income group, needed to take out a loan of 400 GH₵ ($296) in June 2009 for their son's university education, drawing on their resource networks in Ghana. This was possible because her family had links with both Liberian refugees and Ghanaians inside and outside Buduburam camp, and these people had access either to remittances or to formal employment in Ghana. Moreover, the fact that Jennifer had some biological siblings who lived in developed countries and would have been able to remit her worked as tacit collateral, thus making it easier for her to secure relatively larger loans from people.

On the other hand, the resource networks of Olivia, the female head of one of the poorest sample households, were confined to a handful of refugees with similar socio-economic status. She earned a living braiding hair and washing clothes for others. As Tripp (1997: 123) has commented, this type of small-scale informal business is highly embedded in personal relations. According to her data record book, Olivia's customers were made up of several refugees who were close to her – mostly those sharing the same ethnic background in Liberia. Later, I found out that her regular customers were also her helpers in the camp, because in her data record books the same names appeared again and again as sources of food and cash. This meant that Olivia's support network consisted of a group of five or six other refugees in the camp. Her family received support from these 'strong ties' but the amount of resources that she could obtain from them was limited – just some food items and petty cash – because no one in her support network had sufficient assets to share with Olivia's family.

As the examples of Jennifer and Olivia make clear, in the context of the Buduburam refugee community, refugees' social networks are best conceptualized as the aggregate of numerous individual and organizational connections that a refugee possesses at different levels, from local to international. While a possessor of networks may access resources owned by each of these connections through personal routes, the amount of resources drawn from these connections will inevitably be differentiated by the quality of each contact within a person's network.

Conclusion: Inequality behind the Façade of a Vibrant Economy

The analysis of household economy provides useful insights into the economic life of the Liberian refugee population. First, the study has confirmed the significance of overseas remittances for the daily lives of refugees in Buduburam camp. On the other hand, the cash-generating capacity of camp-based businesses was far more limited than that of remittances. Given the reduced refugee population after the large-scale repatriation, most refugee entrepreneurs faced declining sales from their enterprises.

As the data in Chapters 2 and 3 show, the image of Buduburam's refugee population as self-reliant due to an economy sustained by refugee businesses proves to be unfounded. A more accurate description of refugees' economic life in the camp is that it was a remittance-reliant economy sustained by the Liberian diaspora. Given the number of formal and informal restrictions on livelihoods and decreasing aid from UNHCR, the refugees inevitably sought survival through securing financial help from their contacts abroad.

Above all, the quantitative data presented in this chapter reveals considerable economic inequality in this supposedly model camp; the 'decent life' existed alongside grinding poverty. This gross economic division was slightly moderated by the redistribution of remittances via remittance clusters. But crucially, more than half of the camp's residents lived in extreme poverty at only bare subsistence levels. Households in the low- and very-low-income groups were definitely not 'self-reliant' by UNHCR's definition. This finding in turn suggests the limited fungibility of remittances. In Buduburam camp, the secondary distribution of remittances inside the camp population was undeniably important but did not transform the entire population into a self-sufficient community.

This chapter has shed light on the 'dark side' of Buduburam – acute impoverishment – behind the façade of a flourishing economy. In contrast, a small group of the wealthiest households, such as Grace's, did exceptionally well due to the constant assistance of remittances. Strictly speaking, only these households in the high-income category lived up to the reputation of 'exemplary and self-reliant' refugees. As I continued in my field research, I became increasingly curious about what was behind such sharp divisions among the refugee population. The next chapter will delve into the roots of economic inequality among the refugees.

Notes

1. However, not all participants managed to accurately record the data. Initially, more than twenty households participated in the household economy study, but due to significant inconsistency and frequent omissions in the data recording of several households, I have decided not to use their data in my analysis.
2. The proportion of high-income households in the entire Liberian refugee population was estimated to be about 10 per cent. Therefore, the inclusion of four better-off households out of the eighteen sampled slightly over-represents their number compared with their actual presence in the entire refugee community.
3. Interview, Buduburam, March 2009.
4. Interview, Accra, July 2009.
5. Interview, Buduburam, April 2009.
6. In the middle-income group, 36.3 per cent of household income came from assistance from others. This relatively higher reliance on others was mainly due to the fact that a member of one household in this group mobilized substantial sums of cash from other refugees for his education expenses during the data collection period. Consequently, this fluctuation increased the total percentage of assistance from other refugees in the middle-income category. In turn, this suggests that it is generally easier for households with access to remittances to obtain resources from other refugees since their connection with the diaspora implies the potential of future reciprocity vis-à-vis other refugees.
7. Interview, Buduburam, June 2009.
8. Interview, Buduburam, June 2009.
9. I triangulated this information with medical staff working inside the camp. According to a Ghanaian nurse who worked at a clinic in Buduburam, it is not recommended to practice this type of self-medicine in high doses over a long time.
10. Interview, Buduburam, July 2009.
11. Interview, Buduburam, July 2009.

4

The Roots of Economic Stratification

A Historical Perspective

My remitters in the United States aren't refugees. My family started migrating to America since the 1950s. Most of them are now US citizens ... They are working as nurse, government official, and shop manager. They are doing well.

—Remittance recipient in Buduburam

Given the significant economic divisions within the Buduburam refugee population, this chapter explores the roots of this considerable inequality. In earlier chapters, I demonstrated how high-income households, perhaps constituting no more than 10 per cent of the camp population, had benefited from their constant remittances. Who were these 'privileged' refugees? Why were they able to access these large amounts of financial assistance from abroad over many years whilst other Liberians had no access whatsoever to financial help or struggled to maintain what help they did have?

Answering these questions necessitated employing historical and holistic approaches. Murray (2001) states that the economic differences between rich and poor households have to be understood in terms of their social relations in a particular historical context. In the case of forcibly displaced groups, their livelihood assets and strategies not only relate to their displacement but also to the broader context of life prior to the time of conflict (Longley and Maxwell 2003: 17). I therefore had to investigate the pre-displacement background of high-income households and others, and to situate them within the social, economic and political contexts of Liberia. What emerged from the research was that the recipients of 'robust' remittances generally shared particular traits: Americo-Liberian ethnicity, an economically and often politically powerful ancestry and a long history of family migration to the United States.

In this chapter I shall also examine the prewar life of impoverished refugees in the camp and illustrate the structural inequalities between richer and poorer refugees within the Buduburam refugee population. Drawing upon a historical approach, the chapter unveils the hidden implications of privilege and oppression that were embedded in refugees' economic well-being and livelihood strategies in their current camp life.

Well-Off Refugees in Buduburam: The Offspring of Ruling Elites

As I described in Chapter 1, Liberia was founded in the early nineteenth century for the repatriation of freed American slaves to Africa. These emancipated settlers – called Americo-Liberians – had been brought up in Western culture and possessed some knowledge of modern political organization and technology. Because of this memory, they regarded themselves as superior to the indigenous people of Liberia (Akpan 1973; Dalton 1965; Lubkemann 2004; Saha 1998). Political power in Liberia rested solely with these ruling elites until well into the late twentieth century (Railey 1997: 271). This process of monopolization by a powerful minority resulted in the marginalization of the masses and meant that indigenous Liberians were largely excluded from economic and social progress (Mayson and Sawyer 1979: 145).

Throughout my research in Ghana in 2008 and 2009, I conducted one-to-one interviews with over twenty refugee households belonging to the high-income bracket. Except for one household, all of these families had roots in the ruling elite in Liberia.

Americo-Liberians in Buduburam: Signs of Wealth

Historical privileges based on ancestry were clearly observed in the camp life of descendants of freed American slaves who had moved to Liberia. The following remark was made by a camp-based Liberian refugee whose mother was Americo-Liberian:

> If you were born as a member of an Americo-Liberian family, your starting point in Liberia is very different from natives. Even in the camp, the difference is visible. Americo-Liberians are clearly having better living standards [than indigenous refugee groups] even though they are living in the same camp. They normally don't have survival problems like others.[1]

In Chapters 2 and 3, I mentioned some tangible features of the economic well-being of the most affluent Liberian households: wearing more expensive clothing, owning electronic gadgets and consumer durables, and having higher levels of education. For instance, one of my interviewees of Americo-Liberian origin in the highest economic group had his own second-hand car in the camp. Many of the people in this category owned a laptop, a digital camera, an iPod and an expensive mobile phone. I met several refugees who had been sent to boarding schools in Sierra Leone and Ghana for a better education when they were of school age in Liberia. Some of them were attending universities in Ghana. Often, those who had received their education outside Liberia spoke fluent English without a Liberian accent. During my interviews with refugees in the high-income category, some of them said that they were buying or planning to buy land or a house in Liberia using remittance resources from other family members abroad.

Whereas I mainly focused on camp-based refugees, I should note that there were also a considerable number of Liberians with Americo-Liberian backgrounds living outside Buduburam camp, mostly in Accra, Ghana's capital. Although these urban Americo-Liberians maintained their contacts with the Buduburam refugee community, they had never lived inside the camp. These self-settled refugees had their own social circle and often got together to maintain communication. Although I interviewed only about ten of them during my research, it did seem that they had much better living standards than the camp-based refugees with an Americo-Liberian background. Most interviews with them took place at their houses, which were usually spacious and equipped with home appliances. Some of them ran sub-regional trade businesses and guesthouses in Accra. In addition to this material wealth, their responses to my questions during the interviews hinted at their better access to financial capital and wider social connections.

Ancestry with Economic and Political Power

Through a series of life-history interviews with some of the wealthiest households in Buduburam, I realized that these families were often closely linked to influential statesmen and/or successful businessmen, and some even had ties to previous Liberian presidents who had come from their lineage. For instance, in the previous chapter I mentioned Jones, a 36-year-old head of a well-off household, which included his wife and four children. He came to Ghana in 2000 and had been living a decent life thanks to substantial remittance support from family members living in the United States. Jones was very proud of his renowned family background and, without prompting, he occasionally talked about his ancestors:

> My grandfather [on my mother's side] was a very reputable statesman who served many high rank posts in the Liberian government before he died.

He was Americo-Liberian. The former [Liberian] President Tolbert called him 'father' [although they were not directly related]. On the Liberian Independence Day, my grandfather was invited to the national ceremony and delivered his speech in front of the public. He was also a big businessman involved in the diamond and gold trade. He owned a missionary school in Maigibi county [in central Liberia]. He was an extremely influential person. I am really proud of him.

My uncle [on my mother's side] was also a powerful man. He studied in the US for his Bachelor and Master degree. He served as vice-president of City Bank in Monrovia until 1980. Then he moved into his real estate business.[2]

Among those in receipt of the largest remittances with origins in the ruling elite, there were similar stories pointing to their famous lineage. These testimonies indicated that they were the descendants of traditionally wealthy and privileged families.[3] These influential family backgrounds from the prewar period contrasted sharply with those of Liberian households in the poorer economic groups whose parents were mostly small-scale traders, farmers and hunters. I shall return to the relationship between prewar life and current exile later in this chapter.

Family Migration History: 'They Are Migrants! Not Refugees!'

Liberian Migration to the United States

Another distinctive feature of the high-income households in Buduburam was their familial migration patterns over generations to countries overseas, predominantly to the United States. This meant that these families had been sending their members to America as migrants even before the outbreak of the Liberian war in 1989, rather than through refugee resettlement programmes. I first became aware of this prewar migration culture when I interviewed Josh, who had a relatively comfortable life in the camp assisted by constant remittances from his wife and children in both the United States and Canada. Josh came to Ghana in 1990 in the very initial stages of the war, and as soon as he arrived he started receiving financial help from his Americo-Liberian wife, who had already moved to the United States before the outbreak of the civil war.

N.O.: When did your wife and children move to the US?

JOSH: 1987.

N.O.: Why did they leave Liberia before the war?

JOSH: We were planning to migrate to the US. It was our family strategy to gradually move there. We couldn't [all] do it at once so my wife and two children first left in 1987. Also I then had a good job in Liberia. So my youngest son and I stayed in Liberia but were planning to join them in the US later ... But the war broke out. It changed our migration plan completely. I fled from Liberia with my son in 1990.

N.O.: Did you have any other relatives in the US before your wife moved?

JOSH: Yes, my wife's family has a long migration history to North Carolina. I think she had eight relatives there.[4]

Among refugee families with several decades of family migration history, I discovered a chain of migration to the United States going back generations. As Lubkemann (2008b: 48) comments, throughout the twentieth century, the Americo-Liberian elite sent their children back to the United States to pursue higher education or further business interests. Typically, the first person from these families to move to the United States went as a government scholarship student and was followed by other members later. According to my interviews with refugees in Buduburam, in Liberia, especially during the prewar period, government scholarships were traditionally granted to children of families with Americo-Liberian heritage.

During field research in Liberia, I sought opportunities to meet Liberian academics to better understand the historical and cultural context of the country in relation to my research project. One of them, Harris, a Liberian history teacher at a high school in Monrovia, explained the following about migration culture in Liberian society: 'Certain Liberian families have a long history of migration to America. But such movement was available only for wealthy Americo-Liberians who could afford it. If you investigate the background of families with many relatives in the US, you will see their privileged family origin'.[5]

Differences between Refugee Resettlement and Migration

In order to receive overseas remittances, the first and foremost condition is that the recipient has at least one person abroad. Recipients can achieve this by having a fellow refugee who has been given refuge in a third country through a resettlement programme or by having one who has migrated to an industrialized foreign country. Although the outcome of these two movements is identical on the surface, many Liberians agreed that they need to be understood as fundamentally different phenomena because the latter option was available only for 'elite' families in Liberia.

Korlison was the principal of the largest refugee school in Buduburam camp and a former history teacher in Liberia. He classified these two groups as 'before' and 'after' war movements.

Before war started in 1989, some Liberians travelled to the US. Let me call this privileged people as a 'before war group'. The characteristics of this group are [that they are] well-educated and mostly from a wealthy family in Liberia. Of course, they didn't move to [the] US as refugees but as immigrants. The majority of these people are of Americo-Liberian origin.

On the other hand, we have an 'after war group'. Most of these Liberians went to the US as refugees after the Liberian civil war broke out. These Liberians are not from rich families and normally have [a] weak educational background. I think 90 per cent of resettled Liberians from Ghana are belonging to this group. These people were never able to travel to [the] US or abroad without resettlement programmes. In other words, the civil war gave them an opportunity to move to the Western world as a refugee.[6]

Lubkemann (2008b: 48–49) has also identified differences between the 'before' and 'after' groups. According to him, the socio-economic elite was more highly represented in the years prior to 1990, when the Liberian diaspora in the United States largely comprised those who had come as students from particular wealthy families. During this prewar period, the scale of migration from Liberia to the United States was relatively modest and Americo-Liberians were disproportionately represented among Liberian diaspora in the United States. In contrast, more recent immigrants – many of whom have suffered persecution – represent a much broader spectrum of Liberia's population and, if anything, are socio-economically skewed in exactly the opposite direction from the earlier waves of migration (ibid.). Lubkemann estimated that the descendants of the American-born settlers are now actually a fairly small minority among US-based Liberians, probably representing between 10 per cent and 15 per cent of the entire Liberian diaspora in the United States.

Differences in Remitting Capacities among the Liberian Diaspora

While the previous chapters have highlighted access to remittances as a chief determinant of economic well-being within the Buduburam refugee population, I have also emphasized the considerable differences in the quality of remittances in terms of amount, frequency and regularity among recipients. These differences can be largely attributed to the socio-economic conditions of the senders of remittances. Therefore, I expanded the scope of the research from the remittance recipients in Buduburam to their remitters in developed countries, predominantly in the United States.

As illustrated in subsequent sections, those who had migrated to the Global North had a much greater capacity to remit to their relatives in

Buduburam than resettled refugees did. Those sending remittances to high-income households had the following three distinctive aspects in common: more stable employment; a larger number of economically functioning members; and existing relatives in the Global North that were able to support them when they arrived and to integrate them.

The Stable Profession of Remitters

Mercer et al. (2008: 18–19, 148–49) suggest that there are considerable disparities in economic standing among members of the African diaspora. For high-income households in Buduburam, their overseas remitters normally had professional and specialized full-time occupations that generated a larger income compared to those who sent sporadic remittances to recipients in the camp.

For instance, Akua, a forty-one-year-old female remittance recipient in Buduburam, was an Americo-Liberian who had four elder siblings and more than twenty relatives who had been living in the United States for decades. During the Liberian civil war, some members of her family escaped to Guinea, and others, including Akua, fled to Ghana through Ivory Coast. Since her arrival in Ghana in 1999, Akua had received financial support totalling about $300 every month from her siblings in the United States. She explained the occupations of her remitters:

> N.O.: What are your siblings doing in the US?
>
> AKUA: Elise, my eldest sister, is a medical doctor. Josephine, the second one, is a beauty-care technician. She owns her salon in the US. Markey and Otabias [her third and fourth siblings] are both working for the US government. Both of them were diplomats in Liberia.
>
> N.O.: They all have good jobs.
>
> AKUA: Yes, all of them are well established [in the US]. They have been in the US for a long time.[7]

The occupational status of remitters to ordinary recipient families was sharply contrasted with those of well-to-do Liberian households. These remitters had moved relatively recently to industrialized countries in the North through refugee resettlement programmes and were mostly engaged in less specialized (manual labour) occupations, working as carers and cleaners for example. Many of them found it difficult to send remittances to their relatives living in the camp because of their own relatively low-paid employment.[8]

In Chapter 2, I mentioned Victoria, whose husband had moved to Norway in 2005 through a resettlement programme, and how a remittance cluster was set up between her and other refugees. Whilst Victoria's husband was committed to assisting his wife, it seemed quite challenging for him even to remit $50 to $100 every month because of his limited salary as a hotel cleaner. According to Victoria, after his resettlement in 2005, he first had to spend two years learning Norwegian. In 2007, he got his first job as a hotel cleaner and finally started remitting to Victoria. But in late 2008, due to the world economic crisis, his job was cut to a part-time post (two full working days a week), reducing his salary accordingly. Since early 2009, he had been searching for a more lucrative job in Norway but there seemed to be very limited employment opportunities for him with his high school diploma, limited command of Norwegian and lack of specialized vocational skills. Although Victoria admitted that the amount of his remittances was insufficient, she was aware of her husband's difficulties. During an interview with her, Victoria expressed her sympathy for him:

> I know he is having hard time there [in Norway] ... He even struggles to pay his own bills ... I can't ask too much from him ... He is searching for better job because his salary is small now. But it is not easy for him. He doesn't have good education. Because of the war [in Liberia] he had to stop schooling. Since he left Liberia, he never had a chance to go to higher education like university ... He said that there are very few Liberians in Norway so he doesn't have friends [who may assist him] there.[9]

The Multiplicity of Money Senders

Another important factor in the long-term financial support of wealthy refugee households was the large number of economically functioning family members overseas, often due to a history of migration over more than one generation. If a recipient household has only a single sponsor abroad, over time, remitters might lose their jobs, retire, become ill or die, resulting in the loss of remittances. The advantage of having multiple remitters was that it diversified the sources of remittances. What I often heard from families receiving large remittances was that over a long period of time their relatives who had migrated to the North agreed to rotate the obligation to send money to those in Buduburam.

Take the case of Florence, a refugee in her early forties. Her eldest brother had moved to the United States in the late 1980s for his studies, and other siblings had followed him later. Florence was the youngest child in her family. During her refugee life in Ghana she was entirely dependent on a monthly stipend from her older family members abroad. Florence explained: 'I have six siblings in the US. I receive $200 every month from one of them ... It is a rotation between them. Their [remitting] turn is once in six months [since there are six immediate relatives]'.[10]

With respect to Florence's case, this rotation had worked well for almost a decade because she had multiple remitters who had already reached an economically functioning age due to the family's migration to the United States since the 1980s.

Obviously, reliance on a single remitter is precarious over the longer term. Among the high-income households whom I interviewed there was one exception – that of Terry – which did not meet each of the three criteria mentioned earlier: Americo-Liberian background, economically and politically eminent family background, and multi-generational migration to the United States. In Chapter 3, I briefly described his remittance-based life in the camp. Although Terry regularly received some $200 from his spouse, who had settled in Delaware in the United States, he shared his concern with me about his heavy dependence on his wife:

> My wife is a nursing assistant. During the credit crunch last year [2008], her salary was reduced. Her rent and other bills cost total $950 per month. She also supports other family members in Liberia. Her salary from the hospital is not enough so she is also doing part-time work to make ends meet … [S]ometimes I become so concerned for her … [I]f she becomes ill …[11]

Akuei (2005: 6–7) discusses the case of a Sudanese refugee resettled in San Diego, who was single-handedly responsible for assisting sixty-two people, directly and indirectly, across a number of locations. Even though Terry's wife in Delaware did not assist as many as that, she was still solely responsible for helping more than twenty people in both Liberia and Ghana. Given the amount she worked in order to be able to remit money to her family, Terry's concern about her becoming ill was quite realistic. If his worry unfortunately were to become a reality, his remittance would be halted immediately as his wife was a single remitter for Terry.

Existing Relatives in the North Able to Support a Migrant

In migration studies, the importance of having contacts prior to movement has been well established as a key facilitator or cushion for newcomers upon arrival (Brettell 2008: 125; Castles and Miller 2009: 28–29; Hardwick 2008: 172). These already-established contacts, based on family connections or common origin, make the migratory process safer and more manageable for new arrivals by providing shelter, work, finance and material and psychological assistance (Faist 2000: 53). Thanks to support from family members who had previously migrated, the remitters to high-income households had moved to the North with less transitional stress and tended to be able to build their economic foundation quickly.

On the other hand, members of the Liberian diaspora who moved to the industrialized world via resettlement programmes had very little or no access to family assistance and seemed to have suffered to a far greater degree in securing employment and housing in their adopted country. For example, Joseph, one of my research assistants and in his mid thirties, had two biological sisters who had moved from Ghana under resettlement programmes to the United States and Australia in 2004 and 2006 respectively. According to Joseph, his remittance requests had often been refused by his sisters, especially during the early days in the country they had moved to, as they had been struggling to establish their own economic foundation in an unfamiliar environment. Being cognizant of their plight abroad, he pointed to the effort required by those who had migrated, highlighting differences between resettled refugees and long-time immigrants:

> If a person has established hosts abroad, I think it will be easier for him to make a transition to a new country than one who just got resettled from a refugee camp. But the ones without helpers have to start everything from scratch. It will perhaps take a long time for them to really establish themselves. I think this is why my sisters have been struggling there.[12]

Without existing support networks, the transition process is likely to be longer and challenging. As in the case of Victoria's husband, it may even take several years for someone to be able to remit even specific sums of money regularly, since they need to establish themselves in an unfamiliar environment with very little social capital to support them.

Selectivity in Accessing 'Robust' Remittances

Grace: A High-Income Remittance Recipient

Thus far, this chapter has elucidated some characteristics common to high-income groups of refugees – recipients of robust remittances. Here I illustrate these characteristics through the case of Grace, whom I introduced in Chapter 3 as one of the most affluent refugees in the camp due to her access to stable remittances. Her life trajectory embodies the confluence of the features specific to recipients of robust remittances.

At the time of my interview with her in 2009, Grace was living alone in a nicely decorated small house in the camp. Her surname was White, an apparently non-indigenous name in Liberia. Grace was born and raised in Arlington in Monrovia, which has been traditionally a place where many Americo-Liberian families live. Grace had two mothers. When she was born, her aunt, who was unable to bear any children, adopted Grace. Grace's mother's side was half Americo-Liberian and half indigenous, but had produced some high-ranking diplomats and major business people in Liberia. Her foster mother, whom I shall call her mother from hereon, ran a trading business between Liberia and the United States, and her husband was a diplomat whose last post was as the Liberian ambassador to France.

According to Grace, the migration history in her family dated back to the 1960s. Before Grace was born, one of her aunts on her mother's side had moved to the United States on a scholarship from the Liberian government. After completing her Bachelor's degree, the aunt remained in the United States and obtained employment there. In the 1970s, her mother emigrated to the United States with her Liberian diplomat husband. Over the subsequent decade, a few other family members joined those already established in the United States. At the point of this interview, all of these migrants had obtained US citizenship, got married and constructed their own livelihoods there.

Since her arrival in Ghana in 1996, Grace had always been financially assisted by her relatives in the United States. As soon as she reached Ghana, her mother started remitting $100 to $200 per month. Later, Grace's former boyfriend who became her current husband took over this role. Grace met her husband in Liberia before her displacement and they promised to marry. During the war, they were physically separated but they were formally married in 2006 when he came to Ghana to visit Grace.

Grace's husband had previously migrated to the United States from Liberia in 1997 with a Diversity Immigrant Visa. Like Grace, he was from a powerful business lineage with an Americo-Liberian background and a history of family migration to the United States since the 1960s. After his arrival in the United States, and with support from family members who had already settled there, he completed university and graduate law school, and subsequently became a lawyer. When I interviewed Grace in 2009, he was working as a lawyer in the United States and was sending at least $300 to $400 to her every month.

Due to regular financial assistance from her husband, Grace had a very decent life in the camp. Even after spending substantial sums of money on helping other refugees and donating to her church, she could still use a significant amount of the remittances she received for her own entertainment and comfort, such as having her hair braided and nails fixed. When I asked her whether she had ever had any problems in making a living in exile, she responded 'never', thanks to the consistent financial assistance she had received for years.

Since 2007, Grace's husband had been preparing to bring her to the United States as his spouse. At the time of my interview, her visa was being processed and Grace was looking forward to joining him.

The Preconditions of Being a High-Income Remittance Recipient

A study of the households of Grace and other affluent refugees in Buduburam highlights some of the preconditions necessary in order to receive relatively large financial remittances on a regular basis over a period of years. First, a refugee needs to have still-living immediate family members, since most regular remittances come from parents, children or spouses. Second, they need to have some family members who have moved to industrialized nations. Third, these family members must feel obliged or at least willing to assist someone left behind. Fourth, those abroad must be economically functioning. Finally, these family members overseas need to have durable means of generating income that enable them to remit a specific proportion of their earnings regularly and for a long time.

Evidently, it is not easy to satisfy all of these criteria from individual efforts, in that most of them are highly contingent on a multi-generational family background and assets prior to displacement. In other words, considering the nature of these requirements, rather than being arbitrary, the possibility of being a recipient of large and constant remittances is more or less dependent on previous living conditions and one's social background in Liberia. Most of the refugee interviewees in the lower economic divisions were aware of this harsh reality. Samuel, a twenty-year-old Liberian who had come to Ghana with his brothers and had experienced a series of survival challenges, told me:

> If you observe very rich Liberians in the camp, you will see that they already had strong contacts prior to the war. If you go to a good high school or university, you will meet many good educated schoolmates from rich families. If you are in a good post in the government, you will again meet influential people there. Wealthy people in the camp built their contacts with abroad in Liberia and carried them to Ghana.[13]

Samuel was right. In the current study, all direct beneficiaries of robust remittances, with one exception, were part of the former Liberian elite and received financial assistance from these networks, which already existed before their exile.

The selectivity in accessing remittances has been highlighted by other researchers. Using case studies from Ghana and Sri Lanka, for instance, Van Hear (2002, 2011, 2014a) points out that migrants in wealthier countries are increasingly the better off. Usually they already have with links with people abroad, and they can also afford the substantial outlays incurred by migration by deploying their existing social and economic capital (also see de Haas 2005: 10; Kapur 2004: 11; Massey et al. 2008: 48). My own research adds empirical evidence to this issue, and shows that such selectivity largely applied to remittance recipients in the Liberian refugee population in Buduburam.

In turn, these findings on the preconditions for being a recipient of robust remittances indicate the cruel reality that full economic self-reliance in the environment of Buduburam was unlikely to be attained by refugees' individual efforts alone. I have made a clear distinction between access to 'robust' remittances, which are sent in larger volume in a consistent manner, and smaller amounts of sparse and unreliable remittances. This differentiation is essential because an income of roughly $100 per month was necessary to enable a refugee household to have a decent life – a self-sufficient life in UNHCR terms – in Buduburam. Given the limited profitability of refugee enterprises in the camp, access to robust remittances was almost the only way of constantly generating $100. However, the highly selective nature of being a recipient of robust remittances further elucidates the slim possibility of accomplishing self-reliant status in the refugee camp.

The Pre-Displacement Life of Poorer Households

The obvious counterpart to the historical background of the wealthy refugees is understanding how the pre-displacement lives and experiences of impoverished households in Buduburam camp differed.

Rural Life in the Pre-Displacement Period

Many Liberian refugees agreed that if someone had been poor in Liberia, they would be likely to remain poor in exile due to a lack of access to external financial assistance. In the first place, almost all of the refugee households in the poorer quartiles had no relatives who had migrated abroad. Thomas, the Liberian senior pastor of the largest church in Buduburam, had been living in the camp since 1990. With his years of observation, he described the background of refugees with lower economic status to me:

> Poor Liberians (or their parents) in the camp are mostly from the hinterland [in Liberia]. In rural sides of Liberia, there are very few important social and economic activities. Most of these Liberians are either peasants or hunters. They are not educated at all and don't have very strong family background. It is hard to imagine that such families actively send family members to abroad.[14]

In line with the statement of the pastor, I discovered through life-history interviews that the vast majority of the refugees in the poorer economic categories had challenging pre-displacement lives in the Liberian interior. Most of them had never been to Monrovia or had never even left their home county. In the hinterland of Liberia, there used to be very few schools. Thus, most of these Liberians had limited education or no schooling at all, which consequently left them with limited literacy and weaker English skills. Samuel explained his family's lifestyle prior to displacement: 'My family was living in a rural village, almost like bush. Our family members were traditionally farmers or hunters. I went to school only for a few years there but most of the time I was working. My job was collecting rubber seeds and selling them'.[15]

In addition, even before the civil war, sometimes families were split up due to insufficient economic capacity to feed all the household's members. In Chapter 3, I wrote about Stephanie and her malnourished daughter who were denied the WFP/UNHCR free food ration and were surviving on an income from selling oranges and perhaps from commercial sex work. When I asked her about her prewar living conditions, Stephanie recalled her tough life in rural Liberia:

N.O.: Where were you living before the civil war?

STEPHANIE: In Liberia, I was living in a village in Bomi county [a rural county in west Liberia].

N.O.: With whom?

STEPHANIE: My grandmother.

N.O.: You were not living with your parents?

STEPHANIE: No, my parents sent me to my grandmother when I was three-months old.

N.O.: Why?

STEPHANIE: I don't know … I have never met my parents.

N.O.: How was your living environment?

STEPHANIE: We were living in a small village in a bush area. My grandmother was catching fish in the pond and selling them in the market.

N.O.: Were you in school?

STEPHANIE: I was in school only for very short time [due to lack of means to pay for tuition]. I had to help my grandmother.[16]

Among households in the very low income group, this type of prewar lifestyle was not uncommon. Some previous research on Buduburam camp (Agyeman 2005; Owusu 2000) has emphasized the well-educated character and urban background of camp-based Liberians. Although there were such residents, during my field research I also identified a significant number of Liberians like Stephanie who had been poor, rural dwellers with little education.

Crucially, after their arrival in Ghana, refugees from the countryside could no longer pursue their previous livelihoods – farming, fishing and hunting – due to the lack of access to farmland, lakes, rivers and forests in the semi-urban environment of Buduburam camp. Abandoning their existing livelihood skills created additional livelihood challenges for those from under-privileged backgrounds.

Victims of Direct Assault during the Civil War

Another commonality in the pre-displacement life of these impoverished households was that many of them had experienced direct assault by rebel groups. The following is Stephanie's reply when I asked her how she had fled from her rural village in Bomi county:

> In 1996, the rebel groups captured our village. We [Stephanie and her grandmother] managed to flee from the village during night time. We walked to a next village. In this village, my grandmother paid some money to a rebel member who was arranging a vehicle for his own family. He joined the rebels from Bomi and my grandmother knew him well. He wanted to send out his parents from the village to a safer place. We got a ride and drove through Bongo and Nimba [counties] and finally reached to Ivory Coast.[17]

Since similar traumatic stories were repeated in other interviews with many poorer refugees, I asked them why they had not left their village in advance of the rebel invasion. Their common response was: 'We didn't know war was coming to our place'. According to Carney (1999), rural poor people, especially in Africa, are isolated not only from economic opportunities but also from access to information due to poor communications infrastructure. Esther, a war widow in her mid-forties who had been living deep in Montserrado county, described how her family and neighbours had not fully grasped the war context: 'In 1990, we were hearing, "Taylor is coming", but we didn't know who Taylor was and why he was coming. My neighbour said, "Taylor is rebel", but none of us understood what rebel means. We finally got it when the rebel[s] attacked our village'.[18]

Apparently, for these families with limited access to information and financial resources, making any 'anticipatory' movement (Kunz 1973, 1981) from their village or sending family members to safer zones in advance of armed conflict was simply not an option. Having been exposed to an unexpected assault by the rebels, during their flight many households lost family members or were forcibly dispersed. This family disruption was particularly harmful to younger individuals. Many of those who were separated from their main breadwinners at a very young age faced more difficulties as unaccompanied minors. During their flight and exile, these refugees often had to resort to undesirable coping techniques such as commercial sex or unwanted sexual partnerships to ensure their survival.

No Escape from One's Economic Plight

A Poverty Trap

As the examples presented above suggest, most of those in economic difficulty in Buduburam were socio-economically underprivileged in the prewar period, were forced to face more challenges during their flight, and had to start life in exile with a meagre portfolio of assets and limited social connections.

Earlier in this book, I highlighted an over-concentration of refugees in 'easy' livelihoods such as selling drinking water and fruit, and picking up discarded plastic bags for resale. With their fractured asset profile, their livelihood strategies in the camp were naturally confined to economic activities and businesses which were easier to start but not lucrative. On the surface, they were engaged in their own enterprises, which had perhaps contributed to creating the image of 'bustling Buduburam'. But in reality, these unprofitable economic activities would not enable them to fundamentally improve their economic status and to attain the same living conditions as those who had access to overseas remittances through transnational networks.

In her study of refugees in Dadaab camp, Kenya, Horst warns about over-emphasizing the transnational lifestyles of refugees:

> By stressing that Somali refugees in Dadaab are part of a network of 'transnational nomads', I do not want to deny the fact that many of the poorer refugees have to depend solely on the refugee camps for their livelihoods. Many refugees do not have an alternative, neither in the form of a remittance-sending relative nor in the shape of a migration dream. Instead, they survive through marginal income-generating activities and strategies of gaining additional rations, or through the help of those refugees who do have relatives outside the camp. (Horst 2006b: 211)

Similarly, indigent refugee households in Buduburam lived on the margins, with no access to transnational mobility or connections. For instance, Emily and her children, whom I mentioned in Chapter 3, worked from early morning to late evening for six or seven days a week to pick up discarded plastic bags to sell to recycling shops. Her household had a very abstemious lifestyle and often even compromised on basic necessities such as food and medicine. With their tiny income – 25 GH₵ to 35 GH₵ ($19 to $26) per month on average – it was very hard for me to imagine that Emily's family would be able to achieve decent living conditions in the future, notwithstanding their remarkable efforts. And thousands of camp residents from lower economic categories in the camp were in a similar situation to Emily's household.

Providing Vocational Training: Strengthening Livelihoods and Self-Reliance?

Earlier in the camp's history, UNHCR and other refugee-supporting agencies had provided some assistance to strengthen refugees' economic capacities but were largely unable to improve the economic well-being of underprivileged households in Buduburam. Among the support for refugee livelihoods, the provision of vocational training was one of the few initiatives available for refugees during my research in Ghana. However, what struck me was that some UNHCR staff members in Ghana tended to think that the provision of skills-training programmes alone will automatically lead to refugees attaining self-reliance and subsequently to their economic empowerment. When I presented some findings on the challenges facing impoverished refugees to UNHCR's senior programme officer, his questions concentrated on what technical skills are needed for these refugees to achieve self-reliance. He said to me:

> You suggested that there are a large number of Liberians in the camp who are just surviving every day. If so, my inquiry to you is what skills are needed or would be useful for making these refugees self-sufficient? We identified IT [information technology] can be an area of support but we need to know more about other potential areas. I am hoping that your research can identify some other areas.[19]

However, the provision of vocational skills failed to sufficiently strengthen the subsistence of poorer refugees and consequently to alleviate their dire poverty. The following is a comment from Vivian, a female refugee in her fifties who used to work as a public relations officer at an NGO providing training for refugee women such as hairdressing and interior decoration:

> Vocational training has very limited impacts on beneficiaries. Even after the training, many women cannot use their skills because they don't have access to start-up capital. Also, they cannot sell in local markets outside the camp either. Without access to capital and market, what can they do? Every year, many students graduated from our training programmes but they remained jobless. What they can do is only table-markets inside the camp. They may be educated but not empowered. UNHCR is not understanding this.[20]

In earlier chapters I discussed some of the structural obstacles for refugee livelihoods in Ghana, including the xenophobic attitude of the locals, the lack of financial capital and limited access to formal employment. No matter what types of business skill refugees acquired, without solving these hurdles they would not be able to transform their human assets into productive livelihood strategies.

Conclusion: The Importance of a Historical Approach

This chapter has explored the roots of economic stratification within the Buduburam refugee population and situated the difference vis-à-vis the social, economic and political contexts of Liberia. What has emerged from the analysis is the reproduction of historical inequality from the pre-displacement period into people's exile. Again, Korlison, the Liberian historian and school principal quoted occasionally in this book, gave me an insight when we were discussing the correlation between the pre-displacement status and the current economic conditions of Liberian refugees: 'You cannot analyse the economic differentiation in this camp by looking at only the camp population in front of you. Do you understand what I mean? This camp is a microcosm of Liberia. You cannot separate Buduburam from Liberia's social and historical context'.[21]

He was correct. In order to understand why some households were better off due to access to strong remittances, I needed to investigate their family background in Liberia as well as their remitters in the developed North. The triangular nexus between prewar Liberia, Buduburam camp in Ghana and the United States was a key element in understanding the considerable economic division between refugee households in the same camp population.

These findings also contribute to advancing the theoretical understanding of transnational networks and international remittances. Some studies have described the situation as if remittance recipients are lucky people who have won a lottery (see Jacobsen 2005), implying a randomness or arbitrariness to receiving remittances. However, the research findings from Buduburam have demonstrated that robust remittances to a well-off household are more like a product of a recipient's familial social networks and assets. These financial products do not happen in one day. Rather, they have accumulated over generations of the recipient's parents, grandparents or even more distant ancestors, and have eventually resulted in steady financial assistance to a refugee living in the camp. In other words, the nature of consistent remittances is similar to the inheritance of family assets by the current generation.

In turn, the research findings in this chapter point to critical deficiencies in many of the analytical approaches to livelihoods that pay little attention to the origin of livelihood assets possessed by an individual or household. In the Introduction, I pointed to the static understanding of livelihoods as a weakness of the sustainable livelihoods framework and of other analytical approaches to exploring livelihoods in disrupted circumstances. As the empirical evidence indicates, people's livelihoods are often constructed with capital and assets that have been inherited from their families or accrued over years of family privilege. Without a historical analysis of the roots of assets, studies of livelihoods will fail to capture the hidden implications of social inequality, privilege and marginalization in the formulation of specific livelihood strategies, which is critical for providing meaningful scholarly insights and analysis.

Notes

1. Interview, Buduburam, July 2009.
2. Interview, Buduburam, April 2009.
3. However, having Americo-Liberian parentage did not always guarantee special access to resources. For instance, in the case of one female half-Americo-Liberian refugee, her parents were divorced and she had been taken by her indigenous mother, who was from an ordinary family background. Since the divorced father refused to support his former spouse and biological children, she did not benefit from any privileges on her father's side.
4. Interview, Buduburam, June 2009.
5. Interview, Liberia, May 2009.
6. Interview, Buduburam, June 2009.
7. Interview, Buduburam, June 2009.
8. See also Akuei (2005), Hammond (2006) and Lindley (2007) for similar findings.
9. Interview, Buduburam, August 2009.
10. Interview, Buduburam, June 2009.
11. Interview, Buduburam, February 2009.
12. Interview, Buduburam, April 2009.
13. Interview, Buduburam, April 2009.
14. Interview, Buduburam, March 2009.
15. Interview, Buduburam, April 2009.
16. Interview, Buduburam, June 2009.
17. Interview, Buduburam, June 2009.
18. Interview, Buduburam, July 2009.
19. Interview, Accra, August 2009.
20. Interview, Buduburam, July 2009.
21. Interview, Buduburam, June 2009.

5

Repatriation to Liberia
The 'Best' Solution for Refugees?

I think repatriation is not for everyone. At least it didn't work with me at all.
In Ghana, I was not too worried about my daily life. But in Liberia, I have
to first secure daily basics like food and shelter. Now it is very hard for me to
think about my future here.

—Female returnee from Ghana to Liberia

This chapter turns to refugees' experiences of repatriation and economic
reintegration in Liberia as part of a broader, though often neglected, con-
tinuum of protracted displacement. As described in the Introduction, the
socio-economic status of refugees in the camp and their networks influenced refugees' decisions about repatriation, and even affected the process
of their economic adaptation in Liberia. By following those repatriated
from Ghana to Liberia, this chapter reveals their varied experiences of
economic readjustment, which were – again – largely differentiated by
returnees' access to resource networks in Liberia. Drawing on empirical
evidence, this chapter challenges the idealization of repatriation as a glori-
ous homecoming, as often advocated by the international refugee regime.

The Dilemma of Return after Prolonged Exile

Between 2008 and 2009, Liberian refugees in Ghana were placed under
intense pressure to repatriate by both national and international refugee
authorities. As explained earlier, after the 2008 protests by 'ungrateful'
refugees against the promotion of local integration, the furious minister of the interior (who is in charge of refugee issues in the country)
publicly announced in April 2008 that all Liberian refugees should go

back to Liberia. The minister also expressed his intention of breaking up Buduburam camp into more manageable, smaller units and of dispersing the remaining Liberians to other parts of Ghana.

UNHCR took advantage of the tension between the Liberian refugees and the Ghanaian regime and used it as leverage to decrease the number of remaining refugees in Ghana via the mechanism of repatriation in order to facilitate its subsequent local integration scheme. The agency continually placed announcements on the bulletin boards inside the camp to remind refugees 'to make sound decisions about their future' before the closure of the repatriation programme in March 2009. The Liberian refugees in Buduburam had to make significant decisions within a short period of time under strong pressure from non-refugee stakeholders about whether to repatriate or to stay.

Family Splits and the Decision to Return

Even under intense pressure to repatriate, however, making the decision to go back or not was never straightforward for the refugees, but rather a complex interplay of social, political, personal and economic factors (see Fagen 2011). Also, decisions about whether to repatriate were often dependent on broader family and household strategies, rather than on decisions made at an individual level. To illustrate the challenge of making a collective decision in a household, I take the example of the family of one of my research assistants: Jack and Shetha, both in their mid thirties, and their six-year-old son, Lucas. As I have already described in a previous chapter, Shetha was a respected female refugee in Buduburam and supported my research until her departure for Liberia in 2009. Shetha left Liberia in 1996 because of the chronic insecurity there, and came to Ghana alone. Jack first fled from Liberia to Ivory Coast in 1996, but in 2002 he was forced to move again due to the instability there; he escaped to neighbouring Ghana. Jack and Shetha met as members of the same church in Buduburam and married in 2005.

Around October 2008, Jack and Shetha had a major disagreement about whether to return to Liberia or not. In the absence of information about the future of Buduburam and with her memory of being chased by the Ghanaian police during the refugee protests still fresh, Shetha insisted on repatriating to Liberia: 'I am tired of my life here. We are just wasting time. I think our life will be much tougher in Ghana. The Ghanaian government will again do brutal things against Liberians. There will be no opportunities for us in this country. It is better to restart our new life in Liberia'.[1]

But Jack did not support Shetha's view. He insisted that Lucas should at least finish elementary schooling in Ghana. He also raised the challenging issues of securing shelter and new sources of income in Liberia. Jack had lost most of his immediate family during the civil war and had no reliable contacts who could temporarily accommodate him and his family in Liberia. In the refugee camp, he earned 50 GH₵ ($37) per month from his job teaching at a refugee school. He was very unsure about whether he would be able to find employment in Liberia if he returned there. In addition, Jack had not yet fully given up pursuing hopes of future resettlement opportunities, although neither he nor Shetha had any relatives living abroad.

To persuade her reluctant partner, Shetha decided to make a so-called 'go-and-see visit' to Liberia in December 2008. The go-and-see visit is sometimes employed by repatriating refugee households as a risk-reduction strategy; returning households send some family members to their homeland first to check out the conditions in the country of origin and to prepare for the subsequent return of the rest of the members of the family (see e.g. AREU 2006: 46; Korac 2009: 127).

During her one-month stay in Liberia, Shetha made significant preparatory efforts using her networks and siblings, who had remained in Liberia throughout the civil war. Her older brother offered her a free room in his house in the capital, Monrovia, until Shetha's family could find their own housing. She also secured a teaching job for Jack at the elementary school at which one of her siblings was working. Meanwhile, she contacted her resettled refugee friends in the United States and Australia and succeeded in eliciting a few hundred US dollars of remittances from them to cover the cost of resettlement.

Eventually, the family rift over whether to return to Liberia or not was resolved, and Shetha finally persuaded Jack to return. Another factor which prompted Jack's decision to return was that his monthly salary from his teaching job had been reduced by 30 per cent to 35 GH₵ ($26) in January 2009 as a consequence of the reduced number of students at his school caused by the ongoing repatriation programme. With the prospects for survival in Ghana clearly dwindling, Jack had to put aside his dream of resettlement to the Global North and prioritized looking after his family.

'*I Chose Repatriation by the Process of Elimination*'

As the case of Shetha and Jack's family suggests, when refugees make a decision about whether to repatriate or not they also must take into consideration the availability of other durable solutions – namely third-country resettlement and local integration. During the repatriation period between April 2008 and March 2009, however, Liberian refugees in Ghana were given virtually no access to other durable solutions. As already mentioned, despite it being the most popular choice for Liberian refugees, the option of third-country resettlement was closed to the majority of the remaining refugees.

Meanwhile, for Liberian refugees, the option of local integration remained an uncertain 'black box'. As explained in Chapter 1, there were tensions between the Ghanaian government and UNHCR over this durable solution. Given decreasing donor support for the remaining Liberian refugees, the UN refugee agency was trying to hand them over to the host government. Without any financial commitment from UNHCR, however, the Ghanaian administration was extremely reluctant to accept remaining Liberians and did not propose a scheme to integrate them into the country. During fieldwork, I asked staff members at UNHCR and the Ghana Refugee Board about any plans for implementing local integration, but they were consistent in stating that no plans had been made yet (see also Byrne 2013: 55).

Given the dearth of relevant information, a male refugee who decided to repatriate to Liberia in 2009 expressed his frustration over the ambiguous nature of local integration:

> In this refugee camp, none of us knows about the real meaning of local integration. Does it mean we will become Ghanaian? Or does it mean we will remain in Ghana without refugee status? What is it? UNHCR says we should make an 'informed decision' but how can we make it if they don't tell us what it is? I can't take something which I don't even know what it means, so I ruled it out [as an option] and decided to go back to Liberia.[2]

More importantly, even before the introduction of stringent policies after the refugee protests, the living environment surrounding refugees in Ghana had become increasingly inhospitable. In Chapter 1, I explained that Liberian refugees in Buduburam had been concerned about their uncertain legal status and the limited economic capacities of Ghana. Also, refugees had been virtually excluded from gainful employment opportunities in the formal sector. To make matters worse, in recent years the general relationship between Liberians and local people had been deteriorating. In the absence of information on local integration, many Liberians interpreted this undefined durable solution as a means of completely abandoned them in Ghana without any assistance from the international community. This fear led many refugees to passively choose repatriation.

A Side-Effect of Repatriation: Economic Impacts on the Local Economy

While this chapter focuses almost entirely on refugees' experiences of return to Liberia, it is perhaps worth noting the impact of the large-scale repatriation on the neighbouring Ghanaian villages around Buduburam camp. Under intense pressure for repatriation from the national and international refugee regimes, between 2008 and 2009 more than 9,000 Liberians chose to return to Liberia. The exodus of a large number of refugees not only significantly destabilized the camp economy but also had a severe negative impact on local Ghanaian business communities near the camp.

As explained above, Liberian refugees had been important customers for Ghanaian shops in the camp area for many years. Because Buduburam camp is located in a very poor district of Ghana, indigenous Ghanaians did not have the same purchasing power as Liberian refugees. The departure of refugees, especially wealthier remittance recipients, eroded the livelihoods of hundreds of local villagers who sold food and other daily necessities to refugees. A Ghanaian owner of a retail shop near the camp expressed his frustration and lamented:

> This repatriation is hitting us hard. So many Liberians left the camp because they were chased out [by UNHCR and the Ghanaian government]. Before repatriation started, I used to receive almost thirty Liberian customers per day. My daily sales were then about 50 GH₵ [$37]. Now I cannot make even 20 GH₵ [$15]. This is a crisis for our local businesses.[3]

As Phillips (2003: 14) notes, in the case of entrenched refugee camps, the departure of refugees often generates a downturn in the host economy. Over nearly two decades of prolonged exile, the refugees' economic lives and their purchasing power had become completely incorporated into the host economy, although UNHCR and the Ghanaian administration were both unaware of the likely side-effect of the rapid departure of refugees due to repatriation.

Is Repatriation a 'Homecoming'?

From this section onwards, the chapter focuses on the post-repatriation life of Liberian returnees from Buduburam. I followed refugees who had repatriated from Ghana to Liberia in 2009. In Liberia, I conducted more than eighty interviews. These were mostly with returnees whom I had already met in Buduburam, but I also interviewed members of the Liberian government, UNHCR Liberia staff and Liberians who had stayed in the country throughout the war.[4]

Warner (1994: 162) points out that voluntary repatriation implies a return to a place and a community in which refugees were residing before their flight into exile. Repatriation is also closely linked to a myth that centres around an assumed nostalgia for 'home' and memories of a past associated with return (Chetail 2004: 2). As a corollary of these perceptions, institutions dealing with refugees tend to depict repatriation as a 'homecoming' (Bakewell 2000: 357): a fairly straightforward way of restoring pre-displacement life in familiar and comfortable settings (Stefansson 2004: 171).

However, the repatriation of Liberian refugees from Ghana did not necessarily conform to this notion of homecoming. The term 'homecoming' is certainly misleading if 'home' is understood as a place of refugees' former housing before their exile. A considerable number of returnees did not have a house any more as it had been destroyed during the fourteen years of war in Liberia. Instead, upon return to their homeland, many repatriates spent the first few nights at a transit centre prepared for them near the international airport in the capital, Monrovia.

With permission from UNHCR Liberia, I accompanied some UNHCR staff to meet a returnee flight from Ghana. As soon as they arrived in the country, returnees were sent to the transit centre for screening by the immigration bureau of the Liberian government. Once they had completed the screening process, repatriates who had accommodation with relatives left immediately for their places. On the other hand, those who did not have accommodation to go to stayed over in the centre. Returnees were allowed to stay there for a maximum of 72 hours. After three days, they had to move on whether or not they had somewhere to stay.

Even after having been obliged to move out of the transit centre, the majority of repatriates did not go back to their home towns or villages. Regardless of where they had been living in their pre-displacement life in Liberia, they decided to stay in Monrovia. Some repatriates from Buduburam remained there to take advantage of better educational opportunities for themselves or their children, since there were very few schools in the interior of the country. Many chose to stay in the capital to look for work. Francis, one of the returnees from Ghana, told me: 'In Liberia, living in the capital or in rural area is a very different thing. In this country, everything is in Monrovia. The country is not decentralized at all. My home town is in Nimba [a county in the hinterland]. If I go back there, I won't find any job. I will stay here [in Monrovia] until I find something'.[5]

The Liberian government, as well as UNHCR Liberia, was aware of this urban concentration of returnees due to the ability it gave them to access economic and educational opportunities. According to a high-ranking official with the Liberia Refugee Repatriation and Resettlement Committee (LRRRC), the government body responsible for returnees, Monrovia is over-congested, as 1.1 million people out of the national population of 3.4 million reside in the capital, where socio-economic opportunities are concentrated.

The Significance of Personal Connections in the Initial Phase of Return

Existing studies suggest that, rather than the romanticized homecoming, the repatriation and reintegration of returning refugees in their country of origin is almost as complicated as the experience of exile, involving adjustment to a new culture and society (Black and Koser 1999; Hammond 2004, 2014; Harrell-Bond 1989). As in other types of migration, the importance of personal connections upon return emerged in my case studies of returnees in Liberia. Whether or not returnees could secure shelter and daily food through personal connections made a significant difference in the initial phase of the transition process.

Mobilizing Familial Support Networks

Among the various types of contact, immediate linkages such as family and kinship are particularly crucial in the migration process in that these networks often serve as the most reliable sources of assistance (see Long 2004; Pantuliano et al. 2008; Pilkington and Flynn 1999). Similarly, Liberian repatriates who were able to draw support from immediate family members had much better access to housing and food upon their return.

For example, Gloria was a twenty-two-year-old female returnee whom I had interviewed a few times in Ghana. She repatriated to Liberia in early 2009 under the UNHCR repatriation programme after ten years of exile. During the Liberian war, Gloria's family had taken a decision to send some family members outside the country. In the early stage of the civil war, one of Gloria's aunts had resettled in the United States. Gloria and her three sisters moved to Ghana with the expectation of being taken to the United States by her aunt. However, as this intended family resettlement scheme did not materialize, they finally abandoned the plan and made up their minds to go back to Liberia after the 2008 refugee demonstrations. Because Gloria's parents and other older siblings had remained in Liberia, her repatriation was very much a return to her 'home'.

When I met up with Gloria in Monrovia in April 2009, less than two months after her repatriation, her life was quite settled thanks to her family's assistance. She had been given accommodation and food by her elder sister. She also occasionally received sums of money from her siblings as an allowance. Gloria was about to start university studies in Liberia when the new academic year commenced with financial help from her family. Like Gloria, returnees who could access familial support in Liberia stayed at a relative's place, normally with food provided, upon their return, and were able to settle gradually into their new environment in the country of origin.

Depending on Buduburam-Based Networks

Not all returnees were blessed with access to kin support in Liberia. In particular, for those who had lost immediate relatives in the civil war, the lack of familial assistance made their return daunting. These returnees depended upon their repatriated friends from Buduburam camp, as they had done when they were living in Ghana. For instance, Caroline, a twenty-six-year-old female returnee, lost her parents and got separated from her siblings during the civil war and fled to Ghana alone. During an interview in April 2009 in Liberia, with no family accommodation, Caroline explained to me about her 'camping life' after her repatriation:

> I am moving around my friends' places for the last several months. They are all friends from Buduburam camp. First I stayed at Nora's place between September and October 2008. But her boyfriend came in so I had to move out. Then I spent several weeks at different places. In February [2009], I moved to Tito's place and I am still with her. I am not paying rent.[6]

Caroline was exceptionally lucky as her friends had generously accommodated her for several months. Whilst other returnees had in some ways extended their Buduburam-based networks to Liberia, once their stay became prolonged they were normally pressurized to move out of their initial accommodation or required to put some money into the host household. For example, Yonnio, a male former unaccompanied-minor refugee, went back to Liberia in March 2009 and found temporary shelter at a friend's place. But from the second week of his stay, he felt silent pressure from the host family:

> I am staying at George's [family's] place. He is my best friend from Buduburam. I am also getting food there ... But I can't rely on them for good. I know his parents are complaining about my extended stay because I am not contributing to them. Also, they themselves are constrained by limited resources. I need to move out as soon as possible.[7]

Caroline and Yonnio were both only very tenuously connected with other relatives in Liberia and had had barely any communication with them during their exile, so they were unable to draw substantial support from these extended kin upon their return to Liberia.

High Transition Costs for Those without Reliable Networks

In conflict-affected countries where state welfare provision is often absent, securing an initial provider of assistance is the first step for successful reintegration (Pantuliano et al. 2008: 63). As the evidence presented above shows, support from family members (and friends) cushioned returnees' transition by providing shelter, food and even some finance.

These forms of assistance had clear financial implications. If a refugee could not utilize these personal connections, their starting costs upon return would be much larger. For instance, monthly rent in Monrovia, even for a small room with a communal kitchen and toilet, was about $20, and it was common practice to demand advance payment for at least six months. Renting a house in the capital could cost at least $100 per month. Expenditure on food was also a burden for many repatriates without immediate assistance networks. In my own experience, a small meal from a market in Monrovia normally cost $1 or $2.

If a refugee returned without help to secure the basic necessities of living, such as shelter and food, they had to use the $100 repatriation grant provided by UNHCR just for rent and food, whereas a more fortunate returnee with familial support was able to save or invest it.

Constructing New Livelihoods

Once a physical foothold such as shelter is established, the next integration challenge for a returnee is to establish an economic footing. But as with their socio-economic lives during exile, significant differences emerged regarding their economic adjustments upon return; while some well-off returnees managed to establish an economic base relatively smoothly, many others were confronted by a series of difficulties. According to the case studies of Liberian repatriates, the transferability of livelihood strategies from exile and, again, access to meaningful networks in Liberia were key determinants in the degree of returnees' economic integration.

Transferability of Livelihood Resources

If returnees can transfer the livelihood assets and skills they have acquired in exile to the country of origin, this can be a positive factor in the integration process. On the other hand, when no or limited livelihood resources are transferable, returnees are likely to face economic hardship upon return (Rogge 1994: 45–46).

One of the few portable economic coping strategies for returnees was receiving overseas remittances, which were the most crucial livelihood resource for refugees in Buduburam camp. For instance, Charles's household, consisting of himself, his wife and two school-aged children, was one of the wealthiest families in the camp as they had access to large volumes of remittances from abroad. During their exile, Charles's household received a few hundred dollars every month from his siblings in the United States. Charles and his family decided to return to Liberia from Ghana in November 2008. Even after repatriation, the main income source of the household was the financial assistance it received from the United States. At the time of my interview with Charles in April 2009, he received at least $100–$150 per month from his relatives. This financial support continued to sustain his family and covered the transition costs from Ghana to Liberia, including housing, furniture and school fees for the children. Simultaneously, using the remittances as starting capital, Charles was discussing with some business partners setting up a vocational school that would provide computer-skills training in Monrovia.

In contrast, for most of the Liberian returnees from Ghana, their livelihoods in exile were of limited transferability because their previous subsistence strategies were deeply embedded in the camp environment. In Chapter 2, I analysed the livelihood trajectory of James, a twenty-five-year-old former unaccompanied minor. He had been making a living by doing housework for other Liberian households in Buduburam camp. When his client households repatriated in 2008, James lost his main income sources and eventually decided to go back to Liberia himself in early 2009. His original plan of survival upon his return was to find new households for which he could do the same work. When I met James in Liberia in May 2009, however, he was struggling to find new 'client families' in an unfamiliar environment. He said: 'I cannot find families who can give me cleaning or washing work … To do this kind of work, you have to have trust and good relation with them. I have not established them yet … I left Liberia at eleven years old. I don't know many people here [in Liberia]. It is hard for me to survive here'.[8]

In addition to the loss of his key source of income, James lost his informal economic safety net upon his return. In the camp, sharing resources between kindred, friends and neighbours was a common survival strategy for many households. James frequently obtained food and small cash from other residents in the camp, but after repatriation he could no longer rely on his 'friends in need' (Devereux and Sabates-Wheeler 2004: 15). He explained how he had been surviving during exile: 'In Buduburam, I had many helpers. When I was in trouble, I could run to someone for emergency. Buduburam camp was like a big family. People were sharing resources and assisting each other. But here [in Liberia] I can't do the same. I no longer have such people'.[9]

James had forged his social networks during his long exile in Ghana. His personal connections, however, comprised of his friends and neighbours residing within minutes' walking distance within the camp. In the process of multiple dislocations, his personal connections formed during exile were disrupted. Unless returnees moved to Liberia together with these helpers, the ties were severed or significantly circumscribed upon repatriation. Even if they did retain some of their camp connections, returnees were scattered all over the capital's county of about 1,900 square kilometres. The dispersed locations of returnees made it difficult for mutual assistance to function in the same way as it had in Buduburam.

The Importance of Social Networks in Job Seeking

If returnees were unable to transfer their coping strategies from Ghana, they needed to construct new income-generating strategies from scratch. Because they had returned to the capital city, where agricultural subsistence was unavailable, most returnees had to seek employment either in the private or the public sector.

As other scholarly works have noted (e.g. Poros 2001: 245; Vertovec 2009: 39), new arrivals often become linked to local labour markets through specific networks of interpersonal relations. Likewise, in Liberia, personal contacts, particularly with the former ruling group, the Americo-Liberians, played a key role in facilitating returnees' job-seeking activities. As described above, the country's power and resources rested entirely with this group until 1980. Even a few decades later, the descendants of ex-slaves still possessed economic and political privileges. With the inauguration of an Americo-Liberian president, Ellen Johnson Sirleaf, in 2005, this elite regained power over the country's economy and politics, according to my interviews in Liberia. Using two contrasting cases, I shall illustrate the extent to which access to strong networks differentiated the job-seeking activities of returnees from Ghana.

Leonard: 'My Uncle Always Found a Job for Me'

Leonard was a thirty-five-year-old, single, former Buduburam-based refugee. He came from an eminent Americo-Liberian family. He had some former high-ranking military officials among his ancestors, and several relatives occupied senior government positions at the time.

Leonard left Liberia for Ghana in 1997. His main purpose in moving there was to migrate to the United States through refugee resettlement programmes. Several members of his extended family had moved to New York State before and during the Liberian civil war. Leonard had been interviewed by the US embassy in Ghana in 2001, but following the terrorist attacks of 11 September 2001 in the United States, his application had been suspended.

With his dream of migrating fading, he gave it up entirely and repatriated in late 2006. Some of his older brothers had stayed in Liberia during the civil war, so Leonard was given accommodation by them upon his return. During his exile in Ghana, he had been mainly living on regular remittances from relatives in the United States. Even after his repatriation, his relatives continued remitting to him until Leonard established his life financially in Liberia.

Leonard had few problems in finding gainful employment in Liberia as his uncle always played a facilitating role in getting him a job. When I interviewed Leonard in May 2009, he was working for one of the major bilateral donor agencies in Liberia. His uncle on his father's side was then a senior administrative officer in the central government and was well-connected with all the donor agencies because of his high-ranking position. The uncle was also politically affiliated with the incumbent Liberian president and was a key member of her party. When I asked Leonard how he had obtained his current position, he explained to me that it was due to his uncle's strong connection with the donor agency.

When I talked to the director of the bilateral donor organization subsequently, he frankly admitted that Leonard's post had been 'created for' him, and given to him without any competition since it was not advertised. Leonard's monthly salary was roughly $400, which was considered very good pay in the economic climate of Liberia at the time.

The case of Leonard appears to be an extreme one, but among returnees who had close links with Americo-Liberian elites in the government or in companies, job hunting based on nepotism was commonly observed. By contrast, for the majority of returnees without good connections with the privileged class, finding lucrative employment became an extremely onerous challenge, as illustrated by the case of Comfort.

Comfort: 'No Contact, No Jobs'

Born in 1982, Comfort was twenty-seven years old at the time of my interview with her in Monrovia in 2009. Her parents used to farm in rural Liberia but they had migrated to Monrovia for better jobs. Comfort recalled that their prewar life had been financially very tough. Before her displacement, she had been in and out of school due to lack of money for tuition fees.

In 1996, her town was destroyed and other members of her family were all killed by a rebel group, and Comfort managed to flee from Liberia to Ghana alone. She survived in Buduburam camp by combining multiple casual income sources. She did not have any relatives abroad and so had no access to overseas remittances. During her exile in Ghana, she gave birth to a son, although her partner did not provide any material support for them.

Comfort had no plan to repatriate to Liberia until 2008. But between February and April 2008, she participated in the refugee protests in Buduburam and was arrested and detained by the Ghanaian police. Frightened by the brutal reaction of the Ghanaian administration, Comfort immediately registered with the UNHCR repatriation programme.

Since her repatriation in late 2008, she had faced various challenges in her attempts to settle in Liberia. She received a $150 repatriation grant from UNHCR ($100 for herself and $50 for her son). With no accommodation, however, she had to use most of this money to rent a room in Monrovia. Among all the difficulties, finding a job had been the toughest for her. Over the six months prior to our conversation, she had applied for about twenty jobs in banks, government offices and private companies but had got none of them. When she was in Ghana, she had learned computer skills at a vocational training school, but this did not help her to get a job in Liberia. Comfort lamented that in Liberia the quality of contacts determines what kind of job you can get. Without any close connections with 'someone who can put her into the system', Comfort felt that she had no hope of finding gainful employment in Liberia.

Comfort came back to Liberia with her six-year old son but she found it very hard to keep sustaining life for herself and her son. Without any stable income-generating means, Comfort struggled to secure adequate daily food for her household and increasingly depended on charitable support from her friends who returned from Buduburam. Furthermore, Comfort was unable to send her son back to school as she could not afford tuition and other expenditures for his schooling. Due to these daunting financial challenges, she had to give her son to another Liberian family. When I interviewed her in Liberia, her biggest and most immediate concern was accommodation, as her housing contract would end soon but she had not yet been able to find money to extend it.

The case of Comfort is in sharp contrast to that of Leonard. According to my observations, most returnees from Ghana had at least some contacts in Liberia. As Vertovec has emphasized, however, the quality of networks matters: 'dimensions of social position and power, such as the class profile of ... networks, have been shown to have considerable conditioning impact on the migration process' (Vertovec 2009: 39). In postwar Liberia, where the employment market had not been organized, connections with economic and political elites generated access to important livelihood opportunities, especially for institutional employment.

Returning with Bad Timing? Reintegration without Institutional Support

Through my research it became apparent that there were conspicuous disparities in the degrees of returnees' integration into Liberia. Evidently, some repatriates faced daunting challenges regarding economic reintegration. But how did non-refugee stakeholders perceive the situations of the returnees? Their views varied. The staff members of UNHCR and the LRRRC in general viewed the reintegration of ex-refugees from Ghana as gradually moving in a successful direction, which was perhaps a predictable response given their official position and responsibility.

When I challenged them about this by raising some concrete cases of returnees' struggles to settle in, some of the officers of UNHCR and LRRRC commented that because these returnees had not taken advantage of educational and vocational training opportunities in Ghana, they could not find work back in Liberia. They almost made it sound as if these repatriates had been lazy about investing in their futures. But it was evident to me that most of the repatriates suffered from the lack of meaningful connections in their search for jobs, not from any lack of, or failure to develop, vocational skills.

Conversely, staff members of UNHCR's partner agencies in Liberia gave me different comments. In an anonymous interview, an experienced field officer at one agency shared his personal view: 'We hear very few success stories of returnees. UN support for returnees is phasing out although there is so much to be done for their reintegration in Liberia ... Reintegration is not an automatic process. Their struggles need much more attention from donors. Reintegration is not just dumping people back to the country of origin'.[10]

As the comment above suggests, notwithstanding the number of challenges to integration facing returnees from Ghana, the level of support for them between 2008 and 2009 was very limited when they arrived in Liberia. Before their departure from Ghana, the refugees were informed of various forms of assistance awaiting them on their return. On one of the main streets in Buduburam camp, there was a big UNHCR banner saying 'Come home! Liberia is back on her feet!' Upon their return, however, returnees faced realities completely different from what they had expected. For instance, Dekontee, a twenty-eight-year-old female repatriate, commented in frustration that: 'I made enquiries to UNHCR [Liberia] about support schemes for us but they said that they are setting them up. When I called again, they said "We will get back to you", but I have never heard of any response from them for the last five months. In Ghana, we thought some assistance programmes are prepared for us but not really'.[11]

I shared these complaints of returnees with UNHCR Liberia staff members throughout the research period in Liberia. At one of these meetings, one of the senior programme officers, with obvious annoyance, explained that very little remained in the organization's budget for recent repatriates:

> We carried out the large-scale repatriation programme between 2004 and 2007. After the closure of the programme in 2007, reintegration support had already scaled down. But suddenly there was a big influx of returnees from Ghana after refugee demonstrations in 2008. We [UNHCR Liberia] were not prepared for such a large-scale repatriation at all.[12]

In war-torn countries in developing regions of the world, refugee repatriation and reintegration often occur before states have been able to establish
adequate social and economic capacity or infrastructure to support large
numbers of returnees (Long 2013). In this case, the Liberian government
was unable to provide any meaningful support for the integration of its
returning citizens. According to an LRRRC programme officer, in 2009
the ongoing assistance for returnees was limited to employment referral
services, the provision of advisory services for the retrieval of property,
and scholarship programmes for returnee students. The officer candidly
admitted that these services were being provided on a very limited scale
(for example, only two scholarships were given in the 2008/9 academic
year). He also acknowledged that there was almost no assistance for returnees in the area of livelihoods, due to lack of funds.

Observing the absence of effective governmental interventions, I began
wondering whether the government of Liberia was really ready to accept
its citizens repatriating from neighbouring states. With my findings on
the severe challenges facing returnees in Liberia in mind, I discussed
the absorptive capacity of the country with the director of the LRRRC.
Whilst she denied that the country was not prepared to receive returnees,
she also emphasized the necessity of external support for the repatriates:
'Liberia is on our way to recovery. We still need external assistance for
reintegration of returnees in the country. There is massive demand for
funding to enable them to kick-start their life in their new environment.
But now there is a huge funding shortage. This is a big issue for LRRRC'.[13]

As these testimonies from LRRRC and UNHCR staff suggest, repatriation from Ghana between 2008 and 2009 was an ad hoc initiative
and lacked adequate coordination between the sending and the receiving sides at government level and, equally importantly, at UNHCR level.
Despite some announcements about assistance upon return, repatriates
from Buduburam were going back to their country of origin where integration support was being phased out. With a dearth of external assistance, adjustment in a new environment was left almost entirely to returnees' individual capacities.

'Successful' or 'Failed' Repatriation?

One of the biggest problems in current discourses about repatriation is
the absence of a working definition of 'success' in relation to repatriation
and reintegration in the international refugee regime (Hammond 2014).
Despite the lack of official criteria for assessing repatriation or reintegration, I have attempted to appraise the repatriation of Liberian refugees in

relation to returnees' socio-economic conditions and their own feelings of satisfaction.

Degrees of Self-Reliance after Repatriation

After obtaining the 'optimal' solution for refugees, did the self-reliance of returnees improve in the country of origin? UNHCR's guide to repatriation (UNHCR 2004d) underscores the importance of self-reliance upon repatriation – defined as a state in which an individual, household or community depends on their own resources, judgement and capabilities with minimal external assistance in meeting basic needs. As illustrated with the case of Leonard, those who were already doing well in Ghana may have improved their already self-reliant lifestyle upon their return, because many of them obtained gainful formal employment in Liberia. On the other hand, a good number of Liberian returnees experienced severe setbacks in their living conditions upon repatriation; they said that their levels of self-sufficiency significantly decreased in Liberia as they lost peer assistance for food and other necessities.

Earlier in this chapter, I wrote about Yonnio, who had been temporarily hosted and fed by his friend from Buduburam. He told me that he had become worse off in Monrovia because upon return he had to worry about securing even absolute basics, such as accommodation and daily food, which he used to have when he was living in Buduburam. He did not have to pay any rent in Buduburam as he was living in a house with his friends in a rent-free zone of the camp. When he did not have money for food, he was occasionally able to obtain meals from his friends and neighbours. He could not carry any of these assets with him back to Liberia, however.

At the time of my interview with Yonnio in Liberia it was less than a year since he had repatriated, so the decline in his self-reliance could have been a temporary effect, in an initial stage of his new life. But could Yonnio improve his situation without external intervention in the subsequent year? Would he be able to construct effective networks and mobilize them to obtain gainful employment in Monrovia? Unfortunately, during fieldwork, I did not see any concrete clue that his life would improve dramatically given his limited asset profile and the lack of personal connections in his country of origin.

Refugees' Perspectives on Their Return

Even with worse economic conditions, if some former refugees feel happy or satisfied to be back in their motherland, we may still be able to call repatriation a 'success' or an 'achievement'. For instance, Bascom (2005: 176) reports in his study of Eritrean repatriates that they preferred poorer economic conditions in their homeland to a better situation in exile, and were sanguine about their future too.

With respect to their levels of satisfaction, again there was significant variation among returnees. As expected, those who were managing well were generally satisfied with their decision to repatriate. Meanwhile, many of those who faced severe adjustment challenges regretted their decision. As I mentioned above, Comfort had been suffering a great deal since her arrival in Liberia in late 2008. She complained to me about her situation:

N.O.: How are you seeing your repatriation now?

COMFORT: I am regretting my decision so much. No matter what UNHCR says, repatriation is neither any achievement nor solution for me.

N.O.: What do you want to say to UNHCR?

COMFORT: If UNHCR still says repatriation is the best solution, I really want to ask why so? 'Home sweet home' or 'nothing like home' ... but home is a place where you can find life easier, right? Since I came back to Liberia, everything is going worse. Can I still call this place home? I am only facing problems and my life is deteriorating so much. Why is it the best solution for me?[14]

Similar comments were echoed by other returnees who were daunted by a series of survival challenges in Liberia. These former refugees remained jobless for several months or longer after their repatriation and had to beg for charity, using the limited networks that had been forged in Buduburam. Some of these returnees began to see their Buduburam life as the 'good old days', although they had not necessarily embraced their life of exile in Ghana when they were living there.

'Re-Returning' to Buduburam

During fieldwork in Liberia, many of those who had encountered challenges in integrating expressed to me their intention to return to Buduburam. In fact, some managed to do so. When I concluded fieldwork in Ghana in late 2009, there was a noticeable number of returnee Liberians back in Buduburam camp. They had shared more or less similar livelihood challenges in Liberia and had decided to go back to Buduburam, where they believed that they would be able to survive.

Paul, a twenty-one-year-old former unaccompanied minor, repatriated to Liberia under the UNHCR programme in 2008, but went back to Ghana in 2009. Without any relatives abroad, his principal survival techniques in Buduburam comprised of portering goods with a wheelbarrow and peer support from his friends and neighbours. After a decade of exile, Paul had decided to leave Ghana because of his diminishing prospects for survival in the country. But, unfortunately, his life in Liberia turned out to be even more difficult. With few reliable contacts in Liberia, he continued 'camping' around his Buduburam friends' places and occasionally slept outdoors. He lived on the charity of his friends as long as they were willing to help him. Paul attempted to resume his portering work but could not purchase a wheelbarrow, which cost $75 in Monrovia. For almost a year, he had not been able to find any gainful employment there. He begged some cash from his friends for travel and luckily managed to make his way back to Buduburam. The following excerpt is from my interview with him upon his return to Buduburam camp.

N.O.: Why did you come back to Ghana?

PAUL: In the camp, at least I can find some helpers. They can give me small work and also some food. Marcus, Joanna, Fiona ... they can save my life. But there was no one like them in Liberia. I didn't really know many people there.

N.O.: How are you managing now [in Buduburam]?

PAUL: I wash someone's clothes.

N.O.: Do you want to go back to Liberia in the future?

PAUL: No, I don't want to go back there anymore. I don't like this camp life but at least [it is] better than Liberia.[15]

There is evidence that returnees will go back to their country of asylum if repatriation fails to offer viable protection and access to livelihood resources (see Bryan and Cocke 2010; Carr 2014; Crisp et al. 2008). Long has called this phenomenon 're-emigration' (Long 2010: 36), but among refugees in Buduburam, this return movement to Buduburam was referred to as 're-returning'. Whilst the term 're-emigration' does not necessarily suggest returning to a specific place, for these Liberian 're-returnees', it would mean moving back to the Buduburam refugee camp. By the time of their return to Ghana, most of the support provided by UNHCR had already ended, and thus going back to Buduburam did not give them any direct material benefits. Rather, their return was specifically to do with going back to the Buduburam refugee community in which they had experiences and memories of survival along with their fellow refugees. Even though the mutual assistance networks in the camp were significantly undermined, they still thought that they had a better chance of survival there than remaining in Liberia where they had few connections.

There were some commonalities among the 're-returnees', and they were similar to the shared characteristics of the poorer refugees in Buduburam. Most originally came to Ghana alone or with only a few immediate family members, as many of them had been separated from their family before or during their escape. None of them had any close relatives abroad, and therefore they had not received remittance assistance during their exile. In Buduburam, they had constantly relied upon other refugees. The departure of their principal supporters from Ghana often led to a decline in their living conditions. Due to dire survival challenges and little prospect of improvement in Ghana, they decided to go back to Liberia in despair.

Because their official refugee status was deleted from the UNHCR database when they left Ghana, the 're-returnees' were not to be found in any UNHCR statistics. According to Liberian refugees in Buduburam camp, however, there was a constant influx of these 'failed' repatriates into the camp. As I suggested above, there were others in Liberia who intended to return to Ghana provided that they could find the resources.

Conclusion: Repatriation and the Continuation of Socio-Economic Differences

This chapter has challenged the idealization of repatriation as an unproblematic homecoming. For several years, UNHCR had been strongly promoting repatriation to Liberia as the best solution for the remaining refugees in Ghana. But UNHCR now needs to answer a fundamental question: Is repatriation really the ideal solution for all of the Liberian refugees?

Evidently, there were considerable differences in the degree of reintegration among returned Liberians, despite them having opted for the same durable solution. Following returnees from Ghana to Liberia revealed the continuity of socio-economic inequality that prevailed in exile. As discussed, upon their arrival in Liberia, some wealthier returnees from privileged backgrounds, such as Leonard and Charles, settled in with relatively little stress by utilizing their individual and family networks in Liberia. In particular, personal contacts with the Liberian elite emerged as a key factor in facilitating their economic integration. Most of these repatriates had belonged to the high-income category when they were living in Buduburam camp, sharing Americo-Liberian origin, an eminent family background and a long history of family migration to the United States. Upon return, once again these repatriates mobilized their social capital to facilitate economic reintegration in their country of origin.

On the other hand, many other 'ordinary' returnees faced daunting hardships and often experienced severe setbacks in their living conditions due to the disruption of their subsistence and social networks. I presented the integration challenges of James in Liberia earlier in this chapter. Despite his desperate efforts to subsist in Liberia, he met with repeated failure and again had to depend on the charity of his friends from Buduburam. During one of my interviews with him in Monrovia, he pointed to structural inequalities between returnees with potent social assets and those without:

> If you know good rich people in Liberia, you can start from a much better position. You will find a job easily and may be able to still receive remittances. These people can be easily reintegrated ... When they were in Ghana, they were always assisted by their family abroad ... No matter [whether] you are in Ghana or Liberia, you will be better off if you are well linked with good rich people.[16]

For returnees without specific personal connections in Liberia, successful economic reintegration was not readily attainable by the efforts of an individual or a household. Given these research findings, refugees' return and reintegration ought to be understood as a highly selective process which is contingent upon their resource networks in the country of origin and abroad.

These empirical findings also indicate that it would be difficult to conclude that their 'refugee journey' (BenEzer and Zetter 2015) had really ended with repatriation to Liberia. In recent years, tens of thousands of Liberians from Buduburam decided to return to their country of origin due to the extensive promotion of repatriation by UNHCR. Making physical movement onto the terrain of their homeland was not a challenging task for them. However, except for a handful of privileged cases, building meaningful livelihoods and attaining self-reliance after protracted exile turned out to be an onerous challenge. As this chapter has demonstrated, for a considerable number of returnees from Ghana, their lives did not necessarily improve – in fact, they worsened – despite the fact that they had obtained the 'ideal' durable solution for them.

Notes

1. Personal communication, Buduburam, October 2008.
2. Interview, Buduburam, February 2009.
3. Interview, Buduburam, May 2009.
4. In order to meet more repatriates from Ghana, I also asked my research assistants to put me in touch with their friends and relatives who had returned to Liberia before my fieldwork.
5. Interview, Liberia, April 2009.
6. Interview, Liberia, April 2009.

7. Interview, Liberia, April 2009.
8. Interview, Liberia, May 2009.
9. Interview, Liberia, May 2009.
10. Interview, Liberia, May 2009.
11. Interview, Liberia, April 2009.
12. Interview, Liberia, May 2009.
13. Interview, Liberia, May 2009.
14. Interview, Liberia, May 2009.
15. Interview, Buduburam, July 2009.
16. Interview, Liberia, May 2009.

6

The 'End' of Refugee Life?
When Refugee Status Ceases

No-one should remain as a refugee forever. Refugee status cannot be
permanent.
—UNHCR protection officer in Ghana

The camp life is being tougher and tougher ... but returning to Liberia can
be even more difficult ... Even in worsening conditions, I will stay here [in
Buduburam].
—Female refugee in Buduburam

This chapter addresses Buduburam camp from 2012 onwards. Although
I completed thirteen months of fieldwork in West Africa in late 2009, I
remained connected with the refugees who participated in my research.
At the end of my time in Buduburam in 2009, in collaboration with camp
residents and some researchers who worked in the camp, I co-founded a
small-scale community-based organization that aims to improve food security for vulnerable families. For this reason, I maintained regular communications with the Buduburam refugee community by e-mail, Skype
and telephone.

Around the beginning of 2012, communications with my former refugee interviewees became more frequent. This was because in January
2012 UNHCR announced that refugee status for the remaining Liberian
refugees worldwide would cease at the end of June 2012. After this announcement, I received numerous e-mails and phone calls from my refugee interviewees who were concerned about whether they should remain
in exile or return to Liberia. Although I had already collected a substantial amount of data about their decisions to return or not during 2008
and 2009, I learned about their latest views on repatriation or remaining
in exile in the face of their ending refugee status. Drawing upon phone

and Skype interviews during 2012 and 2013 with some thirty households who had actively participated in the previous research, this chapter investigates how remaining Liberian refugees in Ghana responded to the sudden cessation of their 'formal' refugee life.

Invocation of the Cessation of Refugee Status

As noted earlier, in 2015, the majority of the world's refugee population lived in protracted refugee situations and the average length of their exile amounted to more than two decades. The frequency of protracted exile, however, does not mean that refugee status is granted permanently. According to the 1951 UN Refugee Convention, when the circumstances under which people were recognized as refugees no longer exist, the Cessation Clause is invoked by the international refugee regime to end their refugee status. For example, in recent years, the Cessation Clause has been invoked for refugees from Angola, Sierra Leone and Rwanda.

The vast majority of Liberians in Buduburam had become refugees due to the Liberian civil war. As nearly a decade had passed since the 2003 peace accord, the international community deemed that the situation in Liberia had greatly improved and that the cause of displacement no longer existed. This was the background of the invocation of the Cessation Clause for Liberian refugees in 2012.

In January 2012, there were still approximately 11,000 Liberian refugees living in Ghana. They were left with two options: either repatriate by the end of June 2012 before the invocation of the Cessation Clause, or remain in Ghana to be locally integrated as citizens through an agreement among members of the Economic Community of West African States (ECOWAS). One male refugee who had been in Ghana since 1998 described his registration interview with UNHCR staff as follows:

> I was told [by UNHCR staff] that I have only two choices; either repatriate or locally integrate. I told them I don't want to take any of them. But they told me to choose one ... For me, going back to Liberia is not an option so I had to take local integration. I did not really choose it but I was forced to take it'.[1]

In early 2012, UNHCR began the 'final call' for repatriation of the remaining refugees and pressed them to go back to Liberia before the termination of their refugee status. To encourage their return, UNHCR provided free transportation from Ghana to Liberia and an increased cash grant ($300 per adult and $200 per child) for repatriates. In order to access UNHCR's logistical support and repatriation grant, the refugees were required to register their repatriation decision with UNHCR by the end of March 2012 (this deadline was later extended to the end of April 2012).

UNHCR stated that after June 2012 it would no longer be able to assist remaining refugees to return to Liberia, and as banners they produced show (see Illustrations 6.1 and 6.2), it urged refugees to take advantage of this last offer of assisted repatriation. As in 2008 and 2009, the Liberian refugees were again forced to make a critical life-determining decision within the space of a few months about whether to return to Liberia or stay in Ghana.

The Sub-Regional Integration Scheme: Ambiguity and Uncertainty

What will happen if I stay in Ghana? What is ECOWAS integration? How does it change my life? These questions were frequently posed to me during my interviews with the remaining Liberians in Ghana. I could not answer these questions because of lack of detailed information about the sub-regional integration scheme that drew on the ECOWAS treaty.

ECOWAS is not a refugee-protecting body but a regional confederation of fifteen West African states, which was founded in 1975 to promote economic integration and trade activities across the region. Since roughly 2007, in the absence of the foreseeable attainment of any durable solutions, UNHCR had been focusing on the ECOWAS treaty not only as an instrument of regional economic integration but also as an 'innovative solution' for protracted refugee situations in West Africa (Fresia 2014).

The gist of this sub-regional approach is based on the 1979 Protocol on Free Movement adopted by ECOWAS, which confers on community citizens the right to enter, reside in and establish economic activities in the territory of any member state (Adepoju et al. 2007: 1). Even after the end of their formal refugee status, those who do not want (or cannot) go back to their country of origin are allowed to stay in their current country of asylum or to seek better opportunities in other ECOWAS member states. Boulton, a UNHCR legal officer, states that:

> Ordinarily, migration is not a 'solution' in the sense used by UNHCR. It is more often a temporary measure resorted to in order to overcome a deficit in the protection or assistance available to refugees. In West Africa, however, the provisions of the Protocol relating to the Free Movement of Persons, Residence and Establishment and four supplementary protocols adopted by ECOWAS may provide a solution for refugees from one member state residing in another. The rights to residence and employment at the heart of the 'solution' of local integration are available to refugees as to any other citizen of an ECOWAS state – at least, in theory. (Boulton 2009: 32)

Illustration 6.1 Banner posted inside Buduburam camp in early 2012.

Illustration 6.2 Banner posted inside Buduburam camp in early 2012.

During my fieldwork in 2008 and 2009, it was very clear to me that UNHCR Ghana staff members were keen to bring in this sub-regional scheme as a final remedy for Liberians trapped in Ghana. In fact, I was asked by some UNHCR international staff members in Ghana if I could assemble some supportive findings on the importance of mobility for refugees' livelihoods from my research in order to promote the ECOWAS scheme.

The substance of what the sub-regional integration scheme entailed, however, has remained unclear since then. To obtain more details about the integration scheme, in 2012 I contacted Allen, a Ghanaian who had worked for a UNHCR implementing partner for several years, and who was at that time working for a local NGO operating inside Buduburam camp.

N.O.: Do you know anything about ECOWAS's local integration scheme?

ALLEN: Nothing is clear about this. No information at all.

N.O.: Why?

ALLEN: I think the [Ghanaian] government is still reluctant about accepting many refugees in the country. In the meantime, UNHCR is departing from here. I am not sure whether there is any consensus between them about the remaining Liberians.

N.O.: What will happen after June 30?

ALLEN: I don't know. The government and UNHCR announced that after June 30 there will no longer be Buduburam refugee camp. The government is saying they will return this land to local chiefs but I do not know whether it will really happen.[2]

Almost all the refugees I interviewed complained about the dearth of information on the ECOWAS scheme. A male refugee in his twenties expressed his frustration, saying sarcastically: 'Well, at least, we know what it means by "repatriation"; we carry 30 kilos of items and receive $300 to start our life in Liberia. We still don't understand what it means by local integration as ECOWAS citizens. It is a black box. No one knows what is inside this box'.[3]

'Black box' – I repeatedly heard this term during my research in 2008 and 2009 from refugees to criticize the absence of information about the local integration plan. Even three years later, the ambiguity of the integration scheme for refugees remained unsolved, making rational decision-making extremely difficult, if not impossible.

Returning Refugees: What Had Changed Since 2009?

During the 2012 UNHCR repatriation programme, approximately 4,000 Liberians chose to go back to Liberia. Many of these refugees had changed their minds since 2009, and decided to return in the face of continuous announcements by UNHCR that it was the 'last call' for assisted repatriation.

Diminishing Economic Opportunities in Ghana

The most frequently cited reasons for refugees' decision to leave Ghana were related to the diminishing economic opportunities and support in Buduburam. According to Crisp (2000: 172), repatriation can be induced by a general deterioration of living conditions in countries of asylum, resulting from reductions in the level of international assistance and declining economic opportunities. As mentioned earlier, the general environment for refugees in Ghana had been increasingly onerous. After 2009, while aid for Liberian refugees was virtually cut off, the livelihoods of refugees in Ghana continued to be constrained by various obstacles.

In Chapter 2, I briefly introduced John, a refugee and owner of an internet café in the camp. He set up this popular business with the help of $2,500 from his relatives and friends living in North America. At the time of my interviews with him in 2009, his internet café was one of the most lucrative businesses in Buduburam, and he had no intention of returning to Liberia. When I spoke to John in February 2012, however, he gave me the following explanation of his decision to repatriate that year:

> I have been concerned that my business would slow down in the near future. As you know, the population of the camp has been shrinking in recent years. This year, I am sure that again many more refugees will leave [due to the cessation of refugee status]. With a reducing number of customers, it will be much harder to continue running my business. It is better not to wait until the last minute.[4]

In previous chapters I discussed how, between 2008 and 2009, the Buduburam refugee economy was significantly undermined. During my interview with John in early 2012, he emphasized the dwindling capacity of Buduburam camp economy more generally, stating: 'After you left in 2009, I think the general camp life got worsened. I know some wealthy families decided to go back to Liberia on their own. I am sure the percentage of poorer people is increasing inside the camp'.[5]

Although I did not collect quantitative data on refugees' income levels and well-being between 2012 and 2013, there was a firm consensus among all refugee interviewees that the overall socio-economic conditions of the

Buduburam refugee community had further deteriorated since my departure in 2009.

Abandoning the Resettlement Dream

Liberian refugees in Ghana were well-known for their desire for third-country resettlement (see Dick 2002b: 48; Essuman-Johnson 2011: 117). At the end of my previous fieldwork in late 2009, a considerable number of refugees continued to stay in Ghana primarily to pursue this solution. By 2012, however, some had abandoned this elusive dream and repatriated back to Liberia.

One of the interviewees introduced in previous chapters, Jones, was from an eminent family, one which had produced several statesmen and influential business people in prewar Liberia. A number of Jones's relatives, including his siblings, had migrated to the United States before and during the civil war, and Jones's household had a decent life in the camp due to constant remittances from them. Initially, Jones came to Ghana to try to find a way to join his relatives in the United States. For the last few years, he continued to extend his exile in order to pursue resettlement in the United States. When I interviewed him during the previous repatriation period between 2008 and 2009, his determination to pursue this 'dream' was firm.

Illustration 6.3 Refugees registering for repatriation.

Jones's quest for resettlement, however, was still unsuccessful three years later. During an interview with him in February 2012, Jones told me that, given the upcoming cessation of refugee status, the possibility of being resettled in the United States was no longer realistic, and he expressed his desire to repatriate. Because some of his siblings had remained in Liberia throughout the civil war, Jones quickly secured a place to live upon his return. He used savings accumulated from previous remittances for his family's transportation without waiting for the UNHCR repatriation programme to begin. With additional remittance support from his relatives abroad, at the beginning of March 2012, Jones's family spontaneously left Ghana to begin their new life in Liberia.

The 'Unfixedness' of Decision Making

Of course, there were many respondents who struggled to make up their minds about whether to stay or whether to repatriate, mainly because of the dearth of information about their future prospects if they chose to remain in Ghana. Victoria, the head of one of these households, which I described in Chapter 2, expressed her frustration to me in early 2012:

> The current situation is very confusing. Right now, UNHCR says, 'Register, register, register!' We were told that this would be the last opportunity to use the UNHCR repatriation package. So I started feeling like I should go back to Liberia this year. But I want to know what would happen to us if we stay in Ghana. This is why I cannot make up my mind.

Although Victoria did not register herself for UNHCR's repatriation programme by the end of March 2012, she changed her mind and decided to go back to Liberia in early 2013. The following is an excerpt from a conversation with her in 2013.

N.O.: Why have you decided to go back to Liberia?

VICTORIA: There is no future [for me] in Ghana. I cannot tolerate this uncertain life.

N.O.: What do you mean about 'uncertain life'?

VICTORIA: If I continue to stay in Ghana, what will happen to me? Since the end of June [2012], more than eight months passed but still we do not know the detailed contents of local integration plan.

N.O.: What did your husband [living in Norway] say about your return?

VICTORIA: He agreed with me.

N.O.: Have you told Justina and Anita [those who were part of Victoria's remittance cluster] about your decision?

VICTORIA: Not yet ... But in any case, I cannot carry them with me to Liberia.[6]

When Victoria changed her mind and decided to repatriate in 2013, the UNHCR assisted repatriation programme had already come to an end. In Victoria's case, her husband in Norway sent remittances to prepare for her return to Liberia.[7] Victoria's return to Liberia, in turn, meant the departure of another remittance recipient in Buduburam and the dismantling of a remittance cluster which included at least two other refugees.

As the example of Victoria shows, after the invocation of the Cessation Clause, some remaining households in Ghana decided to go back to Liberia. One of these was headed by Mariana, a single mother in her early thirties with two children of school age. She chose to stay in Ghana because she wanted her children to complete their elementary school education, and she had some 'hope' in a future local integration programme. However, when I interviewed her in early 2013, she regretted her decision, saying: 'I initially opted for local integration in Ghana but now I want repatriation ... We waited for many months but still the Ghanaian government is not giving us the contents of integration scheme. Also, day by day, living in the camp is getting tougher'.[8]

Mariana went to the UNHCR office in Accra to express her intention to return to Liberia but she was unable to receive assistance: 'I went to UNHCR in November [2012] and told the protection officer that I want to go back to Liberia. But she [UNHCR protection officer] told me that registration for repatriation is already closed down and UNHCR can no longer assist any Liberians who didn't apply for repatriation by the deadline'.[9]

When I discussed Mariana's case with Allen, the Ghanaian NGO officer mentioned above, he confirmed that Mariana was not an exception and that there were other refugees who had also changed their minds and wished to repatriate. Allen highlighted how problematic the sequencing of cessation and repatriation deadlines were: 'The Ghanaian government and UNHCR should have disclosed the detailed contents and schedule of ECOWAS integration scheme before the closure of repatriation. Without knowing the contents of local integration, how could refugees make an informed decision about their future?'[10]

Returning to Liberia or staying in Ghana were not mutually exclusive options for some refugee households. In the face of the upcoming cessation of their refugee status, some of my interviewees used family dispersal strategies between Ghana and Liberia in order to keep 'room to manoeuvre' given their uncertain future.

For instance, Christiana, a fifty-three-year-old female head of household, sent her husband, who was suffering from a chronic illness, along with one of her two sons back to Liberia in 2012 using UNHCR's repatriation package. But she remained in Buduburam with her younger son to pursue any opportunities that might arise from their ECOWAS migrant status.

While the decision to split up Christiana's household was based on a shared decision among all the family members, some households could not agree on whether to repatriate or continue to live in exile. Randy, a 27-year-old refugee, got separated from his unmarried partner and child in 2012 because of a difference of opinion on repatriation.

N.O.: Why didn't you go back to Liberia with your family?

RANDY: I cannot go back. No house, no relatives to help us, no jobs ... it is too risky.

N.O.: But your wife returned, right?

RANDY: Yes, she left [with their child].

N.O.: Why did she leave?

RANDY: She could no longer tolerate the camp life. I explained [to] her how difficult [it is] to live in Liberia but she didn't listen to me.

N.O.: Did you speak to her after her return?

RANDY: Only once, she called me. I also called her but my phone call didn't come through.[11]

Reasons for Staying in Ghana

Even with the intense promotion of repatriation, coupled with the imminent ending of their refugee status, the majority of Liberians remaining in Ghana – approximately 7,000 refugees – continued to remain in exile at the end of June 2012. With very few benefits or future prospects in Ghana, why did they remain in exile? As this section makes clear, these refugees did not embrace camp life in Buduburam. Rather, most of them were 'stuck' in exile due to concerns about security, psycho-social issues, lack of capital and access to livelihoods, as well as issues regarding documentation and registration.

Worries about Insecurity upon Return

The perception of (in)security after repatriation is closely related to personal experiences during the conflict in the country of origin. The formal signing of a peace treaty does not necessarily mean that the home country has become a safe and comfortable place to return to for all displaced people (also see Hardgrove 2009; Lindley 2011).

Among the refugees who chose to stay in Buduburam, especially those who had been involved in Samuel Doe's administration, some were particularly concerned about the risk of persecution in Liberia. This concern was amplified by the inauguration of President Ellen Johnson Sirleaf in 2005, since she had been persecuted by Doe and thus had initially supported Charles Taylor, who launched the rebellion against Doe's regime. For example, Nathalie was a fifty-six-year-old widow who had lost some of her immediate family in the initial stage of the Liberian war but had managed to flee to Ghana in 1990. Because her husband was a county superintendent in Doe's administration, her family had been deliberately targeted by rebel groups. Her fear of being persecuted, coupled with lingering acute trauma, prevented her from wanting to repatriate even after two decades of exile. When I asked her whether she would return or not in February 2012, she gave me the same reply that she had given three years earlier:

> You know what happened to my family ... My husband was very close to President Doe during his regime. This is why we were targeted by rebels. We were tortured, raped ... These rebels have not been arrested. The Liberian war is not over ... My face and name are well known to them [the former rebel groups]. If I go back, they will hunt me.[12]

In addition to Nathalie, among my respondents there were a few other households who had undergone similar traumatic experiences as a consequence of their family's deep involvement in the Doe regime. For these refugees, who had experienced gross human rights violations, Liberia was still a place to be feared. They were determined not to go back there regardless of claims about the general stability of post-conflict Liberia and the cessation of their formal refugee status.

Lack of Confidence in Establishing New Livelihoods upon Return

Whether refugees can ensure their economic security upon return or not was one of the principal concerns of Liberian refugees during my earlier field research, and it remained so in 2012. Almost all of my respondents who did not repatriate mentioned a lack of confidence about obtaining gainful employment or building new income-generating strategies in Liberia as a major reason to stay in Ghana.

This was not an unfounded fear, as there is a strong correlation between poor socio-economic status and difficulties in establishing a new economic basis upon return. In Buduburam camp, impoverished refugees with few marketable livelihood skills had been surviving by combining multiple meagre income-generating activities, such as selling water and fruit, braiding hair and doing housekeeping jobs for other refugees. Also, most of the indigent refugees had been reliant on charity and mutual assistance from other camp residents. As demonstrated in Chapter 5, since their income sources were built upon their Buduburam connections, the transferability of these sources to Liberia was significantly restricted. Despite their deteriorating living conditions in Ghana, these poorer households thus had to remain in exile.

In Chapters 3 and 4, I wrote about the difficult living conditions of Stephanie and her malnourished daughter. At the time of my study in 2009, her household was surviving on a very small income from selling oranges in the camp and probably from commercial sex. During an interview in 2012, Stephanie explained her current means of survival and expressed her concerns about constructing a new livelihood in Liberia if her household chose repatriation:

> I stopped selling oranges last year [2011]. I had to use money for my daughter's medical expenses because she got malaria recurrently, so I could not buy oranges ... I am now making a little money by selling water inside the camp. I also wash others' clothing for some money. I sometimes get food from my neighbours. This is how my daughter and I have been managing [in Ghana]. I know I cannot live in the same way in Liberia [because we do not have such helpers].[13]

Stephanie's concern about establishing an economic base in Liberia was well-founded. In Chapter 5, I discussed the 're-returnees' who repatriated to Liberia but came back to Buduburam because of the harsh challenges of economic integration. Refugees who had remained in Buduburam knew about these 're-returnees', and were aware that many of them had had a similar economic status while they were living in the camp. Naturally, remaining refugees in poorer economic categories came to think that the possibility of economic survival upon return was very slim for them too.

Non-Registered Refugees: Trapped in Exile

Many refugee households without UNHCR ID cards were stuck in the camp. As described in earlier chapters, there were said to be more than a few thousand non-registered Liberian refugees in Ghana. These had not been recognized by UNHCR and thus had not been able to benefit from UNHCR's repatriation programme, including logistical support and financial payments. According to my refugee interviewees, in 2012, transportation to Liberia with several pieces of luggage cost nearly $100 per person, which was a considerable amount for most camp residents, who did not have access to transnational remittances.

An example would be Emily's household, whose difficult life in the camp I described earlier. She and her children were living at a bare subsistence level and heavily reliant on charitable support from neighbours, in particular Kevin and Samantha, who also faced survival challenges in Buduburam. As explained below, despite increasing uncertainty surrounding their future in Ghana, Emily and her four children were trapped in exile.

Emily: 'Hard to Stay Here but Impossible to Return'

At the time of my research in 2009, Emily's household was living hand-to-mouth by gathering and selling discarded plastic bags and with support from other refugees. According to an interview in 2012, she stopped collecting plastic bags due to increasing competition as other poorer refugees had taken up the same means of subsistence. The previous year, she began selling drinking water, which gave her a meagre profit.

In early March 2012, Emily said she was not planning to go back to Liberia for multiple reasons. During the civil war, her village was attacked by the rebels and her household was dispersed. Since then, she had completely lost contact with her parents and siblings (in fact, she did not know whether they were still alive or not), and therefore she would be unable to rely on family assistance for housing and food in Liberia. With limited literacy and no special livelihood skills, Emily believed that it would be extremely difficult, if not impossible, for her to sustain her current household if she returned to Liberia.

Meanwhile, she was increasingly concerned about her future survival in Ghana. With a diminishing number of refugees in the camp, she had been barely able to make significant income from low-profit livelihoods requiring a large number of customers. Also, more importantly, Emily was particularly worried about the repatriation of Kevin's family, who had been regularly assisting her and her children. As Kevin and his wife Samantha were considering the option of repatriation in the face of the cessation of their refugee status, Emily might lose the most crucial helper for her household.

Emily's worst case scenario was being left alone in Ghana without any other refugees on whom she could depend. Without a UNHCR ID card, however, her household could not avail themselves of the UNHCR repatriation package. Thus, if they were to change their mind and go back to Liberia, they would have to cover the cost of transportation and other necessary expenses, which was unrealistic with her meagre income and lack of savings.

As Emily's case illustrates, many of those who continued to stay in Buduburam were not only reluctant to return but in fact unable to do so, given that they had very little or no access to shelter, reliable support networks, marketable livelihood skills and sometimes no access to repatriation support because they had no UNHCR ID card. These various impediments created a complex situation in which these households were 'forcibly immobilised' (Lubkemann 2008a: 455) in Ghana.

A Future in Limbo: Life Post-Cessation

The ECOWAS Integration Scheme: A 'Solution' for Former Refugees?

For those who opted to remain in Ghana (or were unable to repatriate), the idea was that their situation would be dealt with through the ECOWAS sub-regional integration scheme. This 'solution' was predicated on the assumption, held by UNHCR, that increasing refugees' mobility through the scheme would be a means of ensuring their enduring access to sustainable livelihoods and meaningful employment opportunities by providing regularized long-term residency and better access to labour markets in ECOWAS countries (UNHCR 2012b). However, the feasibility of this new scheme deserves careful scrutiny.

First, notwithstanding the increased focus on the mobility of refugees, evidence points to the differentiated levels of access to mobility among different groups in relation to their socio-economic class. Bauman, for example, states that mobility has become the most powerful and most coveted stratifying factor between 'the mobile elite' and the poor in the current world: 'certain people can move out of the locality at will. Others watch helplessly the sole locality they inhabit' (Bauman 1998: 18). As the cost of migration has multiplied with the increasingly restrictive migration regime, socio-economic status has become ever more important in differentiating levels of access to specific forms, patterns and degrees of mobility.

Also, successful livelihoods cannot be established through mobility alone, but require access to other resources such as business knowledge, personal trade connections and start-up capital. But, as repeatedly emphasized, most remaining Liberian refugees had extremely limited resources, few marketable livelihoods skills and no access to financial capital with which to embark on new enterprises. Therefore, without the provision of a holistic support package, granting former refugees in Ghana sub-regional mobility would perhaps make little or no difference – making the ECOWAS scheme a less than optimal solution.

Furthermore, we cannot ignore the limited absorptive capacities of the West African region. Most ECOWAS member countries are among the least-developed nations, and suffer from stagnant economies and high unemployment. It is hard to imagine that many Liberian refugees would be able to access meaningful employment in such an economically weak region. Even if they could move freely to markets in neighbouring states, newcomers are likely to face language barriers and discriminatory practices from locals, as Liberian refugees occasionally experienced in Ghana.

Most importantly, as Long (2014) warns, advocating that refugees become (economic) migrants risks diminishing much needed protection space in host countries, allowing states to evade their responsibilities under the 1951 Refugee Convention. If migrant status is seen as an acceptable alternative to durable solutions, such schemes will disguise the failure to provide a solution by substituting the label of 'refugee' with that of 'economic migrant'. In any case, follow-up research is necessary to find out whether this sub-regional scheme can constitute a 'solution' for Liberians who continue to live in exile. Without this investigation, this quasi-durable solution can blur responsibility for this population's protection, and even be used as part of broader containment measures of refugees by the Global North within West Africa.

The Increasing Invisibility of Remaining Liberians

Even more alarming was the observation that the remaining Buduburam refugee population was slowly becoming 'invisible'. Polzer and Hammond (2008: 417) note that invisibility in forced migration is essentially relational to and dependent upon the power dynamics and interests connecting those who see and those who are seen – or not. Thus, an issue of invisibility necessarily entails answering questions about who is 'invisible to whom' and 'why', as part of a broader understanding of the political context.

In the context of Ghana, non-registered refugees without UNHCR ID cards had always been invisible to UNHCR, regardless of their vulnerabilities and dire need for protection. Also, the agency refused to recognize the presence of 're-returnees' in Buduburam, because this would mean acknowledging that these refugees had experienced unsuccessful repatriation and reintegration in Liberia. Finally, after the invocation of the Cessation Clause in 2012, those who did not choose to repatriate were effectively rendered invisible to UNHCR, as they were stripped of refugee status.

Zetter (2007) warns of the creation of various 'labels' attached to refugees, such as 'bogus' or 'economic', because these degraded labels can lead to the deterioration of refugee protection. However, even this pejorative labelling at least gives recognition to the existence of forced migration. In this instance, the Liberian refugees who remained in Ghana after 2012 experienced a process of 'invisibilization' that goes beyond even labels. Through the process of invisibilization by non-refugee stakeholders, issues related to refugees in effect 'disappear' from the agenda as if they no longer exist. Invisible people lose their legitimacy to belong to any state or institution and are inherently excluded as outsiders, reminiscent of Bauman's concept of 'human waste' or 'wasted lives' (Bauman 2004). Bauman describes this as an inevitable outcome of the modernized world, made-up of 'the population of those who either could not or were not wished to be recognized or allowed to stay' (ibid.: 5) because they are 'supernumerary, unneeded, of no use' (ibid.: 12). In Ghana, the very existence of ex-refugees was buried without much notice by human rights observers, the media, advocates or researchers.

Andrews's (2008) study of Sierra Leonean ex-refugees in Boreah camp in Guinea is potentially very illuminating regarding the future of Buduburam. She showed how refugees and refugee camps in Guinea had become invisible to the refugee assistance regime and the host government once assistance was rescinded and refugees refused to avail themselves of the option of voluntary repatriation. Despite the increased vulnerability and protection needs of the remaining Sierra Leonean refugees, they had been abandoned with no alternative durable solutions and ambiguous legal status. Is this the situation that Liberian former refugees will find themselves in in the near future? Since the ECOWAS framework is unlikely to generate meaningful changes in refugees' lives, the example of Boreah camp is a plausible scenario for the remaining refugees in Buduburam.

Conclusion: Diversity in Responses to the End of Refugee Status

This chapter has shown how refugee households reacted to the cessation of their refugee status. In general, refugees who are wealthier or more resourceful tend to repatriate or leave a camp earlier, especially in the face of insecurity or trouble. Crisp notes that 'the strongest members of a refugee population are usually the first to repatriate, leaving the weaker members behind' (Crisp 2003b: 8). The responses of Liberian refugees to the Cessation Clause and the announcement of the subsequent closure of the camp support this observation; better-off households had more options and usually decided to eventually depart from Ghana, whereas those with scarce resources were left immobile in Buduburam.

Alarmingly, this, in turn, means that a growing proportion of the camp population is made up of vulnerable people. In other words, this fact suggests that the refugees who were the most vulnerable and therefore the least well-suited to taking advantage of the ECOWAS integration scheme were the ones left abandoned in exile to survive as 'economic migrants.'

Before my departure in late 2009, I interviewed the senior programme officer of UNHCR Ghana to ask what UNHCR would do for the Liberian refugees who continued to stay in exile. With obvious annoyance, he replied: 'Those who are staying in Buduburam camp are predominantly [doing so] for seeking socio-economic betterment in Ghana, not because of persecution or threat [in Liberia]. Assistance for socio-economic development is not UNHCR's mission. I don't think UNHCR will have to take any responsibility to help the residual Liberians'.[14]

However, as shown above, this assessment of the reasons why refugees continued to remain in exile was patently wrong. Observing what types of households were left behind in Buduburam, it is obvious that, far from pursuing socio-economic opportunities in Ghana, these refugees were unable to think realistically about return to Liberia and were forced to continue their tough camp life despite very few prospects in Ghana.

Different responses to the cessation of refugee status among refugees again highlight the risk of homogenizing a specific group of refugees (also see Al-Ali 2002; Allen and Turton 1996; Turton 2003). My follow-up study with the same households over an extended number of years demonstrates that the meaning of exile was often very different for each household within the Buduburam refugee population. Like Jones, some refugees chose exile in order to increase their options, often access to resettlement opportunities in the developed regions of the world. These 'proactive refugees' (Van Hear 1998: 44) have normally maintained a foothold in Liberia, and repatriation is a secondary option in case the ideal scenario does not work out. Alternatively, for those who left the country to flee from physical violence, and particularly for those with family units broken before and during displacement, the decision to stay in Ghana continued to be based on a need for refuge, in part because of concerns that return to Liberia could be the beginning of 'new suffering', as discussed in Chapter 5.

Furthermore, significant diversity among refugees points to the necessity of micro-level analysis in pursuit of solutions. Van Hear (2014b) underlines the importance of the socio-economic backgrounds of migrants in shaping patterns, processes and outcomes of migration. More specifically, he explores how the migrant's capacity to mobilize different amounts and forms of resources results in a range of possible 'choice' in their migration decisions:

> What counts is the degree of choice in moving or staying put ... Sometimes, it may be the privileged who can leave while the less endowed are forced to stay, stuck in involuntary immobility. The well endowed may have the resources to move if they want or need to, while the less endowed have no choice but to stay put because they have insufficient resources to move across borders. At other times, while the less endowed must leave, the privileged may choose to stay. In challenging circumstances, the well endowed may have the resources to stay put ... and it may be that the less endowed have no choice but to move. (ibid.: S113)

This observation generally applies to the example of Liberian refugees faced with the cessation of their refugee status. As shown in this chapter, given their socio-economic resource portfolio, some well-endowed refugees, such as John and Jones, could choose whether to move or remain in exile, and made a deliberate decision to return to Liberia. Meanwhile, less-endowed households, like those of Emily and Stephanie, stayed immobilized in the camp since they could not afford other options due to their limited assets and the restricted nature of the networks to which they had access.

Without disaggregating the refugee population to an individual or a household level, it is hard to explain why some returned and many others refused to go back, even within the same macro-environment. Such a 'bottom-up approach' may pose some practical and logistic challenges for UNHCR and other refugee-assisting agencies on the ground. Nonetheless, given the heterogeneity of refugees' circumstances, the adoption of a 'people-centred approach' (Zetter 2012: 10) is indispensable if refugee policy makers are to tackle the issue of intractable situations of protracted displacement.

Notes

1. Interview, Buduburam, February 2012.
2. Interview, Buduburam, March 2012.
3. Interview, Buduburam, March 2012.
4. Interview, Buduburam, February 2012.
5. Interview, Buduburam, February 2012.
6. Interview, Buduburam, March 2013.
7. Victoria's husband had been trying to bring her to Norway as his spouse for the last few years, but this process had been quite slow. According to Victoria, the absence of official documents to prove their marital status and the inadequacy of her husband's earnings in Norway were delaying the process of family reunification.
8. Interview, Buduburam, January 2013.
9. Interview, Buduburam, January 2013.
10. Interview, Buduburam, January 2013.
11. Interview, Buduburam, July 2012.
12. Interview, Buduburam, February 2012.
13. Interview, Buduburam, March 2012.
14. Interview, Accra, September 2009.

7

Developing a Better
Understanding of Livelihoods,
Self-Reliance and Social
Networks in Forced
Migration Studies

> The global donor community has become increasingly interested in
> strategies that can lead to a further reduction in the levels of relief
> expenditures for long term refugees.
>
> —Karen Jacobsen, *The Economic Life of Refugees*

In this book, I have tried to probe into the diverse realities of refugees'
economic lives during protracted displacement and to critically investigate whether a 'self-reliant' refugee camp can be feasible even in the
absence of enabling conditions. Simultaneously, I have attempted to his-
toricize the lives of refugees in prolonged exile through the lens of livelihoods, including both pre-displacement and post-refugee periods. In so
doing, I have included refugees' voices as much as possible in order to
adequately represent their perspectives as they are seldom reflected in
international refugee policy making.

This chapter synthesizes the findings, and revisits the viability of the
self-reliant camp model. It also offers a theoretically and empirically informed understanding of refugees' livelihoods, remittances, social capital, and the difficulties of return migration from protracted periods of
exile. Finally, drawing upon research conducted over several years, the
book sheds a broader light on what it is like to be a refugee over a protracted period in the Global South.

The Myth of Buduburam: Does the Model of a Self-Reliant Camp Stand Up?

The End of the Buduburam Fairy Tale

'Vibrant refugee businesses', 'thriving camp commerce' and 'economically successful refugees' – these are expressions which had been frequently used by UNHCR and researchers to describe the economic lives of refugees in Buduburam camp. As the findings presented here demonstrate, however, this idealized image is at minimum overstated, and at worst a myth. With a handful of exceptions, most of the visible commercial activities were totally incapable of producing meaningful income for refugee entrepreneurs.

Instead, access to substantial remittances from overseas was identified as almost the sole way to enable refugees to attain a decent standard of living in the camp. On the other hand, those without access to these transnational financial assets often found themselves trapped in a daily struggle for survival. This alarming fact highlights UNHCR's failure both to support refugees' livelihoods to meet their basic needs and to ensure adequate protection for the poorest and most vulnerable.

Despite UNHCR's stereotypical representation of refugees in Buduburam camp as self-sufficient, the camp was in fact a very difficult environment for refugees to achieve economic autonomy. Camp residents had very little access to natural resources such as arable land and water, making agricultural subsistence unfeasible. In Ghana, there were scant formal employment opportunities for refugees due to various bureaucratic hurdles. Even in the informal sector, local markets were not readily accessible to refugees due to discrimination from Ghanaian traders and lack of access to local social networks. Because of these barriers, refugees were forced to operate in the confined market area of the camp, predominantly dealing with other refugees and a tiny number of local villagers.

Remittances provided a perfect 'solution' for perpetuating such a distorted economy in that the remittance-reliant life required no formal job or access to local markets or natural resources. In other words, financial remittances effectively masked the absence of enabling conditions for Liberian refugees to pursue economic independence by creating the veneer of a vibrant economy. When relatively large amounts of remittances were flowing in and were circulating through what I have termed 'remittance clusters', the refugee community was somehow able to survive despite restrictions on their livelihoods. Nonetheless, as I have described, after the large-scale repatriation programme of 2008 and 2009, coupled with the 2008 global financial crisis, the remittance-based economy in Buduburam began to collapse.

This book opened with a vignette of refugee demonstrations against UNHCR's local integration scheme for the remaining Liberian refugees and questioned why these 'successful' refugees so adamantly rejected being integrated in Ghana. As I continued my research and learned about the daily lives and living conditions of refugees in Buduburam, especially those from poorer households, I could see why the idea of local integration was so unpopular among the camp residents. Except for a small number of privileged refugees, many others perceived local integration as the acceptance of permanent suffering and deprivation, without prospects for future improvement or opportunities.

The Politics behind the Promotion of Self-Reliance

Earlier, I pointed to the absence of convincing empirical studies on the economic status of refugees in Buduburam camp. During my research, I increasingly wondered why the self-reliant reputation given to this refugee population had been maintained for many years without plausible data to support it. Voutira and Harrell-Bond state that the refugee-assisting regime has elaborate schemes for targeting aid to refugees with a view towards 'handing over' to the local administration after the desired state of 'self-sufficiency' has been constructed (Voutira and Harrell-Bond 2000: 72). In her study of the Kiryandongo refugee settlement in Uganda, Kaiser has shown how 'UNHCR was involved in a definitive process whereby it sought to "hand over" responsibility for the settlement at Kiryandongo to the Ugandan government, arguing that the refugees were approaching self-sufficiency and it was time for them to be absorbed completely into local government structure' (Kaiser 2000: 1). Before its handover to the host government, UNHCR Uganda had carefully constructed Kiryandongo's reputation as 'the most successful settlement in Africa' (ibid.: 12) so as to justify its own withdrawal. However, Kaiser notes that this transfer of responsibility from UNHCR to the Ugandan government was driven by imperatives of cuts in the budget for the refugee settlement and of demonstrating the putative 'success' of refugees' economic autonomy and sustainability even without UNHCR's continuing presence.

There is significant resonance between the Kiryandongo case and UNHCR's approach to Buduburam. Given the dwindling resources available for Liberian refugees, UNHCR Ghana gradually withdrew its support for the remaining refugees and attempted to pass responsibility for them on to the Ghanaian administration. In its handover scenario, the self-reliant image of Buduburam was essential for the UN refugee agency, as it constructed a fiction of economically successful refugees. What was crucial for UNHCR was the establishment of the claim that the refugees in Buduburam 'appeared' to be self-sufficient, rather than the fact of whether they had actually achieved self-reliance.

In Ghana, UNHCR never conducted any detailed investigations into the socio-economic status of Liberian refugees in the country, even while portraying the Liberian refugee camp as a 'successful and exemplary' model. Given their intention to withdraw support from this long-term refugee population, it seems apparent that UNHCR did not wish to be made aware about the 'realities' of refugees' social and economic conditions, as this could raise ethical or practical concerns around the agency's exit scenario, which relied on the notion that refugees in Buduburam could sustain themselves as economic actors following the ECOWAS integration scheme.

In the meantime, during my first period of research, UNHCR made every effort to minimize the number of remaining Liberians by pressurizing them to repatriate in order to make the reluctant Ghanaian administration feel 'comfortable' about integrating the residual cases. As already stated above, in late 2009, UNHCR stopped subsidizing the camp clinic and schools, halted free food rations for vulnerable families, reduced funding for its implementing partners and handed over most of the camp facilities to the government of Ghana. The UN refugee agency was evidently paving the way for its final departure from this protracted refugee situation, which came about in 2012 with the invocation of the Cessation Clause.

Revisiting the Promotion of Self-Reliance: In Whose Interest Is It?

The Paradox of Self-Reliance and Dependency

In the international refugee regime, aid dependency has been traditionally viewed and discussed in an extremely negative light. It is widely and firmly believed that dependency syndrome generates deleterious effects on refugees by crippling their initiative and responsibility for their own life and leading to a loss of dignity, self-respect and even depression (see Harvey and Lind 2005; Stein 1981; Turner 2010). As I explained in the Introduction, among refugee-policy makers, promotion of self-reliance is typically posited as a remedy for dependency syndrome.

However, the nature of refugees' economic lives in Buduburam represents a paradox of self-reliance and dependency. As the Introduction highlighted, to date there have been no rigorous and systematic criteria for assessing the degree of refugees' self-reliance. In the absence of a clear measurement system, UNHCR often views refugees as self-reliant when they are living without assistance from the refugee-assisting regime. In that sense, the vast majority of residents in Buduburam camp were indeed 'self-reliant' because they were making ends meet with virtually no access to humanitarian or development assistance.

On the other hand, paradoxically, refugees also remained heavily dependent on others, including relatives, friends and neighbours for their day-to-day survival in the camp. Almost all well-off refugees in Buduburam were reliant on overseas remittances for many years. As examples of 'remittance clusters' revealed, a significant number of those not in receipt of remittances relied on the trickle-down benefits of others' remittances. Interdependence was an essential survival strategy among impoverished groups of refugees. The economic lives of Buduburam residents comprised of numerous complex layers of dependency; instead of being dependent on 'official aid' from UNHCR and other relief agencies, however, their survival depended on informal support from their personal contacts.

Interestingly, while aid agencies and policy makers stigmatize refugees' dependency on relief organizations or donors, they seldom criticize refugees' dependency as long as it is on their personal and social sphere. In fact, instead of criticism, the support within refugee communities is generally lauded by aid agencies as a positive sign of 'mutual solidarity' or 'communal resilience'. Yet when refugees rely on external aid from UNHCR and its partner organizations, this becomes symptomatic of a 'dependency mentality'.

The Promotion of Self-Reliance for Whom?

This, in turn, invites a question: For whom is refugees' self-reliance really promoted? Given the intractable and protracted nature of certain refugee situations, the countries and institutions of the Global North have been increasingly keen on reducing their financial spending on refugees, *inter alia* for those in prolonged displacement. The discourse of self-reliance fits well with the interests of the international donor community.

Among refugee-policy makers, refugees' ability to achieve self-reliance and escape from dependency is commonly framed as an inverse function. This inverse correlation leads to an ungrounded assumption that the promotion of self-reliance can be automatically achieved by reducing assistance for refugees. By framing self-reliance as a way to empower refugees and as a panacea for aid dependency, UNHCR and the international donor community can justify reducing costly assistance programmes for refugee populations in situations of protracted exile, and even disengaging from them.

In the face of decreasing financial commitment from the donor community for long-term refugees, promoting refugees' economic independence is a rational direction. However, the uncritical celebration of self-reliance can conceal the underlying aim of the international refugee regime to minimize their commitment to those in protracted displacement under the name of economic empowerment for refugees.

Is self-reliance encouraged because it helps improve the future prospects and well-being of refugee individuals, families and communities
living in protracted limbo? Or, is it encouraged for improving the budgetary situation of UNHCR and global donor states? These fundamental
questions – and the conflicts of interest inherent in them – deserve more
attention from the refugee-supporting regime.

Whose Responsibility Is Attaining Self-Reliance?

Through the promotion of self-reliance, refugees are required to become
independent economic actors and are held almost entirely responsible for
achieving economic autonomy. But, as I have shown, refugees often face
significant constraints on their economic activities – formally and infor-
mally – and these challenges are often beyond what can be overcome at
the level of individual effort. Also, crucially, the vast majority of refugees
reside in asylum countries that are often devoid of conditions that enable
self-reliance even for their own nationals.

The shifting of responsibility for self-reliance to refugees is reminiscent of Duffield's critique of the discourse of 'sustainable development',
which shifts the burden of supporting life from states to people (Duffield
2006: 74). Duffield conceptualizes sustainable development as a biopoliti-
cal technology for containing 'non-insured populations' that are required
to improve their resilience and strengthen their self-reliance within their
given conditions. These populations are valued in terms of their ability to
effectively manage life's challenges at their own risk, largely in order to
reduce the obligation of states and humanitarian actors.

Evidently, the promotion of self-reliance for refugees indicates neoliberal tenets that are built upon the central pillars of upholding the role of
individuals and the market while 'rolling back the frontiers of the state'
(Heywood 2007: 52). The 'nanny state' is seen to breed a culture of de-
pendence – instead, the emphasis is on self-help, individual responsibility
and entrepreneurialism. While these discourses can shed a positive light
on a small number of economically active and entrepreneurial refugees
and underscore their potential as economic actors, the over-emphasis on
the economic elites can also present a risk for the needs and vulnerabilities of many refugees to be overlooked – and for assistance to be with-
drawn from those in plight.

The path to self-reliance is not a homogeneous process. Personal characteristics and background, including previous livelihood skills, social
status, displacement history, family structure, education, gender and age
play a crucial role in determining the level of refugees' economic well-being, as shown throughout this book. The emphasis on refugees' individual
capabilities can risk neglecting those with specific vulnerabilities and can

obscure the duty of the international refugee regime to provide protection for refugees. Given its organizational primary mandate, UNHCR needs to carry a significant part of the responsibility to ensure that the promotion of refugee self-reliance leads to enhancing, rather than compromising, the protection and well-being of refugees.

Questioning the Livelihoods Agenda of UNHCR

UNHCR's Lack of Interest in the Economic Potential of Refugees

'Liberian refugees are running businesses so they are managing well'. 'Reducing UNHCR support propelled refugees to be economically independent'. During my research, I frequently heard these statements from UNHCR staff in Ghana. These comments were almost always based on superficial and unsubtle observations of commerce in the camp. These remarks appear to be indicative of UNHCR's lack of interest in achieving a better understanding of refugees' economic life in Buduburam camp.

During my field research in 2008 and 2009, I occasionally presented some of my preliminary findings, including reports about the existence of extremely vulnerable refugees, to UNHCR staff in Accra. Their reactions and comments were not promising. I recall one conversation at a meeting in which I presented an example about Victoria's remittance cluster (illustrated in Chapter 2). I emphasized that many refugees without direct access to overseas remittances were having difficulties in securing basic needs on their own and were therefore reliant on spill-over benefits from primary remittance recipients. The UNHCR senior programme officer responded: 'An important dimension of self-reliance is mindsetting. If Justina [a secondary beneficiary within Victoria's cluster] indulges herself to rely on Victoria [the head of the cluster, that is the one with access to remittances], she will never be able to achieve self-reliance. Justina must be determined to become self-reliant and independent'.[1]

I disagreed with him. I emphasized that Justina had been making efforts by selling oranges in the camp every day but that with such a livelihood strategy, she could not produce sufficient income to ensure that her own fundamental needs and those of her three children were met. I argued that it was not appropriate to conclude that Justina was merely dependent on Victoria by choice. The senior programme officer then asked what types of skill training would be necessary to enable poor refugees like Justina to become self-sufficient. In response, I pointed rather to more structural livelihood impediments for refugees, such as little access to formal employment and local markets, as root causes of their economic plight. The officer's reply, however, was discouraging: 'assistance for socio-economic development is not part of the UNHCR mandates'.[2]

Such conversations made me doubt the genuineness of UNHCR's interest at the field level in assisting with the development of refugees' livelihoods and economic autonomy. As mentioned in the Introduction, UNHCR's stated attention to refugee livelihoods at headquarters level emerged in relation to the frequency of protracted refugee situations. The importance of self-reliance and development has also been explicitly recognized and documented in UNHCR's Development Assistance for Refugees (DAR) Programme. This handbook states that there is the need for 'better targeting of development assistance to countries hosting large numbers of refugee populations over protracted periods of time' (UNHCR 2005b).

Nevertheless, the interest in refugees' economic potential proclaimed in Geneva was not translated into meaningful action by field staff who were supposed to be working for the protection of refugees. During 2008 and 2009, UNHCR's primary aim was to disengage from Buduburam refugee camp by reducing the number of Liberians remaining there as much as possible and by facilitating local integration. Given the responses and tone of UNHCR staff in Accra, I became increasingly suspicious of how seriously the issue of the economic empowerment of Liberian refugees had been pursued by the organization even before the resumption of the latest repatriation programme. Their comments made me think that UNHCR Ghana had sidelined the livelihood agenda over the years, viewing it as a minor issue and not part of the organization's mandate to provide protection at ground level.

My follow-up research in 2012 and 2013 further highlighted the absence of UNHCR's efforts at enhancing refugees' economic capacity. While presenting the ECOWAS-based integration scheme as a 'solution' for the remaining Liberians, fundamental impediments to integration such as language barriers and xenophobic attitudes among locals remained unsolved. There was little evidence that UNHCR (and the Ghanaian government) were making meaningful efforts to set up a conducive environment for the successful integration of the remaining 7,000 Liberian refugees.

The Need for Different Approaches

If the global refugee regime genuinely aims to facilitate and strengthen refugees' livelihoods and self-reliance, its support for refugees requires a shift from a needs-based approach to a rights-based approach. When refugees are denied access to basic social and economic rights to which they are entitled under international human rights instruments, their ability to achieve a meaningful level of subsistence is largely restrained (Grabska and Mehta 2008: 14). However, UNHCR tends to divorce the issue of livelihoods from access to socio-economic rights. In the current framework of refugee assistance, refugee-supporting agencies normally choose to embark on meeting the practical needs of refugees rather than creating long-term conducive environments in which refugees' socio-economic rights can be realized.

Needless to say, employing a rights-based approach cannot be accomplished by UNHCR alone. In particular, the role of refugee-hosting states is critical since upholding refugee rights is primarily their responsibility. In the case of Ghana, while the country is known as an exemplary model state regarding refugee protection, the Ghanaian administration had done very little to promote the socio-economic rights of refugees in the country. With its own stagnant economy and limited absorptive capacities, the Ghanaian government saw upholding refugees' socio-economic rights as an additional burden on the host country. Indeed, a shift towards a rights-based approach can entail larger commitments on the part of donors, UNHCR, international and national organizations, and host governments. But ensuring livelihood security based upon rights would in the longer term reduce the human, social and economic costs of marginalization (Grabska 2008: 89).

Enhancing refugees' economic capacities also necessitates a renegotiation of the relationship between humanitarian and development strands in policy and practice. One of the most significant barriers to self-reliance has been that the assumption that refugee issues are primarily a 'humanitarian' concern. However, as recent studies highlight, refugees can and do flourish as economic actors when they are given a combination of rights and meaningful support by the international community and host state (see Betts et al. 2014). This requires humanitarian and development actors to work together at both international and national levels; without these fundamental shifts, issues of livelihoods and self-reliance in forced migration contexts will remain unresolved.

Revisiting the Social Network Discourse: Its Limitations and Pitfalls

Towards a Theoretical Understanding of Social Capital and Livelihoods

In the existing body of literature on the livelihoods of displaced persons, the importance of social capital is extensively recognized by many scholars. Nevertheless, given the intangible nature of social networks, this elusive concept is often used uncritically. The empirical evidence here suggests possible improvements in the theoretical understanding of social capital with implications for both academics and policy makers.

First, in the conception of social capital, it is essential to make a clear distinction between the volume of resources and the networks that allow individuals to access these resources. Using the examples of Jennifer and Olivia (see Chapter 3), I conceptualized refugees' social networks in Buduburam as the aggregate of the numerous contacts that a refugee possesses. But the quality and volume of assets that someone can mobilize through each of these contacts are inseparable from socio-economic stratification. Therefore, the sum of the resources drawn from these personal connections will eventually differentiate the potency of the possessor's social capital. In the Introduction, I critiqued the prevailing use of social assets as a 'catch-all' notion, particularly so in livelihood studies. This empirically informed conceptual framework offers a more nuanced understanding of internal differentiations in the quality of different networks, even within a particular population.

Above all, the empirical evidence in this study points to the highly selective nature of access to resourceful and extensive social networks. In particular, the detailed analysis of recipients of robust remittances has illuminated the harsh fact that not everyone is able to draw on transnational connections and become a beneficiary of substantial remittance assistance over a period of years. Chapter 4 revealed that most of the recipients of large and regular remittances are from the privileged ethnic group whose members have traditionally had entitlements to economic, political and social assets in Liberia for generations. Given these research findings, I have argued that access to robust remittances is not a matter of individual efforts or luck, but rather a matter of one's lineage and of privileges accumulated over many decades by one's ancestors.

The investigation of the roots of robust remittances has, in turn, elucidated the correlation between the socio-economic status of refugees in exile and their pre-displacement living conditions. Horst (2006b: 203) emphasizes the importance of a historical approach to the study of forced migration, in that refugees are people with a past. To understand their current economic standing and livelihood strategies, it is critical for researchers to holistically capture the background and origin of refugees, including family members before their displacement, and to situate them in the wider context of the society and country which they are from.

The Perils of Over-Emphasizing the Value of Social Networks

Given significant inequalities in the amount of resources drawn from each network, researchers should be cautious about over-emphasizing the potential of social capital.

According to Bebbington et al. (2004: 36–37), the social networks agenda has gained momentum over recent decades among the Breton

Woods institutions, particularly the World Bank, because of its compatibility with neoliberal discourse. As often observed in these institutions, however, issues of social inequality were given insufficient attention prior to the promotion of social networks. In her study of the African informal economy, Meagher (2010: 21) has alerted us to the fact that enthusiastic proponents of social networks tend to perceive these personal connections as a substitute for state intervention. Hence, their policy stance is to encourage a more 'enabling' business environment, usually involving liberalization, to give these informal networks more space to operate while eclipsing the role of the state, which is fundamentally the same argument as that of neoliberal policy recommendations.

Crucially, in promoting refugees' livelihoods and self-reliance, the neoliberal understanding of social capital is problematic given inevitable differences in accessing robust and resourceful networks. If unequal access to social assets, including transnational remittances and mutual assistance, is glossed over, it could lead to the conclusion that because refugees have social networks they can make ends meet without support from the international refugee regime. Whilst social networks can provide an important temporary fallback in times of crisis, they are unable to overcome the obstacles created by prolonged poverty, social inequality and the dysfunction of humanitarian actors with responsibility for refugees.

Although informal networks of refugees were crucial for their day-to-day survival in Buduburam camp, their communal solidarity should not be celebrated as a panacea. Refugee-policy makers must recognize the sacrifice, stress and burdens entrenched in these mutual assistance practices. In acute destitution, what the international refugee regime calls refugees' 'community-driven responses' can be on the contrary quite disintegrative to their communal solidarity.

Instead, what UNHCR and other refugee assisting organizations ought to target is the 'non-insured' (Duffield 2008: 150); in this case, this specifically means those refugees who had no or very little access to privileged resource networks. In Buduburam, these refugees were surviving in deplorable living conditions, unable to meet their most fundamental needs. Assistance for the non-insured should be ensured by institutionalized aid from aid organizations, not by informal communal networks.

Reconfiguring Refugees' Return Migration and Economic Integration

Selectivity in Repatriation and Reintegration

Drawing upon follow-up research on returnees, this book has challenged another myth in the forced migration policy arena: returning to their homeland is the ideal solution for all types of refugee. As has been demonstrated, the results of returning home for Liberian repatriates varied. In particular, for those who were reliant on Buduburam-based networks during their exile, repatriation normally worsened their living conditions in their homeland because of the disruption to their livelihoods. Put differently, repatriation can undermine or even destroy refugees' subsistence by shrinking their networks due to the dislocation of refugees from a familiar environment to a place where they may have limited access to useful connections.

Importantly, repatriation, especially for protracted refugee cases, should be conceptualized as migration to an unfamiliar environment, not as a homecoming. Given this understanding, access to social networks emerges as an essential issue for facilitating economic adjustment upon return. In the initial phase of return to Liberia, access to supporters who could provide accommodation and food was indispensable for a smooth transition from exile to Liberia. Subsequently, levels of access to economic and political elites largely differentiated the livelihood formation processes of returnees, including access to formal and gainful employment. Due to the historical context of Liberia, intimate ties with the privileged group was more or less the social product of their family-based assets, which had been accumulated over generations. As shown in Chapter 5, those with an eminent family background were much better positioned to adjust to a new setting by drawing on familial support and personal ties in Liberia, as compared with those who returned to the country of origin with limited links.

These findings pose a clear challenge to UNHCR, and to other UN agencies, donors and NGOs that embrace a simple understanding of refugee repatriation. Refugees' return migration and economic integration, especially in protracted cases, ought to be understood as largely dependent on returnees' asset profiles and the quality of their connections in the country of origin. These points highlight the need for providing continuing assistance, particularly for repatriates who are likely to be exposed to new types of vulnerability upon their return. In practice, however, the involvement of UNHCR often ceases and there is next to no investigation of the durability of the ideal durable solution. Notwithstanding the large-scale repatriation campaign by UNHCR, no follow-up research with Liberian returnees about their levels of integration and the challenges which they faced was conducted by any agencies, as far as I am aware. It would clearly not be desirable to see a situation in which UNHCR's interest in refugees ends before the UN refugee regime ensures the achievement of a 'sustainable return' (Black and Gent 2004) of former forced migrants.

Despite the selective nature of successful repatriation and reintegration, maximizing the number of repatriates from Ghana was clearly UNHCR's priority during the large-scale repatriation programme of 2008 and 2009. Under the global 'politics' of the withdrawal of support for long-term Liberian refugees, the perception in the UNHCR Ghana office was 'the more Liberian returnees, the larger the organization's success'. When I asked a UNHCR officer in charge of repatriation of Liberian refugees about the ongoing repatriation programme, he proudly said to me: 'This will be the most successful repatriation programme in Ghana. More than 4,000 refugees already registered for repatriation within four months. By the end of 2008, we aim to send a total of 12,000 refugees'.[3] He put a particular emphasis on 'the target number of 12,000' as UNHCR's organizational goal, as if he was sending 'packages' at a transportation company. Again in 2012, UNHCR's last call for repatriation highlighted its blindness to (or deliberate negligent attitude towards) the complexity of refugees' decision making regarding return and their reintegration challenges upon repatriation from prolonged exile. In the implementation of its exit strategy, the quality of return was put aside, and heterogeneity of circumstances of refugees was not a consideration for UNHCR staff.

Revisiting the Meaning of Repatriation

Repatriation is not just a physical return to the country of origin. It should be firmly conceptualized as a process involving the remaking of citizenship and consequent re-accessing of rights and livelihoods through refugees availing themselves of national protection in the country of origin (Long 2010: 1). UNHCR therefore defines repatriation and reintegration as 'a process which involves the progressive establishment of conditions which enable returnees to exercise their social, economic, civil, political and cultural rights, and on that basis to enjoy peaceful, productive and dignified lives in their homeland' (UNHCR 2004d). The crucial assumption underlying this conceptualization is that a state is willing and able to reassume responsibility for the rights and well-being of its own citizens (ibid.). Nevertheless, when this assumption is invalid or questionable, especially in the case of countries in the Global South where the state's capacity is weak, this entire conceptual framework becomes precarious, and possibly dangerous.

My research findings in Liberia point to the need for a fundamental reconfiguration of the current framework of repatriation and reintegration. During their exile in Ghana, the socio-economic rights of Liberians were constrained by formal and informal restrictions. In theory, the process of repatriation ought to give returnees access to these rights as citizens, enabling their ultimate integration into their country of origin. For Liberian returnees, however, recovery of their citizenship in the country of origin did not necessarily lead all returnees to be able to secure and enjoy their rights and state protection. For those who integrated with less difficulty, the reasons for their relative success were almost entirely linked to their personal asset profiles, rather than guaranteed as inherent rights as citizens of Liberia. Among those who had to struggle for economic survival in Liberia, some refugees even chose to go back to Buduburam camp after repatriation, despite the continued constraints on their economic activities in Ghana.

Because we cannot reliably assume that a state will uphold its responsibility for all of its citizens in all cases, the idealization of repatriation as a solution warrants serious scrutiny. The asset profiles of refugees vary significantly between households even among the same refugee population. Therefore, it is apparent that an optimal durable solution may differ even among sub-groups of a particular refugee population. Moreover, the most ideal options for refugees may even change over time, depending on evolving circumstances or priorities of refugee individuals or households, as well as changes undergone in their 'homeland' during their lengthy exile. Given the evidence presented in this book, more attention should be paid to the complex and nuanced relationship between refugees' socio-economic conditions and priorities and the search for the ideal option for their protection.

Refugees' Lives in and after Protracted Displacement

At the end of 2015, there was a record number of forced migrants globally: 65 million, including 21.3 million refugees (UNHCR 2016). The vast majority of the world's refugees remain in exile in the developing world long after the initial emergency phase of the crisis that forced them to migrate is over, and the average length of exile is currently estimated to be more than a quarter of a century.

Given the daunting scale and unprecedented duration of protracted refugee situations worldwide, the existing framework of three durable solutions is not sufficient to resolve the global refugee problem. Meanwhile, the international donor community shows little interest in providing aid for long-term refugees as their attention is diverted to newly emerging high-profile refugee crises. This current situation represents a failure of the existing paradigm in the international refugee regime.

Against this backdrop, strengthening refugee livelihoods and promoting their socio-economic independence has been spotlighted as a remedy for long-term refugees. But what this really means is that in the absence of effective solutions to prolonged displacement, refugees themselves have been required to make up for the deficits of flawed systems. Put differently, self-reliance discourse shifts the primary responsibility for supporting refugees from aid agencies and states to refugees themselves.

With the universal promotion of self-reliance, therefore, refugees are valued in terms of their ability to embrace risk and effectively manage their lives in the face of various difficulties. As this book shows, the Liberian refugees in Buduburam had to make ends meet despite numerous livelihood restrictions and the lack of meaningful support from humanitarian and development organizations. UNHCR and Ghana played a very limited role in strengthening refugees' economic capacities, and sometimes even disturbed their pursuit of sustainable livelihoods by tightening up refugee policy and implementing large-scale and rapid repatriation.

In Buduburam camp, wealthy Liberian refugees who had access to remittance support were indeed 'ideal refugees' (Fiddian-Qasmiyeh 2014) for UNHCR and the Ghanaian administration because they were able to manage various challenges without bothering these institutional players. More importantly, by bringing substantial remittances to Buduburam, the well-off refugees helped underpin the camp economy and even assisted in the survival of poorer refugees, ironically helping to mask the absence of meaningful intervention by the refugee-supporting organizations.

In contrast, the impoverished Liberian refugees disproved the stereotypical image of self-sufficient refugees, which UNHCR had promoted over the years. Even more problematically for the UN refugee agency, the poorer Liberian refugees refused (or were unable) to repatriate – UNHCR's preferred durable solution for them. The existence of these 'non-ideal' (ibid.) groups of refugees was a huge inconvenience to both national and international refugee policy makers, since they were evidence of the failures and limitations of the existing refugee assistance regime. Ultimately, it could be said that UNHCR and the Ghanaian and Liberian governments had been attempting to avoid responsibility for these 'undesirable' Liberian exiles.

In late 2012, UNHCR declared that the protracted Liberian refugee situation had finally come to an 'end'. Following the invocation of the Cessation Clause, formally ending their refugee status, the Liberian refugees are no longer considered the responsibility of UNHCR. Left without official refugee status but no durable solution, these remaining Liberians – still in their country of exile, now with ECOWAS migrant status – have extremely few opportunities for international or media attention, given their increasing invisibility and 'policy irrelevance' (Bakewell 2008). In UNHCR's global appeal in 2015, there is no reference made to the progress of the sub-regional integration scheme for Liberian exiles in Ghana. UNHCR appears to be unaware that leaving former refugees with ambiguous status in Ghana does not guarantee their local integration. It is imperative that the international refugee regime closely monitors the situation of former refugees in West Africa to find out whether the ECOWAS integration scheme can really constitute a 'solution' for Liberians who continue to live in exile. Otherwise, this invisible population will simply 'disappear', removed from official statistics. Given the ubiquity of protracted refugee cases worldwide, alarmingly we may witness more of these 'forgotten' former refugees in the near future.

It should also not be forgotten that the futures of the returnee refugees in Liberia are perhaps no less precarious. Liberia has received over 150,000 returnees from neighbouring countries over the last several years. Despite a congratulatory attitude towards its social and economic stability internationally, the economy is weak, employment opportunities are scarce and its infrastructure is largely destroyed. The influx of repatriates has further burdened the limited absorptive capacity of this war-torn country, as several Liberian government officers frankly confirmed. It is essential that we continue to observe the future of these returnees within their fragile country of origin. As compelling evidence shows, upon their return from prolonged exile, harsh realities awaited them. There, their homeland gave them different types of survival and integration challenges, rather than welcomed their return and facilitated their integration.

There is a large body of literature arguing that we should recognize that refugees are active, capable players with ingenuity and resilience (Golooba-Mutebi 2004; Harrell-Bond 1986; Korac 2009; Macchiavello 2003). Having worked with refugees as a practitioner and researcher for more than a decade, I agree wholeheartedly with this view in principle. However, over-emphasis on their resilience, agency and capacity can obscure internal differentiations in refugees' economic capacities, and universal celebration of refugees' livelihoods, social capital and self-reliance will continue to disguise the flaws of existing humanitarian responses to prolonged refugee situations. While we should certainly acknowledge and respect refugees' capabilities and resourcefulness in the face of adversity, we should not place all the challenges that arise during protracted displacement on the shoulders of refugees alone.

Notes

1. Interview, Accra, July 2009.
2. Interview, Accra, July 2009.
3. Interview, Accra, August 2008.

Epilogue

Buduburam in 2015

Three years have passed since the invocation of the Cessation Clause for Liberian refugees in 2012. Although their lives as 'formal' refugees ended, approximately 7,000 Liberians remained in exile and have continued living in Ghana under the new label of ECOWAS migrants. Even though the Ghanaian administration officially announced the closure of Buduburam camp in 2012, most of these former Liberian refugees continue to live in the camp and surrounding area. This epilogue is drawn from my continuing communications with former Liberian refugees who stayed – or rather are now stuck – in Buduburam.

In February 2014, almost two years after the cessation of their refugee status, Liberians remaining in Ghana were finally issued with their ECOWAS passports, which included two-year work and residence permits. While these documents have given them legal authorization to stay in Ghana or go to other ECOWAS countries, the provision of migrant status has not brought meaningful changes to the daily lives of most of them. One former refugee commented; 'Even if I have work permit, I cannot get a job in Ghana. I don't speak local [Ghanaian] languages. Xenophobic attitude from locals is strong. I don't have money to go to other places for job search. Nothing has changed in my life [with this new status]'.[1]

In early 2012, some refugees in the camp appealed for exemption from the cessation of their refugee status, but after three years in administrative limbo, most received notifications in June 2015 that their appeal had been rejected by the Ghanaian authorities.

Meanwhile, the Buduburam refugee economy continues to be dismantled. After 2012, the only NGO that was still providing small-scale assistance for former refugees in the camp was forced to halt its activities because of a lack of available funding. Many refugee enterprises have closed down due to the reduced number of refugee customers.

Interestingly, as the number of Liberian residents in Buduburam has decreased, the camp has also received a number of 'new arrivals'. Since around early 2012, a considerable number of Ghanaians started to enter the camp and began to occupy the homes previously occupied by refugees who had been repatriated. In addition, a small number of migrants from other West African states such as Nigeria and Ivory Coast came to Buduburam and took up residence in the former Liberian refugee camp.

Yet, according to the remaining Liberians, there is little interaction and affinity between the Liberian former refugees and these newcomers, in large part because of communication difficulties. Most of the Ghanaian newcomers do not speak English, while the majority of Liberians are unable to communicate in local languages. The Ghanaians who came to the camp started small business in and around the camp area. But these enterprises tend to operate only within the Ghanaian community; as one Liberian put it: 'we don't buy from them [Ghanaian newcomers] but they do not buy from us either'.[2]

There were significant changes in the personal lives of some of my interviewees. For example, Emily and her four children have since joined Kevin and Samantha's household. When Emily stopped being able to pay for the single room she had been renting, she and her children were forced to leave it and they begged help from their main supporter. The economic capacity of Kevin and Samantha's household, however, has been weakened as well. As UNHCR closed down all support for Buduburam camp, Kevin lost his monthly salary from the NGO for which he had been working, a UNHCR implementing partner. Because Emily has no meaningful sources of income, Kevin must now sustain two families. Currently, two households are surviving on donations given to Kevin by some foreign researchers, who previously conducted a study in the camp with support from Kevin. Clearly, their means of survival is highly unsustainable.

Since around mid 2015, refugee issues have drawn considerable attention from the international community and have frequently made the front page of the global media. In contrast to growing interest in refugee issues around the world, these 'invisible' Liberians continue to survive under the radar. The official history of Buduburam refugee camp ended with the cessation of refugee status. But the actual lives of individuals and households have little to do with the phases or cycles that are externally imposed on them by the global and national refugee authorities. Their 'refugee journey' (BenEzer and Zetter 2015) has not really ended.

Notes

1. Interview, Buduburam, May 2015.
2. Interview, Buduburam, July 2015.

References

Adebajo, A. 2002. *Liberia's Civil War.* Boulder, CO: Lynne Rienner Publishers.

Adepoju, A., A. Boulton and M. Levin. 2007. 'Promoting Integration through Mobility: Free Movement and the ECOWAS Protocol'. New Issues in Refugee Research, UNHCR Working Paper No. 150. Geneva: UNHCR.

Agblorti, S. 2011. 'Refugee Integration in Ghana: The Host Community's Perspective'. New Issues in Refugee Research, UNHCR Working Paper No. 203. Geneva: UNHCR.

Agyeman, D. 2005. 'Methodological Lessons: Working with Liberian and Togolese Refugees in Ghana', in E. Porter, G. Robinson, M. Smyth, A. Schnabel and E. Osaghae (eds), *Researching Conflict in Africa: Insights and Experiences.* Tokyo: United Nations University Press, pp. 56–63.

Akpan, M.B. 1973. 'Black Imperialism: Americo-Liberian Rule over the African Peoples of Liberia', *Canadian Journal of African Studies* 7(2): 217–36.

Akuei, S.R. 2005. 'Remittances as Unforeseen Burdens: The Livelihoods and Social Obligations of Sudanese Refugees'. Global Migration Perspectives No. 18. Geneva: Global Commission on International Migration.

Al-Ali, N. 2002. 'Bosnians in the UK and the Netherlands', in N. Al-Ali and K. Koser (eds), *New Approaches to Migration? Transnational Communities and the Transformation of Home.* London: Routledge, pp. 96–117.

Allen, T., and D. Turton. 1996. 'Introduction', in T. Allen (ed.), *In Search of Cool Ground.* Geneva: United Nations Research Institute for Social Development, pp. 1–22.

Al-Sharmani, M. 2003. 'Livelihood and Identity Constructions of Somali Refugees in Cairo'. Forced Migration and Refugee Studies, Working Paper No. 2. Cairo: American University in Cairo.

———. 2004. 'Refugee Livelihoods Livelihood and Diasporic Identity Constructions of Somali Refugees in Cairo'. New Issues in Refugee Research, UNHCR Working Paper No. 104. Geneva: UNHCR.

Amisi, B. 2006. 'An Exploration of the Livelihood Strategies of Durban Congolese Refugees'. New Issues in Refugee Research, UNHCR Working Paper No.123. Geneva: UNHCR.

Andrews, L.A. 2003. 'When is a Refugee Not a Refugee? Flexible Social Categories and Host/Refugee Relations in Guinea'. New Issues in Refugee Research, UNHCR Working Paper No. 88. Geneva: UNHCR.

———. 2006. 'Sustaining Relationships across Borders: Gendered Livelihoods and Mobility among Sierra Leonean Refugees', *Refugee Survey Quarterly* 25(2): 69–80.

———. 2008. 'The Invisible Refugee Camp: Durable Solutions for Boreah "Residuals" in Guinea', *Journal of Refugee Studies* 21(4): 537–52.

Antwi, E. 2007. 'The Truth about Dependency Syndrome'. London: Refugee Aware.

AREU (Afghanistan Research and Evaluation Unit). 2006. 'Afghans in Peshawar: Migration, Settlements, and Social Networks'. Case Study Series. Kabul, Afghanistan: Afghanistan Research and Evaluation Unit.

Ashley, C., and D. Carney. 1999. 'Sustainable Livelihoods: Lessons from Early Experience'. London: Department for International Development.

Bakewell, O. 2000. 'Repatriation and Self-Settled Refugees in Zambia: Bringing Solutions to the Wrong Problems', *Journal of Refugee Studies* 13(4): 356–73.

———. 2008. 'Research beyond the Categories: The Importance of Policy Irrelevant Research into Forced Migration', *Journal of Refugee Studies* 21(4): 432–53.

———. 2014. 'Encampment and Self-Settlement', in E. Fiddian-Qasmiyeh, G. Loescher, K. Long and N. Sigona (eds), *The Oxford Handbook of Refugee and Forced Migration Studies*. Oxford: Oxford University Press, pp. 127–38.

Bascom, J. 1993. 'The Peasant Economy of Refugee Resettlement in Eastern Sudan', *Annals of the Association of American Geographers* 83(2): 320–46.

———. 2005. 'The Long, "Last Step"? Reintegration of Repatriates in Eretria', *Journal of Refugee Studies* 18(2): 165–80.

Bauman, Z. 1998. *Globalization: The Human Consequences*. Cambridge: Polity Press.

———. 2004. *Wasted Lives: Modernity and its Outcasts*. Cambridge: Polity Press.

Bebbington, A., G. Guggenheim, E. Olson and M. Woolcock. 2004. 'Exploring Social Capital Debates at the World Bank', *Journal of Development Studies* 40(5): 33–64.

BenEzer, G., and R. Zetter. 2015. 'Searching for Directions: Conceptual and Methodological Challenges in Researching Refugee Journeys', *Journal of Refugee Studies* 28(3): 297–318.

Betts, A., L. Bloom, J. Kaplan and N. Omata. 2014. 'Refugee Economies: Rethinking Popular Assumptions'. Oxford: Refugee Studies Centre.

Black, R., and S. Gent. 2004. 'Defining, Measuring and Influencing Sustainable Return: The Case of the Balkans'. Working Paper No. 17. Brighton: Sussex Centre for Migration Research.

Black, R., and K. Koser. 1999. 'The End of the Refugee Cycle?' in R. Black and K. Koser (eds), *The End of the Refugee Cycle?* Oxford: Berghahn Books, pp. 2–17.

Bøås, M. 2015. *The Politics of Conflict Economies*. Oxford: Routledge.

Boulton, A. 2009. 'Local Integration in West Africa', *Forced Migration Review* 33: 32–34.

Bourdieu, P. 1986. 'The Forms of Capital', in E.J. Richardson (ed.), *Handbook of Theory and Research for the Sociology of Education*. London: Greenwood Press, pp. 46–58.

———. 2005. *The Social Structures of the Economy*. Cambridge: Polity Press.

Brettell, C.B. 2008. 'Theorizing Migration in Anthropology: The Social Construction of Networks, Identities, Communities, and Globalscapes', in C.B. Brettell and J.F. Hollifield (eds), *Migration Theory: Talking Across Disciplines*. London: Routledge, pp. 113–59.

Bryan, R., and B. Cocke. 2010. 'The Voluntary Assisted Return and Reintegration Programme (VARRP) 2004 and 2004 Extension: Monitoring Report'. Research Report No. 30. London: Home Office.

Byrne, J. 2013. 'Should I Stay or Should I Go? National Identity and Attitudes Towards Local Integration among Liberian Refugees in Ghana', *Refugee Survey Quarterly* 32(1): 50–73.

Campbell, C. 2001. 'Putting Social Capital in Perspective: A Case of Unrealistic Expectations?' in G. Morrow (ed.), 'An Appropriate Capital-isation? Questioning Social Capital'. Research in Progress Series, Issue 1. London: Gender Institute, London School of Economics and Political Science, pp. 1–10.

Carney, D. 1999. 'Approaches to Sustainable Livelihoods for the Rural Poor'. Poverty Briefing. London: Overseas Development Institute.

Carr, H. 2014. 'Returning "Home": Experiences of Reintegration for Asylum Seekers and Refugees', *British Journal of Social Work* 44(1): 1–17.

Castaldo, A., and B. Reilly. 2007. 'Do Migrant Remittances Affect the Consumption Patterns of Albanian Households?' *South-Eastern Europe Journal of Economics* 1: 25–54.

Castles, S., and M. Miller. 2009. *Age of Migration*, 4th edn. Basingstoke: Palgrave Macmillan.

Chetail, V. 2004. 'Voluntary Repatriation in Public International Law: Concepts and Contents', *Refugee Survey Quarterly* 23(3): 1–32.

Clark, C. 2006. 'Livelihood Networks and Decision-Making among Congolese Young People in Formal and Informal Refugee Contexts in Uganda', *First Annual Workshop Households in Conflict Network, 15–16 January 2006*. Berlin: German Institute for Economic Research.

Cleaver, G., and S. Massey. 2006. 'Liberia: A Durable Peace at Last?' in O. Furley and R. May (eds), *Ending Africa's War: Progressing to Peace*. Aldershot: Ashgate Publishing, pp. 179–99.

Codjoe, S.N., P. Quartey, C.A. Tagoe and H.E Reed. 2013. 'Perceptions of the Impact of Refugees on Host Communities: The Case of Liberian Refugees in Ghana', *Journal of International Migration and Integration* 14: 439–456.

Coleman, J. 1988. 'Social Capital in the Creation of Human Capital', *American Journal of Sociology* 94: S95–S120.

Corbett, J. 1988. 'Famine and Household Coping Strategies', *World Development* 16(9): 1099–1112.

Crisp, J. 2000. 'Africa's Refugees: Patterns, Problems and Policy Challenges'. New Issues in Refugee Research, UNHCR Working Paper No. 28. Geneva: UNHCR.

____. 2003a. 'UNHCR, Refugee Livelihoods and Self-Reliance: Brief History'. Geneva: UNHCR. Retrieved 20 October 2010 from: http://www.unhcr.org/research/RESEARCH/3f978a894.html.

____. 2003b. 'No Solutions in Sight: The Problem of Protracted Refugee Situations in Africa'. New Issues in Refugee Research, UNHCR Working Paper No. 75. Geneva: UNHCR.

____. 2004. 'The Local Integration and Local Settlement of Refugees: A Conceptual and Historical Analysis'. New Issues in Refugee Research, UNHCR Working Paper No. 102. Geneva: UNHCR.

____. 2006. 'Forced Displacement in Africa: Dimensions, Difficulties and Policy Directions'. New Issues in Refugee Research, UNHCR Working Paper No. 126. Geneva: UNHCR.

Crisp, J., J. Riera and R. Freitas. 2008. 'Evaluation of UNHCR's Returnee Reintegration Programme in Angola'. Geneva: Evaluation and Policy Analysis Unit, UNHCR.

Dalton, G. 1965. 'History, Politics, and Economic Development in Liberia', *Journal of Economic History* 25(4): 569–91.

Davies, S. 1996. *Adaptable Livelihoods: Coping with Food Insecurity in the Malian Sahel.* London: Macmillan.

de Haan, L. 2006. *The Livelihood Approach and African Livelihoods.* Leiden: African Studies Centre, University of Leiden.

de Haan, L., and P. van Ufford. 2002. *About Trade and Trust: The Question of Livelihood and Social Capital in Rural–Urban Interactions.* Leiden: University of Leiden.

de Haan, L., and A. Zoomers. 2006. 'Exploring the Frontier of Livelihoods Research', *Development and Change* 36(1): 27–47.

de Haas, H. 2005. 'International Migration, Remittances, and Development: Myths and Fact'. Global Migration Perspectives No. 30. Geneva: Global Commission on International Migration.

Devereux, S. 2003. 'Conceptualising Destitution'. IDS Working Paper No. 216. Brighton: Institute of Development Studies, University of Sussex

Devereux, S., and R. Sabates-Wheeler. 2004. 'Transformative Social Protection'. IDS Working Paper No. 232. Brighton: Institute of Development Studies, University of Sussex.

de Vriese, M. 2006. 'Refugee Livelihoods: A Review of the Evidence'. Geneva: Evaluation and Policy Analysis Unit, UNHCR.

DFID (Department for International Development). 1999. 'Sustainable Livelihoods Guidance Sheets'. London: Department for International Development.

Diaz-Briquets, S., and J. Perez-Lopez. 1997. 'Refugee Remittances: Conceptual Issues and the Cuban and Nicaraguan Experiences', *International Migration Review* 31(2): 411–37.

Dick, S. 2002a. 'Liberians in Ghana: Living without Humanitarian Assistance'. New Issues in Refugee Research, UNHCR Working Paper No. 57. Geneva: UNHCR.

———. 2002b. 'Responding to Protracted Refugee Situations: A Case Study of Liberian Refugees in Ghana'. Geneva: Evaluation and Policy Analysis Unit, UNHCR.

Doocy, S., G. Burnham, E. Biermann and M. Tileva. 2011. 'Household Economy and Livelihoods among Iraqi Refugees in Syria', *Journal of Refugee Studies* 25(2): 282–300.

Doron, E. 2005. 'Working with Lebanese Refugees in a Community Resilience Model', *Community Development Journal* 40(2): 182–91.

Dovlo, E., and S. Sondah. 2001. 'Singing the Lord's Song in a Strange Land: Christianity among Liberian Refugees in Ghana', *Studies in World Christianity* 7(2): 199–218.

Duffield, M. 2006. 'Racism, Migration and Development: The Foundations of Planetary Order', *Progress in Development Studies* 6(1): 68–79.

____. 2008. 'Global Civil War: The Non-Insured, International Containment and Post-Interventionary Society', *Journal of Refugee Studies* 21(2): 145–65.

Durand, J., E.A. Parada and D. Massey. 1996. 'Migradollars and Development: A Reconsideration of the Mexican Case', *International Migration Review* 30(2): 423–44.

Dzeamesi, M. 2008. 'Refugees, the UNHCR and Host Governments as Stakeholders in the Transformation of Refugee Communities: A Study into the Buduburam Refugee Camp in Ghana', *International Journal of Migration, Health and Social Care* 4(1): 28–41.

Eastmond, M., and J. Ojendal. 1999. 'Revisiting a "Repatriation Success": The Case of Cambodia', in R. Black and K. Koser (eds), *The End of the Refugee Cycle?* Oxford: Berghahn Books, pp. 38–55.

Ellis, F. 2000. *Rural Livelihoods and Diversity in Developing Countries.* Oxford: Oxford University Press.

Ellis, S. 2007. *The Mask of Anarchy.* New York: New York University Press.

Essuman-Johnson, A. 1995. 'The Refugee Problem in West Africa: Some Responses to Legitimate and Illegitimate Migration', in H. Adelman (ed.), *Legitimate and Illegitimate Discrimination: New Issues in Migration.* Toronto: York Lanes Press, pp. 103–17.

____. 2011. 'When Refugees Don't Go Home: The Situation of Liberian Refugees in Ghana', *Journal of Immigrant and Refugee Studies* 9: 105–26.

Fagen, W.P. 2011. 'Refugees and IDPs after Conflict'. Special Report No. 268. Washington, DC: United States Institute of Peace.

Faist, T. 2000. *The Volume and Dynamics of International Migration and Transnational Social Spaces.* Oxford: Oxford University Press.

Farrington, J., T. Ramasut and J. Walker. 2002. 'Sustainable Livelihoods Approaches in Urban Areas: General Lessons, with Illustrations from Indian Cases'. Working Paper No. 162. London: Overseas Development Institute.

Fiddian-Qasmiyeh, E. 2011. 'Introduction: Faith-Based Humanitarianism in Contexts of Forced Displacement', *Journal of Refugee Studies* 24(3): 429–39.

____. 2014. *The Ideal Refugees: Gender, Islam, and the Sahrawi Politics of Survival.* Syracuse, NY: Syracuse University Press.

____. 2015. *South–South Educational Migration, Humanitarianism and Development.* Oxford: Routledge.

Fine, B. 2001. 'It Ain't Social and It Ain't Capital', in G. Morrow (ed.), 'An Appropriate Capital-isation? Questioning Social Capital'. Research in Progress Series, Issue 1. London: Gender Institute, London School of Economics and Political Science, pp. 11–15.

____. 2006. 'Social Capital', in A. Clard (ed.), *The Elgar Companion to Development Studies.* Cheltenham: Edward Elgar Publishing, pp. 559–63.

Francis, E. 2000. *Making a Living: Changing Livelihoods in Rural Africa.* London: Routledge.

Fresia, M. 2014. 'Forced Migration in West Africa', in E. Fiddian-Qasmiyeh, G. Loescher, K. Long and N. Sigona (eds), *The Oxford Handbook of Refugee and Forced Migration Studies.* Oxford: Oxford University Press, pp. 541–53.

Ghorashi, H. 2007. 'Refugee Voice, Giving Silence a Chance: The Importance of Life Stories for Research on Refugees', *Journal of Refugee Studies* 21(1): 117–32.

Golooba-Mutebi, F. 2004. 'Refugee Livelihoods – Confronting Uncertainty and Responding To Adversity: Mozambican War Refugees in Limpopo Province, South Africa'. New Issues in Refugee Research, UNHCR Working Paper No. 105. Geneva: UNHCR.

Grabska, K. 2005. 'Living on the Margins: The Analysis of the Livelihood Strategies of Sudanese Refugees with Closed Files in Egypt'. Forced Migration and Refugee Studies, Working Paper No. 6. Cairo: American University in Cairo.

——. 2008. 'Brothers or Poor Cousins? Rights, Policies and the Well-Being of Refugees in Egypt', in K. Grabska and L. Mehta (eds), *Forced Displacement: Why Rights Matter*. Basingstoke: Palgrave Macmillan, pp. 71–92.

Grabska, K., and L. Mehta. 2008. 'Introduction', in K. Grabska and L. Mehta (eds), *Forced Displacement: Why Rights Matter*. Basingstoke: Palgrave Macmillan , pp. 1–25.

Griffiths, D., N. Sigona and R. Zetter. 2005. *Refugee Community Organisations and Dispersal*. Bristol: Policy Press.

Halpern, D. 2005. *Social Capital*. Cambridge: Polity Press.

Hamid, G.M. 1992. 'Livelihood Patterns of Displaced Households in Greater Khartoum', *Disaster* 16(3): 230–39.

Hammar, A. 2014. 'Displacement Economies: Paradoxes of Crisis and Creativity in Africa', in A. Hammar (ed.), *Displacement Economies in Africa: Paradoxes of Crisis and Creativity*. London: Zed Books, pp. 3–32.

Hammond, L. 1999. 'Examining the Discourse of Repatriation: Towards a More Proactive Theory of Return Migration', in R. Black and K. Koser (eds), *The End of the Refugee Cycle?* Oxford: Berghahn Books, pp. 227–44.

——. 2004. *This Place Will Become Home*. Ithaca, NY: Cornell University Press.

——. 2006. 'Obliged to Give: Remittances and the Maintenance of Transnational Networks Between Somalis "At Home" and Abroad'. London: School of Oriental and African Studies, University of London.

——. 2014. 'Voluntary Repatriation and Reintegration', in E. Fiddian-Qasmiyeh, G. Loescher, K. Long and N. Sigona (eds), *The Oxford Handbook of Refugee and Forced Migration Studies*. Oxford: Oxford University Press, pp. 499–511.

Hampshire, K., G. Porter, K. Kilpatrick, P. Kyei, M. Adjaloo and G. Oppong. 2008. 'Liminal Spaces: Changing Inter-Generational Relations among Long-Term Liberian Refugees in Ghana', *Human Organization* 67(1): 25–36.

Hardgrove, A. 2009. 'Liberian Refugee Families in Ghana: The Implications of Family Demands and Capabilities for Return to Liberia', *Journal of Refugee Studies* 22(4): 483–501.

Hardwick, S.W. 2008. 'Place, Space, and Pattern: Geographical Theories in International Migration', in C.B. Brettell and J.F. Hollifield (eds), *Migration Theory: Talking across Disciplines*. London: Routledge, pp. 161–82.

Harrell-Bond, B.E. 1986. *Imposing Aid*. Oxford: Oxford University Press.

——. 1989. 'Repatriation: Under What Conditions Is It the Most Desirable Solution for Refugees? An Agenda for Research', *African Studies Review* 32(1): 41–69.

Harvey, P. , and J. Lind. 2005. 'Dependency and Humanitarian Relief: A Critical Analysis'. Humanitarian Policy Group report. London: Overseas Development Institute.

Helmore, K., and N. Singh. 2001. *Sustainable Livelihoods: Building on the Wealth of the Poor.* Boulder, CO: Lynne Rienner Publishers.

Heywood, A. 2007. *Politics.* Basingstoke: Palgrave Macmillan.

Holzer, E. 2012. 'A Case Study of Political Failure in a Refugee Camp', *Journal of Refugee Studies* 25(2): 257–81.

Holzmann, P. , T. Boudieu, J. Holt, M. Lawrence and M. O'Donnell. 2008. 'The Household Economy Approach'. London: Save the Children.

Horst, C. 2006a. 'Refugee Livelihoods: Continuity and Transformations', *Refugee Survey Quarterly* 25(2): 6–22.

———. 2006b. *Transnational Nomads: How Somalis Cope with Refugee Life in the Dadaab Camps of Kenya.* Oxford: Berghahn Books.

Hovil, L. 2014. 'Local Integration', in E. Fiddian-Qasmiyeh, G. Loescher, K. Long and N. Sigona (eds), *The Oxford Handbook of Refugee and Forced Migration Studies.* Oxford: Oxford University Press, pp. 488–98.

Hulme, D., and J. Toye. 2006. 'The Case for Cross-Disciplinary Social Science Research on Poverty, Inequality, and Well-Being', *Journal of Development Studies* 42(7): 1085–1107.

Jackson, J. 1994. 'Repatriation and Reconstruction in Zimbabwe during the 1980s', in T. Allen and H. Morsink (eds), *When Refugees Go Home.* Trenton, NJ: African World Press, pp. 126–66.

Jackson, R. 2006. 'Africa's Wars: Overview, Causes, and the Challenges of Conflict Transformation', in O. Furley and R. May (eds), *Ending Africa's War: Progressing to Peace.* Aldershot: Ashgate Publishing, pp. 15–29.

Jacobsen, K. 2002. 'Livelihoods in Conflict: The Pursuit of Livelihoods by Refugees and the Impact on the Human Security of Host Communities', *International Migration* 40(5): 95–121.

———. 2005. *The Economic Life of Refugees.* Bloomfield, CT: Kumarian Press.

———. 2014. 'Livelihoods and Forced Migration', in E. Fiddian-Qasmiyeh, G. Loescher, K. Long and N. Sigona (eds), *The Oxford Handbook of Refugee and Forced Migration Studies.* Oxford: Oxford University Press, pp. 99–111.

Jacobsen, K., M. Ayoub and A. Johnson. 2014. 'Sudanese Refugees in Cairo: Remittances and Livelihoods', *Journal of Refugee Studies* 27(1): 145–59.

Jamal, A. 2000. 'Minimum Standards and Essential Needs in a Protracted Refugee Situation: A Review of the UNHCR Programme in Kakuma, Kenya'. Geneva: Evaluation and Policy Analysis Unit, UNHCR.

Kaiser, T. 2000. 'UNHCR's Withdrawal from Kiryandongo: Anatomy of a Handover'. New Issues in Refugee Research, UNHCR Working Paper No. 32. Geneva: UNHCR.

———. 2006. 'Between a Camp And A Hard Place: Rights, Livelihood and Experiences of the Local Settlement System for Long-Term Refugees in Uganda', *Journal of Modern African Studies* 44(4): 597–621.

———. 2007. ' "Moving Up and Down Looking For Money": Making a Living in a Ugandan Refugee Camp', in J. Staples (ed.), *Livelihoods at the Margins: Surviving the City.* Walnut Creek, CA: West Coast Press, pp. 302–20.

Kapur, D. 2004. 'Remittances: The New Development Mantra?' G–24 Discussion Paper Series, No. 29. New York: United Nations Conference on Trade and Development.

Kaun, A. 2008. 'When the Displaced Return: Challenges to "Reintegration" in Angola'. New Issues in Refugee Research, UNHCR Working Paper No. 152. Geneva: UNHCR.

Kibreab, G. 2003. 'Displacement, Host Government's Policies, and Constraints on the Construction of Sustainable Livelihoods', *International Social Science Journal* 175: 57–67.

Korac, M. 2009. *Remaking Home: Reconstructing Life, Place and Identity in Rome and Amsterdam*. Oxford: Berghahn Books.

Korf, B. 2004. 'War, Livelihoods and Vulnerability in Sri Lanka', *Development and Change* 35(2): 275–95.

Koser, K. 1997. 'Social Networks and the Asylum Cycle: The Case of Iranians in the Netherlands', *International Migration Review* 31(3): 591–611.

———. 2007. 'Refugees, Transnationalism and the State', *Journal of Ethnic and Migration Studies* 33(2): 233–54.

Kunz, E.F. 1973. 'The Refugee in Flight: Kinetic Models and Forms of Displacement', *International Migration Review* 7(2): 125–46.

———. 1981. 'Exile and Resettlement: Refugee Theory', *International Migration Review* 15(1/2): 42–51.

Leliveld, A.H.M. 1991. 'Social Security in Developing Countries: Some Theoretical Considerations'. Research memorandum. Amsterdam: University of Amsterdam.

Le Sage, A., and N. Majid. 2002. 'The Livelihood Gap: Responding to the Economic Dynamics of Vulnerability in Somalia', *Disasters* 26(1): 10–27.

Lindley, A. 2006. 'Migrant Remittances in the Context of Crisis in Somali Society'. Humanitarian Policy Group, Background Paper No. 25. London: Overseas Development Institute.

———. 2007. 'The Early Morning Phonecall: Remittances from a Refugee Diaspora Perspective'. Centre on Migration, Policy and Society Working Paper No. 47. Oxford: Centre on Migration, Policy and Society, University of Oxford.

———. 2008. 'Conflict-Induced Migration and Remittances: Exploring Conceptual Frameworks'. Refugee Studies Centre Working Paper No. 47. Oxford: Refugee Studies Centre, University of Oxford.

———. 2010. *The Early Morning Phone Call: Somali Refugees' Remittances*. Oxford: Berghahn Books.

———. 2011. 'Between a Protracted and a Crisis Situation: Policy Responses to Somali Refugees in Kenya', *Refugee Survey Quarterly* 30(4): 14–49.

Loescher, G. 2001. *The UNHCR and World Politics: A Perilous Path*. Oxford: Oxford University Press.

Long, K. 2010. 'Home Alone? A Review of the Relationship between Repatriation, Mobility and Durable Solutions for Refugees'. The Policy Development and Evaluation Service evaluation report. Geneva: UNHCR.

———. 2013. *The Point of No Return: Refugees, Rights and Repatriation*. Oxford: Oxford University Press.

———. 2014. 'Rethinking Durable Solutions', in E. Fiddian-Qasmiyeh, G. Loescher, K. Long and N. Sigona (eds), *The Oxford Handbook of Refugee and Forced Migration Studies*. Oxford: Oxford University Press, pp. 475–87.

Long, L.D. 2004. 'Viet Kieu on a Fast Track Back?' in L.D. Long and E. Oxfeld (eds), *Coming Home?* Philadelphia: University of Pennsylvania Press, pp. 65–89.

Longley, C., and D. Maxwell. 2003. 'Livelihoods, Chronic Conflict and Humanitarian Response: A Synthesis of Current Practice'. Working Paper No. 182. London: Overseas Development Institute.

Lubkemann, S.C. 2004. 'Diasporas and Their Discontents: Return without Homecoming in the Forging of Liberian and African-American Identity', *Diaspora* 13(1): 123–28.

———. 2008a. 'Involuntary Immobility: On a Theoretical Invisibility in Forced Migration Studies', *Journal of Refugee Studies* 21(4): 454–75.

———. 2008b. 'Remittance Relief and Not-Just-for-Profit Entrepreneurship: The Case of Liberia', in J.M. Brinkerhoff (ed.), *Diaspora and Development: Exploring the Potential.* Boulder, CO: Lynne Rienner Publications, pp. 45–66.

Macchiavello, M. 2003. 'Forced Migrants as an Under-Utilized Asset: Refugee Skills, Livelihoods, and Achievements in Kampala, Uganda'. New Issues in Refugee Research, UNHCR Working Paper No. 95. Geneva: UNHCR.

Marsden, P. 1999. 'Repatriation and Reconstruction', in R. Black and K. Koser (eds), *The End of the Refugee Cycle?* Oxford: Berghahn Books, pp. 56–68.

Marx, E. 1990. 'The Social World of Refugees: A Conceptual Framework', *Journal of Refugee Studies* 3(3): 189–203.

Massey, D.S., J. Arango, G. Hugo, A. Kouaouchi, A. Pellegrino and J.E. Taylor. 2008. *Worlds in Motion: Understanding International Migration at the End of the Millennium.* Oxford: Oxford University Press.

Mayson, D.T., and A. Sawyer. 1979. 'Capitalism and the Struggle of the Working Class in Liberia', *Review of Black Political Economy* 9(2): 140–58.

Meagher, K. 2010. *Identity Economics: Social Networks and the Informal Economy in Nigeria.* Oxford: James Currey.

Mercer, C., B. Page and M. Evans. 2008. *Development and the African Diaspora.* London: Zed Books.

Meyer, S. 2006. 'The "Refugee Aid and Development" Approach in Uganda: Empowerment and Self-Reliance of Refugees in Practice'. New Issues in Refugee Research, UNHCR Working Paper No.131. Geneva: UNHCR.

Milner, J. 2014. 'Protracted Refugee Situations', in E. Fiddian-Qasmiyeh, G. Loescher, K. Long and N. Sigona (eds), *The Oxford Handbook of Refugee and Forced Migration Studies.* Oxford: Oxford University Press, pp. 151–62.

MoI (Ministry of Interior). 2008. 'Statement by Hon. Kwamena Bartels, Minister for the Interior, on Demonstration by Liberian Refugees at the Buduburam Settlement'. Press Release, 11 March. Accra: Ministry of Interior, Government of Ghana.

Monsutti, A. 2005. *War and Migration: Social Networks And Economic Strategies of the Hazaras of Afghanistan.* Oxford: Routledge.

Moore, M., M. Choudhary and N. Singh. 1998. 'How Can We Know What They Want? Understanding Local Perceptions of Poverty and Ill-Being in Asia'. IDS Working Paper No. 80. Brighton: Institute of Development Studies, University of Sussex.

Mosoetsa, S. 2011. *Eating From One Pot.* Johannesburg: Witwatersrand University Press.

Murray, C. 2001. 'Livelihoods Research: Some Conceptual and Methodological Issues'. Chronic Poverty Research Centre Working Paper No. 5. Manchester: Chronic Poverty Research Centre, University of Manchester.

NCS (National Catholic Secretariat). 2007. 'Nutrition Survey May 2007 Report: Buduburam Refugee Settlement, Ghana'. Accra: National Catholic Secretariat.

Nmoma, V. 1997. 'The Civil War and the Refugee Crisis in Liberia', *Journal of Conflict Studies* 17(1): 1–26.

Olukoju, A. 2006. *Culture and Customs of Liberia.* London: Greenwood Press.

Omata, N. 2011a. 'Forgotten or Neglected? Non-Registered Liberian Refugees in Ghana: Their Rights and Protection', *Oxford Monitor of Forced Migration* 1(2): 12–16.

⸻. 2011b. 'Online Connection for Remittances', *Forced Migration Review* 38: 27–28.

⸻. 2013a. 'Repatriation and Integration of Liberian Refugees from Ghana: The Importance of Personal Networks in the Country of Origin', *Journal of Refugee Studies* 26(2): 265–82.

⸻. 2013b. 'The Complexity Of Refugees' Return Decision-Making in a Protracted Exile: Beyond the Home-Coming Model and Durable Solutions', *Journal of Ethnic and Migration Studies* 39(8): 1281–97.

Orozco, M. 2003. 'Remittances, the Rural Sector, and Policy Options in Latin America', *International Conference on Best Practices: Paving the Way Forward for Rural Finance, 2–4 June 2003.* Washington, DC: World Council of Credit Unions.

⸻. 2004. 'Remittances to Latin America and the Caribbean: Issues and Perspectives on Development'. Report. Washington, DC: Organization of American States.

Owusu, M. 2000. 'Reluctant Refugees: Liberians in Ghana', *Journal of the International Institute* 7(3). Retrieved 18 April 2008 from: http://quod.lib.umich.edu/j/jii/4750978.0007.302?rgn=main;view=fulltext;q1=owusu.

Palmgren, P. A. 2014. 'Irregular Networks: Bangkok Refugees in the City and Region', *Journal of Refugee Studies* 27(1): 21–41

Pantuliano, S., M. Buchanan-Smith, P. Murphy and I. Mosel. 2008. 'The Long Road Home: Opportunities and Obstacles to the Reintegration of IDPs and Refugees Returning to Southern Sudan and the Three Areas'. Research Reports and Studies. London: Overseas Development Institute.

Phillips, M. 2003. 'The Role and Impact of Humanitarian Assets in Refugee-Hosting Countries'. New Issues in Refugee Research, UNHCR Working Paper No. 84. Geneva: UNHCR.

Pilkington, H., and M. Flynn. 1999. 'From "Refugee" to "Repatriation": Russian Repatriation Discourse in the Making', in R. Black and K. Koser (eds), *The End of the Refugee Cycle?* Oxford: Berghahn Books, pp. 171–96.

Polzer, T., and L. Hammond. 2008. 'Editorial Introduction: Invisible Displacement', *Journal of Refugee Studies* 21(4): 417–31.

Poros, M.V. 2001. 'The Role of Migrant Networks in Linking Local Labour Markets: The Case of Asian Indian Migration to New York and London', *Global Networks* 1(3): 243–59.

Porter, G., K. Hampshire, P. Kyei, M. Adjaldo, G. Rapoo and K. Kilpatrick. 2008. 'Linkages between Livelihood Opportunities and Refugee–Host Relations: Learning from the Experiences of Liberian Camp-Based Refugees in Ghana', *Journal of Refugee Studies* 21(2): 230–52.

Portes, A. 1998. 'Social Capital: Its Origins and Applications in Modern Sociology', *Annual Review of Sociology* 24: 1–24.

Putnam, R. 1993a. *Making Democracy Work*. Princeton: Princeton University Press.

———. 1993b. 'The Prosperous Community: Social Capital and Public Life', *American Prospect* 4(13): 1–11.

———. 1996. 'The Strange Disappearance of Civic America', *American Prospect* 7(24): 1–20.

Railey, D.H. 1997. 'Some Impacts of the Liberian Civil War: A Pilot Study of Thirty Liberian Immigrant Families in the United States', *Liberian Studies Journal* 22(2): 261–76.

Rodgers, G. 2004. '"Hanging Out" with Forced Migrants: Methodological and Ethical Challenges', *Forced Migration Review* 21: 48–49.

Rogge, J. 1994. 'Repatriation of Refugees', in T. Allen and H. Morsink (eds), *When Refugees Go Home*. Trenton, NJ: African World Press, pp. 14–49.

Rogge, J., and J. Akol. 1989. 'Repatriation: Its Role in Resolving Africa's Refugee Dilemma', *International Migration Review* 23(2): 184–200.

Saha, S.C. 1998. *Culture in Liberia: An Afrocentric View of the Cultural Interaction between the Indigenous Liberians and the Americo-Liberians*. Lampeter: Edwin Mellen Press.

Salducci, G. 2008. 'Towards the Local Integration of Liberian and Sierra Leonean Refugees in West Africa through Enhancing Self Reliance and Promoting Regional Integration'. Regional Framework. Geneva: UNHCR.

Scoones, I. 1998. 'Sustainable Rural Livelihoods: A Framework for Analysis'. IDS Working Paper No. 72. Brighton: Institute of Development Studies, University of Sussex.

———. 2007. 'Livelihoods Perspectives and Rural Development,' *Journal of Peasant Studies* 36(1): 171–96.

Sesay, A. 1996. 'Civil War and Collective Intervention in Liberia', *Review of African Political Economy* 67: 35–52.

Siisiainen, M. 2000. 'Two Concepts of Social Capital: Bourdieu vs. Putnam', *ISTR Fourth International Conference, 5–8 July 2000*. Dublin: Trinity College.

Sorensen, C. 2000. 'Alebu: Eritrean Refugees Return and Restore Their Livelihoods', in M. Cernea and C. McDowell (eds), *Risk and Reconstruction: Experiences of Resettlers and Refugees*. Washington, DC: World Bank, pp. 184–201.

Stefansson, A. 2004. 'Returns to Sarajevo and Contemporary Narratives of Mobility', in L.D. Long and E. Oxfeld (eds), *Coming Home?* Philadelphia: University of Pennsylvania Press, pp. 170–86.

Stein, B. 1981. 'Refugees and Economic Activities in Africa'. Research report for the United States Agency for International Development. Washington, DC: United States Agency for International Development.

Suleri, A.Q., and K. Savage. 2006. 'Remittances in Crises: A Case Study from Pakistan'. Humanitarian Policy Group Background Paper. London: Overseas Development Institute.

Tanle, A. 2013. 'Refugees' Reflections on Their Stay in the Buduburam Camp in Ghana', *GeoJournal* 78(5): 867–83.

Tapscott, C. 1994. 'A Tale of Two Homecomings', in T. Allen and H. Morsink (eds), *When Refugees Go Home*. Trenton, NJ: African World Press, pp. 251–59.

Taylor, E. 1999. 'The New Economics of Labour Migration and the Role of Remittances in the Migration Process', *International Migration* 37(1): 63–88.

Tete, S.Y.A. 2005. 'Narratives of Hope? Displacement Narratives of Liberian Refugee Women and Children in the Gomoa-Buduburam Refugee Camp in Ghana'. MA dissertation. Trondheim: Norwegian University of Science and Technology.

Tripp, A.M. 1997. *Changing the Rules: The Politics of Liberalization and the Urban Informal Economy in Tanzania*. Berkeley: University of California Press.

Turner, S. 2010. *Politics of Innocence: Hutu Identity, Conflict and Camp Life* Oxford: Berghahn Books.

Turton, D. 2003. 'Conceptualising Forced Migration'. Refugee Studies Centre Working Paper No. 12. Oxford: Refugee Studies Centre, University of Oxford.

UNHCR. 2004a. 'Protracted Refugee Situations'. Executive Committee of the High Commissioner's Programme, Standing Committee 30th Meeting. Document EC/54/SC/CRP. 14. Geneva: UNHCR.

———. 2004b. 'Regional Multi-Year Operations Plan for the Repatriation and Reintegration of Liberian Refugees and Internally Displaced Persons (2004–2007)'. Geneva: UNHCR.

———. 2004c. 'UNHCR Global Appeal 2005'. Geneva: UNHCR.

———. 2004d. 'Handbook for Repatriation and Reintegration Activities'. Geneva: UNHCR.

———. 2005a. 'Handbook for Self-Reliance'. Geneva: UNHCR.

———. 2005b. 'Handbook for Planning and Implementing Development Assistance for Refugees (DAR) Programmes'. Geneva: UNHCR.

———. 2006. 'A Tale of Two Camps: Bustling Buduburam and Quiet Krisan'. Retrieved 18 April 2008 from: http://www.unhcr.org/cgi-bin/texis/vtx/search?page=search&docid=44c7783e4&query=bustling%20village%20 Buduburam.

———. 2007. 'Tertiary Refugee Education Impact and Achievements'. Geneva: Technical Support Section, UNHCR.

———. 2008. 'UNHCR Global Appeal 2009'. Geneva: UNHCR.

———. 2009. 'Liberian Refugees Voluntary Repatriation Statistics'. Internal document. Monrovia: UNHCR.

———. 2012a. 'Livelihood Programming in UNHCR: Operational Guidelines'. Geneva: UNHCR.

———. 2012b. 'The State of World's Refugees: In Search of Solidarity'. Geneva: UNHCR.

_____. 2016. 'Global Trends: Forced Displacement in 2015'. Geneva: UNHCR.

UNHCR and WFP. 2006. 'Joint Assessment Mission, Ghana: Buduburam and Krisan Camps'. Accra/Dakar: UNHCR/World Food Programme.

USCRI (US Committee for Refugees and Immigrants). 2004. 'World Refugee Survey 2004'. Arlington, VA: US Committee for Refugees and Immigrants.

Van Hear, N. 1998. *New Diaspora*. London: University College London Press.

_____. 2002. 'Sustaining Societies under Strain: Remittances as a Form of Transnational Exchange in Sri Lanka and Ghana', in N. Al-Ali and K. Koser (eds), *New Approaches to Migration? Transnational Communities and the Transformation of Home*. London: Routledge, pp. 202–23.

_____. 2011. 'Forcing the Issue: Migration Crises and the Uneasy Dialogue between Refugee Research and Policy', *Journal of Refugee Studies* 25(1): 2–24.

_____. 2014a. 'Refugees, Diasporas, and Transnationalism', in E. Fiddian-Qasmiyeh, G. Loescher, K. Long and N. Sigona (eds), *The Oxford Handbook of Refugee and Forced Migration Studies*. Oxford: Oxford University Press, pp. 176–87.

_____. 2014b. 'Reconsidering Migration and Class', *International Migration Review* 48(S1): S100–S121.

Verdirame, G., and B. Harrell-Bond. 2005. *Rights in Exile*. Oxford: Berghahn Books.

Vertovec, S. 2009. *Transnationalism*. Oxford: Routledge.

Voutira, E., and B. Harrell-Bond. 2000. '"Successful" Refugee Settlement: Are Past Experiences Relevant?' in M. Cernea and C. McDowell (eds), *Risk and Reconstruction: Experiences of Resettlers and Refugees*. Washington, DC: World Bank, pp. 56–78.

Warner, D. 1994. 'Voluntary Repatriation and the Meaning of Return to Home: A Critique of Mathematics', *Journal of Refugee Studies* 7(2/3): 160–74.

Werker, E. 2007. 'Refugee Camp Economies', *Journal of Refugee Studies* 20(3): 461–80.

WFP (World Food Programme). 2007. 'Assistance to Most Vulnerable Refugee Caseloads in Ghana in support of Government Strategy to Promote Repatriation, Resettlement and Self-Reliance'. Protracted Relief and Recovery Operation, Document 10673.0, Accra: World Food Programme.

WRC (Women's Refugee Commission). 2011. 'The Living Ain't Easy: Urban Refugees in Kampala'. New York: Women's Refugee Commission.

Young, H., A. Osman, M. Smith, B. Bromwich, K. Moore and S. Ballosu. 2007. 'Sharpening the Strategic Focus of Livelihoods Programming in the Darfur Region'. Medford, MA: Feinstein International Center, Tufts University.

Zetter, R. 2007. 'More Labels, Fewer Refugees: Remaking the Refugee Label in an Era of Globalization', *Journal of Refugee Studies* 20(2): 172–92.

_____. 2012. 'Unlocking the Protracted Displacement of Refugees and Internally Displaced Persons: An Overview', *Refugee Survey Quarterly* 30(4): 1–13.

Zetter, R., D. Griffith and N. Sigona. 2005. 'Social Capital or Social Exclusion? The Impact of Asylum-Seeker Dispersal on UK Refugee Community Organisations', *Community Development Journal* 40(2): 169–81.

Index

remittances, 40–42, 89–93, 93–96
(*see* remittances); repatriation, 28–
29; re-returning to, 119–21; resource
networks, 9; role of internal
networks in, 51–57; self-reliance,
77–79, 143–45; successful businesses
in, 37–38; as a transit point, 24–25;
UNHCR withdrawal strategy,
31–32; vocational training, 100–101;
well-off refugees, 85–87; Western
Union branch in, 40
Buduburam Refugee Community
School, 23
businesses, 2. *See also* economic lives

C
camp-based organizations (CBOs), 12,
13
Canada, family migration history, 87
capital, social. *See* social capital
carbohydrates, 65
cash, sources of, 68–71
cash grants (UNHCR), 1
Cessation Clause, 3, 14, 125, 156, 158;
2008 refugee protests, 12
cessation of refugee status, 124–41;
deciding on repatriation, 131–33;
invocation of, 125–26; life post-
cessation, 137–39; non-registered
refugees, 135–37; reasons for staying
in Ghana, 133–37; responses to,
139–41; returning refugees (changes
since 2009), 129–31; sub-regional
integration scheme, 126–28
charities, 9; sharing remittances, 49–50
children, 111; diets, 65; food rations,
67; malnutrition, 66
Christianity, 26
churches in Buduburam refugee camp,
26
civil war (Liberia), 20, 29, 105, 125;
victims of, 98–99
clusters, remittance, 45–51. *See also*
remittances
cohesion, 9
commerce, 1. *See also* economic lives
commercial activities in Buduburam
refugee camp, 35–37

communities in Ghana, 55–56
compensation, making a living, 32–34
competition in Buduburam refugee
camp, 39
consumption, 77
corn starch, 65
costs: of basic services, 22, 23; of
education, 23; transitions, 110–11
cross-border livelihoods, 38

D
Dadaab camp, Kenya, 99
debt, 70
demographics, household economies,
63
dependency, 5, 145–46
Development Assistance for Refugees
(DAR) Programmes, 149
diets, 65–66. *See also* food
displacement: cause of, 26–28; new
connections following, 51, 52;
pre-displacement life of poorer
households, 96–99; refugee lives in
protracted, 155–57
Doe, Samuel, 27, 52, 134

E
Economic Community of West African
States (ECOWAS), 32, 38, 125,
126–28, 137, 145, 149, 156, 158
economic integration, 121–22, 152–55
economic lives: in the Buduburam
refugee camp, 35–58; commercial
activities, 35–37; evidence of
success, 39–40; mobility (as a
livelihood asset), 38–39; remittances
(*see* remittances); successful
businesses, 37–38
economic opportunities in Ghana,
129–30
economic reintegration, 10–11
economic stratification, 84–102;
accessing robust remittances,
93–96; family migration history,
87–89; historical approach to,
101–2; poverty traps, 99–100;
pre-displacement life of poorer
households, 96–99; remittances,

STUDIES IN FORCED MIGRATION

General Editor: Dawn Chatty, Refugee Studies Centre, University of Oxford

This series, published in association with the Refugees Studies Centre, University of Oxford, reflects the multidisciplinary nature of the field and includes within its scope international law, anthropology, sociology, politics, international relations, geopolitics, social psychology and economics.

www.ingramcontent.com/pod-product-compliance
Lightning Source LLC
Chambersburg PA
CBHW070930030426
42336CB00014BA/2616